An Informal History of Green Point

From Farm to Community, 1928-2020

by

Jo Currans

> Dedicated to all the volunteers who have resided in Green Point
> over the years and who have given of their time and energy,
> working tirelessly to make the Community what it is today.

An Informal History of Green Point

© Jo Currans

This book is copyright. Apart from any fair dealings for the purpose of private study or research, as permitted by the Copyright Act, no part of this book may be reproduced without permission.

Green Point on Wallis Lake Community Association Inc. - ABN: 39 908 563 484

This book is an initiative of the Green Point on Wallis Lake Community Association Inc., with all proceeds from its sale going to the Green Point Community Association.

For enquiries regarding sales - contact:

Jo Currans (02) 6555 5432

or

gfb1@smartchat.net.au

Published by: The Mickie Dalton Foundation Publishing Company

ISBN 987-0-645534-4-8

Contents

	Page
Preface	
Acknowledgements	
Historical Timeline – within our region since European discovery	
Introduction	1
The First Settlers	4
The Godwin Family	5
Early Development	6
Green Hill Farm	10
The First Farm Dwelling	13
Cattle Grazing	27
The Depression Years – 1929-1936	28
The Lakes Way….*in the early days*	30
Wartime Struggle	31
The Legend of Fraser's Bull	36
Sand Mining	37
Change On the Way	39
Green Point Subdivision	44
Building Problems - Lack Of Electricity	47
Struggle For Services	49
Fire Brigade Formed	52
Noises In the Night	60
Weather Patterns	61
Green Point Craft Gallery and Restaurant	65
The First Children's Playground	67
The Community Planning for the Future	69
A Community Remembers	70
Puppy Dog 'Tales'	72
Memorable Occasions	72
Lake Views Go – As Trees Grow	74
Community Land Made Available	79
Town Water	87
Great Expectations for a Hall of Our Own	90
Association Meeting Places	95
Sporting Complex - Fundraising	98
Sewerage Scheme – Meetings with Residents	106
Community Hall – Building Extensions	111
Fundraising and Repaying the Loan	113
Celebration Fete	114

Contents (Continued)

	Page
Second Children's Playgroup - Green Point Grubs	117
Clean Up Australia Day	120
Bushfire Alert	124
Roads	127
Tidy Towns Awards	129
New Playground Equipment	130
Green Point Park Sporting Complex	139
Tidy Towns Entry	140
Official Opening of the Park	142
Foreshore Cleanup	145
A New Approach - Plans Made	146
Foreshore Plan of Management	147
Tidy Towns Winner	153
Skateboarding at the Park	154
Basketball Half Court	163
Village Mowing and Park Maintenance	165
100 Years of ANZAC (1915-2015)	167
Foreshore Development	169
Coastcare Funding Grants	175
The Community Trailer	178
Coastcare	179
Development Of Foreshore Completed	186
Flora - Wildflower Display	191
Fauna - A Walk on the Wild Side	193
Birds	205
Our Resident Osprey Family	209
Association Becomes Incorporated	211
Bush Fire Brigade	213
Fight to Save Our Brigade	216
'Congratulations' - Green Point RFS	218
Commercial Fishing From Green Point	219
Turtle Tales	222
Formation of a Fishing Club	223
Leadership Changes	226
Roads – The Lakes Way Intersection	227
Major Stormwater Drainage	233
Art In the Park	237
Proposed New Subdivision	239

Contents (Continued)

	Page
Children's Road Safety	247
Green Point Rural Fire Service - Local Fire Danger	249
Early Population Increase	253
Extension To the Community Hall	253
Fundraising – Picnic/Fun Days	254
Green Point Rural Fire Service – The 2013 Bushfire	265
Community Association Goes Digital	268
The Community Hall – A Meeting Place	269
A Caring Community	271
'Artistic Flairs' Of Green Point	275
2014 Green Point Artistic Flairs Event	276
The Green Point Creative Flairs Art & Craft Exhibition	278
Hang'n Glide Park Equipment	279
Green Point Rural Fire Brigade	282
Council Amalgamation	293
Housing Development	295
Public Meeting	296
Tourism	300
Name Change – Barrington Coast	300
Weather Cycles Continue	301
Lake Levels Rise	302
Black Summer Bushfire Season (2019-2020)	305
Changes To Booti Booti National Park at Green Point	310
Epilogue	312
About the Book	313
Index	315

Preface

This work was undertaken to present an historical record of the early development of the Green Point area.

The project started around September 1996 when I was asked to display some early photographs. Some of those photographs included the original Green Point Community Hall being transported from Tuncurry to its present position in Green Point Park. The purpose of this display was to show the local residents attending the upcoming fundraising fete, that by comparison, what improvements had been achieved since then, and how, in order to negotiate proposed additional developments, their help would be greatly appreciated.

I had been taking photos around our area since 1985 and so I decided to include the pictures that had been on display at the fete to develop my story. A pattern was forming and all I needed were a few rough dates to put them in order. As I asked around, residents came forward with more information and old photographs which provided more clues to the past. Next, I referred to earlier residents for information about the early farming days. Before I knew it, the project had become a **Community History**, which I felt should be shared.

An attempt has been made to keep the events as close as possible to the order of occurrence – thus showing the growth and development of the area as it happened over time.

I am hopeful that readers will find it interesting and informative, bring back memories for established residents and enlighten newcomers to Green Point's past.

Jo Currans

Acknowledgements

I wish to express my sincere thanks and appreciation to Margaret Blackwood who generously typed and assisted the compilation of this work and for her reading of the early drafts and her guidance and encouragement.

My thanks also to the members of the Great Lakes Historical Society for their assistance and use of research material and archival photographs.

My sincere thanks to Teresa Siminska and special appreciation to Michael Davies who kindly assisted with the production and publishing of this book.

Special gratitude goes to Owen Mathias who gave us a glimpse into the life of Lachlan Fraser here on 'Green Hill' farm.

I acknowledge the valuable input received from well informed community members through the many phone calls and personal interviews which I have conduced, in order to learn more about the past history and early times of our area.

I am indebted to the Green Point Community Association for allowing access to the Association's records and the Green Point Rural Fire Service for their contribution and support which has given me insight into the 'life and times' of our small community and provided detailed information on many of the significant events and projects undertaken since 1973.

In closing, my thanks to the many early residents of Green Point who have kindly assisted with my gathering of historical information and who submitted stories from the past, together with old photographs, thus helping this project to become a reality.

I gratefully acknowledge the following books and publications, which were consulted for reference or as sources of illustrations.   Jo. Currans

Budge Robin, *Battlers All*
Doust John, *Past Days around Wallis Lake, its Rivers and Villages. Published by Great Lakes Advocate - Forster.* ISBN 0958643415
Greig Denise, *The Australian Gardener's Wildflower Catalogue.* Published by Angus & Robertson 1987. ISBN 0207157839
Feldmann Jules, *The Great Jubliee Book- the Story of the Australian Nation in Pictures, 1951*
McKay Anne & George, *In and About Pacific Palms.* Published by Pacific Palms Graphics, Pacific Palms 2003. ISBN 0975 160001
Rivett Jim, *The Good Old Days (from Barrington to Harrington and around the Great Lakes.)* Published by Anvil Press-Wamberal (2260) 1980. ISBN 0959590641
Wright June, The Historical Society, Tuncurry 1999. ISBN 0958643407

Other Publications --

Coastcare, emblem and brochures.
Focus Magazine article.
Great Lakes Advocate Newspaper articles.
Great Lakes Council, correspondence, information, brochures and use of emblem.
Great Lakes Council, Heritage Study 2007 (pages14-57) -compiled by the Great Lakes Council.
Green Point Community Association, records and past editions of the *Green Pointer* newsletter.

History of Green Point, a report by Liz Meadley c1993

Green Point Rural Fire Services, information, brochures & use of emblems.

Holidays tourist booklet, distributed by Manning Forster Tourist Committee, c1955.

Lakeland Adventure – A History of the Early Days of Forster-Tuncurry, Published by the Forster-Tuncurry Centenary Celebrations Committee, c1963.

Manning River Times article – 1978

National Park & Wildlife Service, correspondence information and brochures.

Shell Tourist Information Guide, c1955

Souvenir Programme to Commemorate the Opening of Forster-Tuncurry Bridge, Published by Forster Chamber of Commerce Committee, c1963.

Photographic Images
courtesy of the following -

Lesley Archer
Chris Baldwin
Margaret Blackwood
Chum & Barbara Bramble
David Buchanan
Jo Currans
C H Degotardi family
Sue Erglis
Great Lakes Advocate
John Hughes
Robin Jones
Sonya Jordan
Marguerite Lamb
Leanne Legge
Craig Mason
Phil McAsey
Col McPherson
Paul Murrell
Doris Perry
Lowell Reardon
Tom Ryan
Bill Shannon
Andrew Stockdale
Noelene Turner
Dr John Van Dyke

Further Contributions
courtesy of the following –

Copy documents - Joyce Bushnell
- Norah Greenwood
- Mick Perry
- RFS Green Point

Diagrams - Jo Currans
- Green Point Community Association

Development & Subdivision Plans
- Lidbury, Summers & Whiteman (Surveyors)

Sketches - Jo Currans
- Ron Davis

Maps - Map No.1 (1928) Liz Meadley
- Surveyor's Map (1950) Grant Mould
- Early Area Map Great Lakes Shire C'cil
- Great Lakes Advocate
- NSW Rural Fire Service

Jo Currans

Historical Timeline – within our region since European discovery

1770 – Captain Cook sailed past our area.

1788 – First Fleet landing and Settlement of Sydney cove established.

1790 – 2nd Fleet: 5 convicts escaped and adopted by Aborigines in Hawks Nest area.

1799 – Matthew Flinders sailed past our area of coastline.

1816 – 2 Ships wrecked off Cape Hawke …. first white settlers lost at sea.

1816 – Cedar getters and their convict servants arrived in Myall and Manning area.

1818 – John Oxley explored the beaches from the Hastings River to Port Stephens. Wallis Lake was named by Oxley when an inland expedition carried a boat from Booti Booti to Boomerang Beach. Timber getters took cedar from the Manning River area and Myall Lakes.

1821 - Governor Lachlan Macquarie established the penal colony of Port Macquarie.

1824 - The Australian Agricultural Company (known as the AAC) was formed in England. One million acres acquired for development. Stroud planned by the AAC.

1825 – 1826 - Hunter River and Port Stephens were surveyed by Henry Dangar.

1831 - Coal mining commenced in the Hunter area.

1832 - AAC withdrawal from our area, as sheep didn't suit Coomba area.

1843 - Wallamba Aborigines left Coomba area campsite.

1850 - The penal settlement of Newcastle expands and more coal mines established.

1850 - Chinese fishermen arrive in our area.

1853 - Land auctioned for development in Newcastle.

1854 - Ex-convict William Bramble became the first settler in Pacific Palms.

1855 - First private Land Grants – Nabiac and Coolongolook.

1856 - 1875 Land Grants in Forster/Tuncurry area. Start of earliest fishing and ship building enterprises, as well as expansion of timber milling.

1859 - to 1862 – George Godwin and family, the first settlers at Cape Hawke settlement and then Smiths Lake.

1866 - The Newman family settled in the area.

1869 - 'Minimbar' changed to 'Forster' by William Forster then Minister for Lands.

1870 - The first foreign migrant, Albert von Ehlefeldt, operated a Bakery and General Store and Shop Boat that traded on Wallis Lake.

1872 - First Public School at Forster. George Underwood – Teacher.

1875 - Sugarloaf Point Lighthouse built at Seal Rocks because of past shipwrecks. John Wright, the first settler in Tuncurry, who along with his workmen built the Shipyards, Mill, Church and a School.

1880 - The Sandbar was settled by one of William Bramble's grandsons.

1882 - The Gogerly family arrived and farmed Booti Booti (now known as The Ruins).

1885 - Cape Hawke census of local farms.

1891 - 1952 Forster Aboriginal school operated.

1910 - The Newmans took up land between Smiths Lake and Elizabeth Beach.

1912 - Newcastle city subdivided.

1914 - 1918 World War I.

1928 – Green Hill Farm acquired by Lachlan Fraser.

1930's-The Great Depression.

1937 - Charlotte Bay school opened, at the south eastern corner of Wallis Lake.

1939 – 1945 World War I I.

1946 - Wally Williams had the first shop at Elizabeth Bay.

1950 - Caravan Parks established at Elizabeth Beach, Santa Barbara and Sandbar.

1959 - Pacific Palms named by their local Progress Association.

1959 - Forster/Tuncurry bridge was opened.

1960 - 1970 Sand mining near Seven Mile Beach and upgrade of The Lakes Way.
1960 - Green Point and Smiths Lake subdivision developments started by C.H Degotardi

1962 - Coomba Park subdivision registered with Great Lakes Shire Council by C.H. Degotardi.

A History of Green Point

Introduction

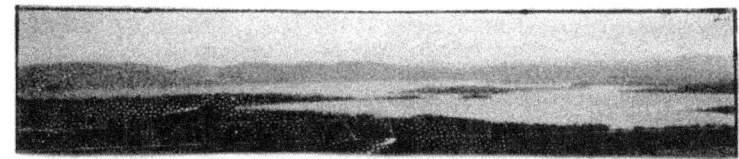

Green Point is a small, picturesque village situated about twelve kilometers south of Forster on the Mid North Coast of New South Wales. The area is beside Wallis Lake to the west and bounded by Booti Booti National Park. Being positioned on a triangular shaped peninsular running out into Wallis Lake, many of its seven hundred or more residents enjoy either beautiful water views of the lake or the unique native bushland nearby.

When driving into Green Point by road, through the coastal forest vegetation of Booti Booti National Park, many varieties of Eucalypts, native trees and under-storey plants can be seen. The most striking are the orange-barked Angophoras which stand out from the green of the forest, especially in the late afternoon light.

The lowland areas of the National Park surrounding the village include a number of important ecological features:- the **wetland**, with its salt marsh areas, and the extensive **sea-grass beds** together with out crops of **mangroves**, (which congregate in places around the edges of the lake and beside the wetland creek), all work together to ensure the growth of new fish stocks and filter the water within the lake. (The sea-grass beds in Wallis Lake account for 20% of the total area of sea-grass growing in NSW. Apart from capturing a large proportion of carbon from the atmosphere, they form a vital part of the lake's ecosystem and are a useful indicator of its environmental health.)

Wet **sclerophyll forest** can be found in low lying areas adjacent to the lake and wetlands. These areas are often dominated by Swamp oaks (Casuarina glauca), and Paperbarks (Melaleucas). Growing beside the lake they help protect the shoreline from wave erosion caused by the action of the strong prevailing winds. Stands of tall Cabbage tree palms (Livistonia australis) can also be found growing close to the lake south of the village.

The **heathland,** situated adjacent to the access road into Green Point, provides a colourful show in springtime with a large variety of flowering native shrubs and wild flowers on display. Being in close proximity to two large swamp areas, the heathland provides a healthy habitat for many native birds and animals, some of which grace the gardens of residents with their presence.

Within the village residential area, many Eucalypts stand tall and proud on the hillside and on ridges, whilst the spreading branches of the very large Port Jackson fig (Ficus rubiginosa moraceae) in Green Point Drive, reminds us of the early days when the area was a dairy farm. This work endeavours to share the history of settlement within the area and how, Green Point in particular, has evolved from earlier farm beginnings – to become the modern residential community it is today!

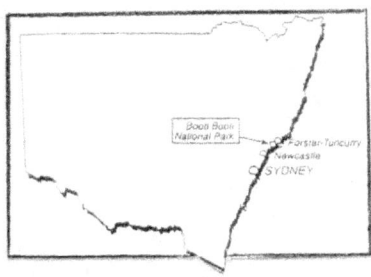

Around 1993 Liz Meadley compiled a report on Green Point as part of her nursing studies. This became the starting point for my investigations. It seemed to be the only history that had been done, to date, on Green Point.

As this previous account was only a brief history, I hoped to find out more details about our area and be able to share with you the more human side of living on the lake and in particular, at Green Point. By visiting the local museum, with its many exhibits and early photographs, I was able to get a feel for how things were in those early days of development. Locally written history books, about the areas around Wallis Lake, whet my appetite for more knowledge.

Learning about other communities around the lake helped place Green Point into perspective. The more I learnt about the past, the more interested I became.

Historical Background

Before European settlement our region was inhabited by the Worimi Aboriginal people and therefore, I acknowledge them as the Traditional Owners of the land on which we stand and also the Worimi elders past and present.

The following is from an extract provided courtesy of Great Lakes Council – Aboriginal History of the Great Lakes District – Narelle Marr 1997: In the Great Lakes district there were two tribes – the Biripi, who inhabited the area between Tuncurry, Taree and Gloucester, and the Worimi who occupied the land between Barrington Tops and Forster in the north and Maitland and the Hunter River in the south. The Worimi were divided into a number of 'nurras'. (nurras were local groups within tribes, each occupying a definite locality within the tribal territory.) The people of Wallis Lake area are called the Wallamba. The Worimi and the Biripi tribes both spoke dialects of the Gattang language. The Aborigines were hunters and gatherers who wandered within their own territory in response to seasonal availability of food so that the land's resources could be naturally replenished e.g. – the coastal tribes would move inland during winter to hunt then back to the coast in spring and early summer to fish.

Captain James Cook noticed the presence of Aboriginals in the Myall Lakes area when he sailed along the coastline in 1770 and named Cape Hawke. However, the first contact that Aborigines had with white people in that area wasn't until 1790, when five convicts escaped from the Second Fleet. They were 'adopted' by Aborigines in the Hawks Nest area, who thought that they were spirits of ancestors who had returned. The convicts lived with them until they were recaptured by Captain William Broughton in 1795. In 1816 cedar getters and their convict servants started arriving in the Myall and Manning areas. Their impact was devastating and caused an early dispersal of the tribes. As a result of this dispersal, the tribal boundaries ceased to be observed and the Biripi and Worimi intermingled and camped in the same territory.

In 1818, Lieutenant John Oxley RN, with surveyor George Evans, Dr John Harris, Charles Fraser (botanist) and party, travelled along the coast from Port Macquarie to Port Stephens, en route to Sydney. After an inland expedition, John Oxley carried a boat from Booti Booti to Boomerang Beach where they spent the night (Lakeland Adventure –a History of the Early Days of Forster/Tuncurry.) Oxley noted that: "The natives are extremely numerous along this part of the coast; these extensive lakes which abound with fish, being extremely favourable to their easy subsistence; large troops of them appear at the beaches while their canoes on the lake are equally numerous. In the mornings, their fires are to be observed in every direction; they evidently appear to shun us, and we wish for no further acquaintance." Oxley named 'Wallis Lake' after the commandant of the penal settlement at Newcastle.

The Cedar Cutters

The cedar cutters and their convict servants arrived in the Hawkesbury River area in 1795 and then the Hunter River area in 1801. It wasn't until 1816 that they ventured up to Port Stephens. The rate of cutting timber intensified from 1817 to 1823. Using suitable anchorages up the coast they systematically sought out the cedar growing areas – cutting down the precious trees for shipment to Sydney; later to be used in furniture making. Cedar trees were scattered throughout much of the Great Lakes area, particularly along the alluvial valleys and in the littoral rainforests along the coastline, but yields were less compared to the major river valleys. Good quality cedar was cut in the vicinity of Bulahdelah and floated to Port Stephens, whilst cedar from the Wollomba Valley was shipped via Nabiac. Little stocks remained and the invading cedar gangs finished by the 1840's. The cedar cutters came, cut the cedar and left – sadly, nothing remains to indicate the importance of cedar cutting as the area's first industry.

The Australian Agricultural Company

In the early days of the colony, the government of the day encouraged settlement up the north coast from Sydney. The Australian Agricultural Company was incorporated by an Imperial Act of the British Parliament, passed in June 1824. Following this a grant of one million acres of Crown Land was approved for the Company's purposes of breeding livestock, establishing a fine wool industry and cultivating crops. The Colonial committee recommended that the grant be obtained in the vicinity of Port Stephens where the availability of a deep water port addressed their concerns regarding transport. Land was selected from Port Stephens to the Manning River in the north and westward from the coast to include the Karuah River and Gloucester River valleys.

The first settlement at Carrington on the northern shore of Port Stephens was established in 1826. Despite the accomplishments of the establishment years the Port Stephens venture was not successful. The soils were of poor quality and agricultural efforts moved north to Booral and Stroud areas. Attempts, initiated in 1830 to surrender the eastern section of approximately five hundred thousand acres in favour of Peel River and Warrah Estates, were approved in 1833. A little over half of this remaining land lay within the present Great Lakes Council area. Much of the grant, particularly the coastal area, reverted to the Crown after a report done by Sir William Edward Perry who surveyed the area in 1830.

The original intention of the AAC was to produce fine wool for Britain's woollen mills, as their main supplier Germany was scaling back production in favour of industrialization. However, the humid coastal climate and inbreeding brought the industry to an end after thirty years. In 1856, the entire flocks from the Port Stephens Estates were moved to the Tamworth area and the Company's headquarters moved from Stroud to Sydney. The sale of land by the AAC for small holdings began after 1860.

The Land Act of 1861 permitted selection of land before it was surveyed and it wasn't long before settlers started to move up north following the rivers and coastal lakes.

(Great Lakes Council Heritage Study 2007)

The First Settlers

George Garlick Godwin had come from England as an emigrant by sailing-ship around 1856 and settled in Gosford. The family travelled from Gosford, blazing their own trail, particularly as they came northwards from Bulahdelah. In 1862 he became the first white man to settle with his family in the Forster area.

The trip north took three months. He was accompanied by his wife and five children. They travelled, with all their possessions in a bullock dray pulled by six bullocks, as well as two saddle horses and five cows. At Bulahdelah a calf was born. It was too valuable to leave behind so it travelled in the dray with the family.

After building on the site, where today it is marked by a Pioneer's Monument and plaque (at the corner of Macintosh and Stanley Streets in Forster), Godwin built a cow paddock for his stock and began a garden to grow crops. He found the Aborigines were friendly and he showed them how to grow corn and till the garden. Later, he taught them how to split shingles and palings. For income, he sent bags of oysters and wild honey to Sydney. Godwin got on so well with the Aboriginals that they called him 'Cohban', meaning 'good fellow'.

During this time the Aboriginals were treated kindly. They migrated towards the settlement, began to learn the white man's ways and language and were employed in many tasks in exchange for food. However, this migration reduced the numbers of Aborigines following a traditional life-style, especially around the lakes.

In 1862, he took up a land grant at Smiths Lake and built a house at Wamwarra. It is thought that Elizabeth Beach was named after one of his daughters. He had fifteen children and the sixth child, Harriet Cape Godwin, was the first white child to be born in Forster.

Harriet later married John Newman who operated the last pulling boat service between Forster and Tuncurry and started the first motor boat service. (Lakeland Adventure – A History of the Early Days of Forster/Tuncurry)

As small settlements developed three mills were built at Bungwahl. Bullock trains needed as many as 20 animals to haul the heavy logs out of the forests. Smaller teams were also used for general transport, both for people and goods. The thriving community provided employment for hundreds of men, either at the mills or in the forests, cutting and transporting the logs. Many families derived an income from the sale of the trees on their property. The prized timber was used in building construction, power poles, railway sleepers and ship building.

Godwin's Bullock Teams

The Godwin Family

George Garlick Godwin & wife Mary Ann

Coach and launch, The Bay Creek

Early Development

During the 1870's Albert von Ehlefeldt, a German migrant, owned and operated the Wallis Lake and Wallamba River shop boat. He also owned a bakery and general store. The boat's shallow draught enabled it to journey to the upper reaches of the waterways for trade with the early settlers. He married Minnie Underwood and they had four children. His shop boat used to be moored in Little Street, Forster. 'The Ehlefeldt Reserve' near the lakeside swimming pool, now honours his past contributions to our area. ('Past Days around Wallis Lake, its Rivers and Villages' - compiled by John Doust, Great Lakes Advocate.)

As Forster grew in population, stores, churches and a school were built. The first Provisional School in Forster was opened in May 1872. It started with only 27 children, but quickly the attendance grew to 30; which meant that the school could then be converted to a 'Public School' and George Underwood became its first teacher. The original school was built on the site of the present day camping ground below Pilot Hill and west of the Forster Surf Club parking area.

The first settler in Tuncurry was John Wright in 1875. He built a timber mill by Wallis Lake. The logs were transported across the lake by barge to his large mill. A ship building industry soon developed and supplied boats for the needs of the people.

By 1878 there was a route through Bulahdelah to Coolongolook and down to the jetty at Charlotte Bay. This route carried mail and supplied to homesteads around the lake and took butter and other produce back. ('In and About Pacific Palms' by Anne & George McKay)

In 1882, John Frederick Gogerly and his family settled at Booti Booti (close to where Tiona is situated today).

Remembering a bush walk, which I did with neighbours years ago, I recall coming across some pioneer grave stones hidden in the undergrowth. We had hiked from The Ruins at Tiona over the coastal track to Elizabeth Beach and back, via the edge of the lake. The grave stones are situated about 200 metres south of The Ruins and well worth a visit. The area is now administered by the National Parks & Wildlife Service.

Later, when compiling this, I decided to look again and get more information as to who were buried there. Luckily the ranger had recently mown the area and the plaques were easier to find.

These details emerged:

Cpt. John F Gogerly	Edward Gogerly	John Burdett Gogerly	Ethel Gogerly	Albert Lionel Gogerly
Drowned 1-8-1905	died in infancy	20-9-1915	4-4-1994	28-9-1910
Aged 61 yrs	1884	22-12-1982	aged 32	25-8-1989
				A 3rd Generation Son of Booti Booti

On my behalf Annette Bramble kindly asked Noel Gogerly about the family resting place.

Apparently, not all are grave stones, two being Memory Plaques ...possibly John Burdett Albert and Lionel Gogerly.

Gogerly's Family Farm

Gogerly's Boatshed Booti Booti

Mrs. June Wright, in her book *'History of Forster'*, gives us an insight into the background of the 'Gogerly' family.

"Charles and Charlotte Gogerly moved from Sydney to Port Hacking in 1844, where they raised their two sons John Frederick and William. Opportunities for a career were rather rare at that time and place, but the Gogerly boys grew up to harvest and live from the waters. With a homemade boat they fished and harvested the shell heaps of the Aboriginal middens, taking the shell out to sea and up to the lime kilns at Milsons Point in Sydney Harbour, where the shell was burned to produce lime to use in mortar of Sydney's buildings.

According to the quarterly bulletin of the Sutherland Historical Society, a Captain Collin and hand Massey, came to the port to also gather shell in 1856, when they were approached by the Gogerly lads who told them of a giant hairy man in the area called 'Yahoo', in an attempt to scare these intruders, for the boys considered the shell of Port Hacking as their preserve. Both lads graduated to superb mariners through the experiences they had gained, and sailed trading and timber gathering vessels along the coast and even to some Pacific Islands. It was on one of such trips that William was caught in a heavy gale and lost at sea.

Eventually in 1882 after the death of his father, John Frederick came north and selected land beside Booti Booti Hill, between Wallis Lake and Elizabeth Beach, a very isolated spot in those days and accessed only by sea. As the Captain was fast wedded to the sea one can well imagine the lonely life his wife and children led, where their only visitors were the occasional Aboriginal group bartering fish for tea and sugar, flour and tobacco.

Captain Gogerly was very confident of his seamanship and the story is told that on one occasion the 'Venture' was anchored fully laden off Elizabeth Beach when the weather began to deteriorate. The only course that could be taken was to up anchor and run bare-poled before it, and as the storm worsened to quite a blow...and indeed it was a memorable one, being 5th May 1898...'The Maitland Storm' as it was called, the Captain sent his companion into the hold, and wrapping himself in oilskins against the weather tied himself to the tiller, and fought the storm for 3 days. Time passed and when the little boat did not return people began to mourn the passing of Captain Gogerly. It was a fortnight later that he sailed back to the coast into Coffs Harbour and eventually Cape Hawke. He was still in possession of his full cargo, to the amazement of the locals. When complimented on his escape he replied 'There's not enough water in the Pacific Ocean to drown me."

However, on 1/8/1905, whilst sailing home with supplies from Forster, in his small boat the St. George, the Captain suffered an apparent heart attack and died. He was only 61 years old. Local fishermen used a 1,000 metre hauling net run across the bay to retrieve the Captain's body. (Noel Gogerly) "After the Captain's death, Mrs. Gogerly staunchly carried on with the farm, raising one daughter and five sons". - 'History of Forster' by Mrs. June Wright. Since this unfortunate incident, the bay south of Smokehouse beach – near Green Point, has been referred to by local fishermen as Dead Man's Bay. (Greg Golby)

Captain John Frederick Gogerly 1843-1905

By 1910, the Godwin family ran a transport business and from old photographs, their passenger coaches resembled that of the Cobb & Co. lines. In their book 'In & About the Pacific Palms', Anne and George McKay wrote that *"Advertisements told of the advantages of a trip by boat and coach from Sydney and Port Stephens to Taree, via the lakes. From Tea Gardens, passenger launches would take people to Bombah Point and then on to Bungwahl, where they would alight and take a 5-horse coach, owned by J.A. Godwin (son of George Godwiin), to get across the 8 miles to Charlotte Bay. Just past Bungwahl they could stop for lunch at Godwin's accommodation house. After skirting the shores of Smiths Lake, they would arrive at Charlotte Bay and re-embark on another launch, to travel to Forster, or just return on the same route, again enjoying the lake's voyage. After crossing from Forster to Tuncurry, the passengers would continue on to Taree by coach."*

As the fishing, timber and ship building industries flourished around Wallis Lake, more cattle and dairy farms developed.

In her book 'History of Forster', Mrs. June Wright gives us details of some early farmers, taken from the 1885 Census, as listed by the Legislative Assembly. The following farms are by no means the total mentioned, but those included will give an insight to the size of the properties and the names of the pioneers.

James Hadley had 100 acres at Bennett's Head. George Underwood, the local school teacher, had 100 acres called 'Sea View'. Later his eldest son set up a dairy on the eastern slopes of Reservoir Hill, down from where the Pioneer Estate is set today. An abattoir was east of the present day golf clubhouse and from there they retailed meat to the public and milk from the dairy. Out at the Hawke, in the valley between the 'two hillocks' as Cook described them, ran Dunn's Creek. Along the northern bank, Thomas Dunn held 100 acres, but being a sick man was not actively farming, merely occupying the place for the owner Tom McBride who finally took it over in 1888. Meanwhile, he was in charge of transport for the Hudson Bros. mill at Narani, and was living at Tarbuck Brush on 10 acres. His 20 horses were no doubt used to tow the trolleys along the rail lines, used to transport the timber up around Booti Booti, to Smiths Lake. William Mulconey held 40 acres on the Hawke and William Fraser held 20 acres. Robert and Thomas Dun grazed large herds of cattle, Robert holding 549 acres at Coomba Coomba (as he called it). Further south at Burrah Beak, Thomas Dun held 1,220 acres.

Back in Forster, John Wylie Breckenridge took over the 40 acres of George Garlick Godwin, on the Mark Street corner. George Godwin meanwhile, having moved to Wamwarra on Smiths Lake, held 120 acres.

Closer to our area and south of the town boundaries Johnathon Piper still held the original 40 acres, selected by his father in 1864 and had five horses, six cows and four pigs. John McQueen, his next-door neighbour, held a total of 680 acres. He had eight horses, fifty head of cattle and six pigs.

In later years, around 1890, Harriet McQueen adopted Agnes Cameron, who later inherited the farm. Agnes married Harry John Mathias and they had 5 children, including Owen Mathias. (O. Mathias).

As previously mentioned, in the 1885 Census records, George Underwood, the local School Teacher, had a 100 acre farm called 'Sea View' east of Forster. Later on, his son J.A Underwood set up a dairy, an abattoir and a butcher's shop. Map No.1 shows that J.A. Underwood owned land at Green Point. According to a family member, this land was used as a grazing area for the cattle before being driven to the Sea View farm. A holding paddock was situated where Baronia Park netball area is today. The cattle were sent to the abattoir for processing and the meat was later sold through the retail butcher's shop, which was situated in the vicinity of Little and Mark Streets, in Forster. (Ted Underwood).

Green Hill Farm

Our area was known as Green Hill; because from the water it stood out as a 'green hill'. All the timber had been cleared out years before and the area was covered in green grass. Little Green Hill was the name for Shepherd Island at that time. Tom Ryan, a long time Green Point resident, used to fish the lake in the 1950's and remembers how unusual it looked compared with surrounding countryside. According to Liz Meadley's 'History of Green Point', records dated June 1928 (map1) show that J.A. Underwood, the London Bank of Australia Limited, the E.S.& A. Bank and Lachlan Fraser, owned the area. J.A. Underwood sold the land to the bank who in turn sold it to Lachlan Fraser. Lachlan's father Thomas, and mother Sarah Beatrice, also had another son Tom and a daughter Gladys. Their farm was closer to Forster called 'One Tree Hill' and backed onto Burgess Beach. Lachlan named his new farm 'Green Hill'.

When I mentioned to a neighbour that I was attempting to do the history of our area, he suggested that I contact his old friend Owen. In the past, Owen Mathias used to live on a farm near Piper's Bay. In the 1930's he became a close friend of Lachlan Fraser. When interviewing Owen, I found him to be a wealth of information as to what the farm was like in the earlier days. Owen, in turn, referred me to another old friend, Chum Bramble who could help with follow-up details after 1940, when Owen went to serve in World War ll.

In the past (around 1870) our area was held by J.A. Underwood, the son of George Underwood, who was the first school teacher in Forster. It was used as a holding paddock for cattle. They were later taken into Forster for slaughter and sale from their butcher's shop. (Ted Underwood).

Lachlan was around 30 years old when he started work on his 'Green Hill' dairy farm. It was only one of many scattered around Wallis Lake. Lachlan was a strong, well-built man and although he was born with a clubfoot, he was an experienced, capable and extremely resourceful farmer. He was able to achieve a good productive farm, from very limited resources. (Owen Mathias) Bev. Bramble and Noel Gogerly both agreed Lachlan Fraser was a big powerful bloke and Bud Degotardi said that he was a great chap to talk to and very kind. Apart from his close friendships with Owen Mathias and Chum Bramble, he also had many long lasting friendships with the local fishermen and farmers.

The chosen position for Lachlan's first dwelling was on the high side of the hill, where Seabreeze Parade and Green Point Drive presently come together. The building faced north and was built on wooden piers low to the ground. It was clad in weather boards and had a corrugated iron roof. There were only two rooms – a bedroom and a dining room. It had a 1,000 gallon rainwater tank and a corrugated iron chimney. Lachlan would wash up at a bench outside near the water tank. There were only two windows in the building. Trees on farms were usually kept to a minimum, but as the harsh southerly wind blew towards the little dwelling on the hill Lachlan chose to allow saplings to grow as a windbreak. (Owen Mathias) Some of these magnificent trees still stand today on the southern side of the hill in Green Point Drive.

The first entrance to the farm was near the turn off to Camellia Place. Charlie Bramble remembers there was evidence of a slip-rail gate being there. Also, Ernie Steel had mentioned this to me years ago. Owen Mathias said that Lachlan had increased his land holdings to include the flats on the southern side of Green Point Drive. Although poor land, this gave him more grazing area in times of drought. In the late 1990's and early 2000's evidence of farm fences, down where the chicane is today, showed that this was probably the entrance to the farm in later years.

A History of Green Point

Green Hill Farm 1928

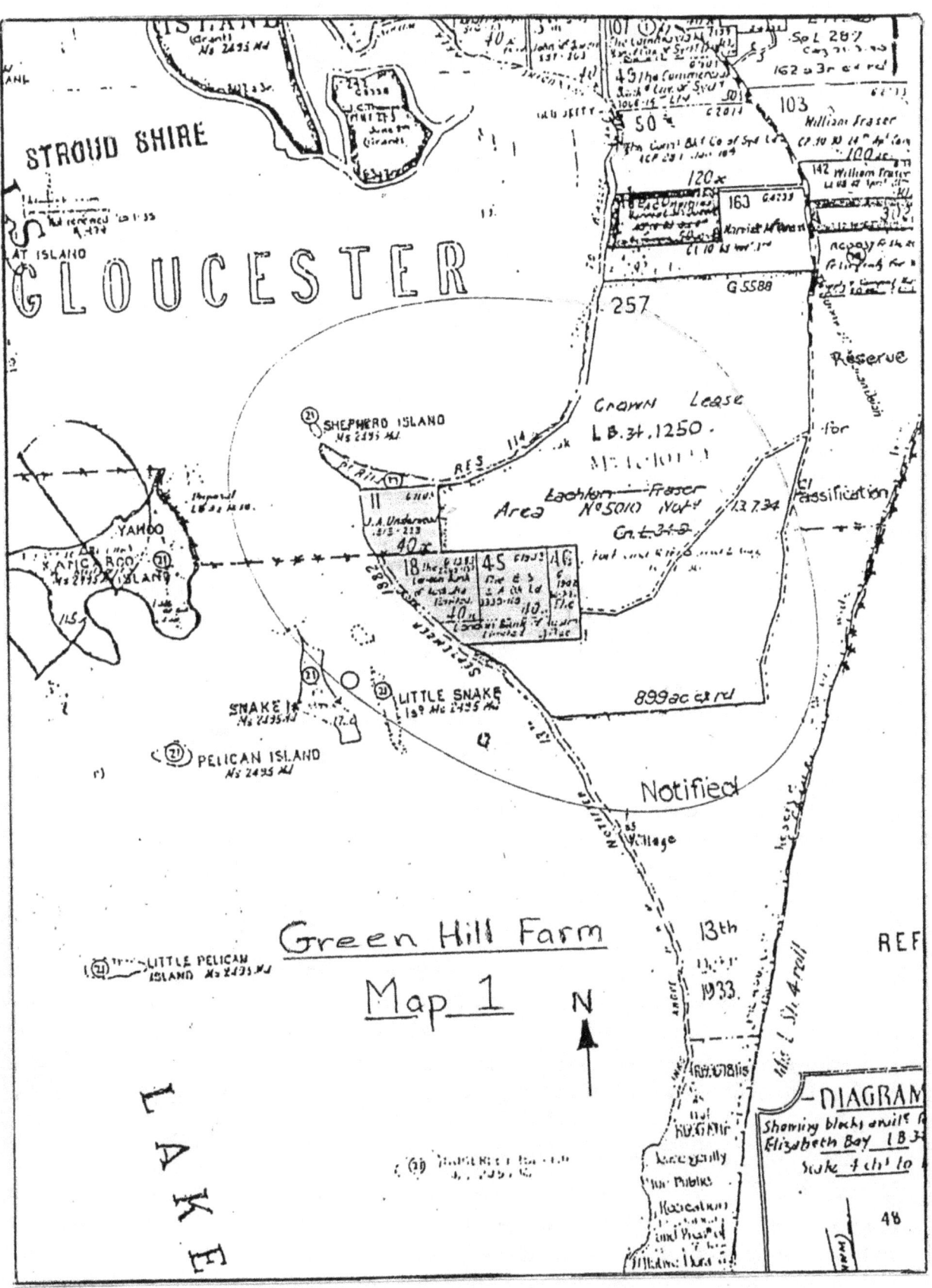

After visiting Green Point, Owen Mathias remarked that the road in, being the present Green Point Drive, didn't go directly up to the farmhouse on the hill but deviated to the southern side. In rainy weather seepage from the hillside made travel with horse and sulky difficult, so the roadway was made a little further over on higher ground. As the ground became firmer towards the hill, the road started to line up with the entrance to the dwelling.

Around 1985, I remember at least two very large round posts standing on the high-side footpath at the corner of Seabreeze Parade and Green Point Drive. When I asked Max Burroughs, who lived nearby, whether he remembered them being there he remarked that he had got sick of mowing around them, so removed them. Possibly they would have been the gate posts in front of the dwelling. In order to have a productive dairy farm, Lachlan Fraser would have had to secure all the fences on the property. Owen Mathias said that most of the fences were posts with wire threaded through them, but where necessary post and rail fences were constructed. Charlie Bramble's dad told him years ago that in the 1940's a top fencer would do a four post and rails in one day.

In the 1990's there were a number of post and rail fences still remaining in Green Point. The most memorable were the ones which were outside the entrance of the Green Point Gallery. Owen Mathias told me that the yards nearby were constructed by Lachlan Fraser and so probably accounted for the fencing being available. Owen added that fences were made using an adze and cut from local wood as they suited the conditions. Chum Bramble said that Corkwood and Angophora were used.

The Chicken Run

In order to find out whether there were any buildings or dams marked on the old maps of the farm property, I visited Lidbury, Summers & Whiteman at Forster, the firm of surveyors which held details of developments run by C.H. Degotardi but unfortunately the map records showed no marked buildings or dams.

When speaking with the office receptionist, Robin Wilcox, I found that she had bought land in Green Point around the mid 1980's As Owen Mathias had mentioned that Lachlan Fraser had kept chickens in the vicinity of where her block was situated, I asked if she remembered any evidences which would substantiate the presence of a fowl yard. Robin stated that, at the end of her block, there was a shed, rolls of chicken wire, old bolts, bits of corrugated metal and a pile of old palings. This was confirmed by Col McPherson and Annette Bramble. The 'chicken run' would have been close to where lot 56 or street No.112 in Seabreeze Parade is today.

Owen Mathias later explained that 5ft. palings were used to board up the fowl-house around the base, whilst the chicken wire was put around the top. This was done to keep the foxes out. Lachlan's two cattle dogs also protected the chickens from the foxes. A stand of gum trees nearby gave shade. In later years when the gums grew very large the trees were either cut down or removed, as houses were built close by. The large chicken run held 50-60 brown leghorns, mostly bred for producing eggs, but the roosters were killed for food or sold.

Once a week Lachlan harnessed his cream mare to the sulky and drove into Forster to sell his produce. He drove via the wetlands track as it was shorter and easier to negotiate. Sand from the sand dunes along Seven Mile Beach used to blow over the road (The Lake Way), and at times made travel impossible, so the track across the moors (as it used to be referred to) became a better option. This track left the northern side of Green Point Drive, near the first hill past the chicane and proceeded at an angle to come out where the Booti sell his produce. He drove via the wetlands track as it was shorter and easier to negotiate. Sand from the sand dunes along Seven Mile Beach used to blow over the road (The Lake Way), and at times made travel impossible, so the track across the moors (as it used to be referred to) became a better option. This track left the northern side of Green Point Drive, near the first hill past the chicane and proceeded at an angle to come out where the Booti Booti National Park sign stands on the Lakes Way.

The First Farm Dwelling

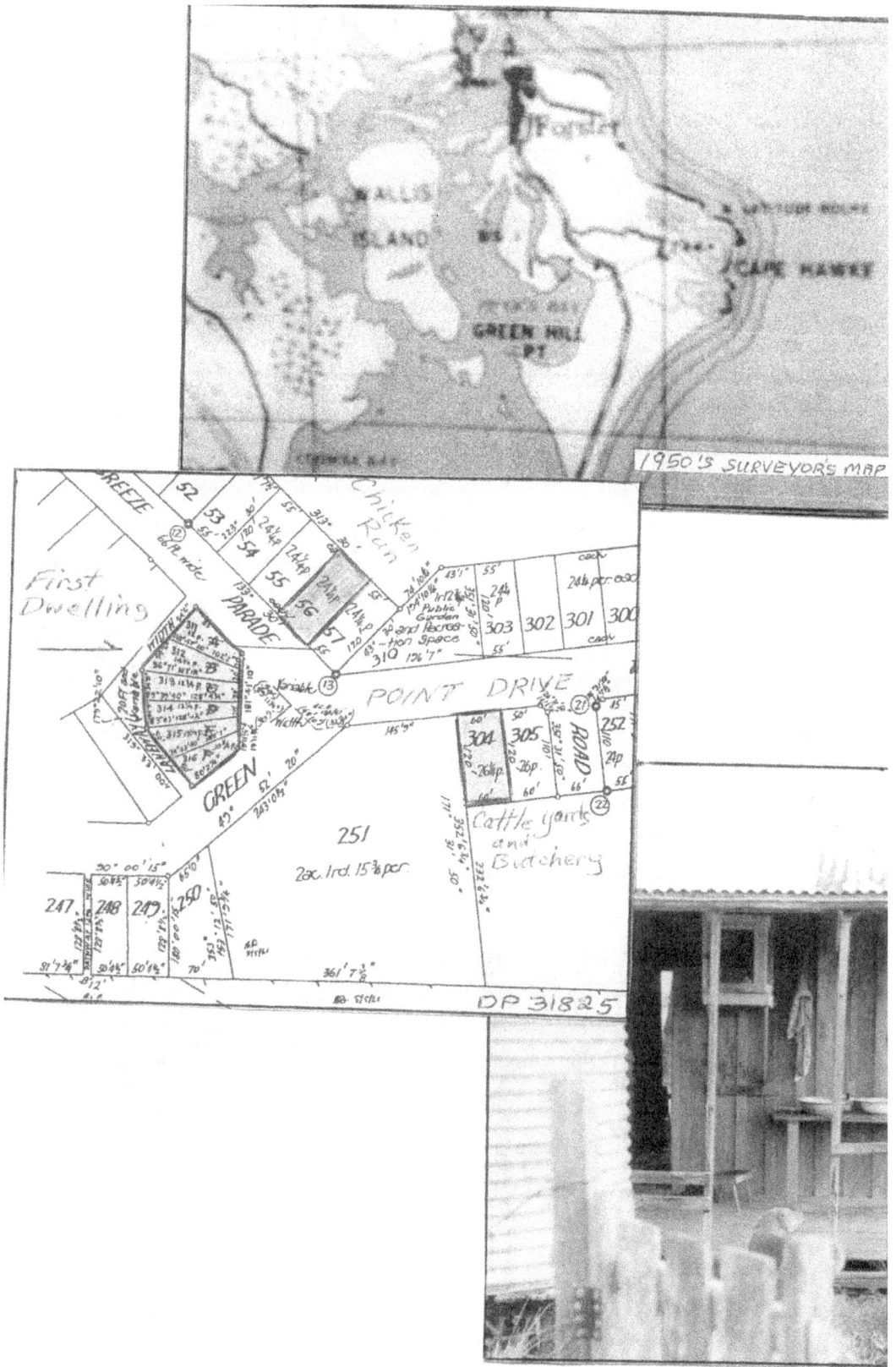

The Orchard

In the late 1980's and early 1990's evidence of cultivated terraces could be seen where the orchard used to be on the slopes of the hillside. They ran parallel to where Seabreeze Parade is today.

Owen Mathias remembered that in the early days Lachlan Fraser grew a large variety of lovely fruit trees – mostly citrus and stone fruit, plus at least one quince tree. He said that most of the fruit was eaten, shared with others, or preserved. Remainders were given to the pigs. Chum Bramble remembers that in poor times the fruit helped supplement a farmer's meagre income.

By the 1950's the fruit trees had become neglected and mainly bush lemons survived. By the 1960's Charlie Bramble recalled seeing mostly lemons and a few peach trees.

Lowell Reardon, a long time resident, explained to me that any wild lemons seen around Green Point would have been throw-backs from the grafted stock. They often have lumpy skins and the branches may have thorns. Some of these old lemon trees remain on properties in Green Point Drive.

The Market Garden

Lachlan Fraser, like most farmers of his time, was self sufficient growing what produce he required. Owen Mathias remembers that Lachlan also kept bees for honey and making mead wine. He had a very productive vegetable garden and practised crop rotation. His garden was located on the flats, behind the dairy building. Draft horses were used for ploughing the sandy loam soil on the north end of the flats – on the low side of where Seabreeze Parade is today. It was a large vegetable growing area of around 4-5 acres for the cultivation of pumpkins, melons, potatoes and tomatoes. Corn (maize) was grown to feed the fowls. Pumpkins were grown to sell in Forster. The rocky area on the top of the hill was no good for crops. Bill Legge was quite young when the farm was in existence. He said that Lachlan was a 'great gardener' and remembers him growing 3ft long watermelons. These were smashed up and fed to the cows who really relished them as an addition to their everyday diet. .

The pigpen was situated close by and discarded produce and watermelons were fed to the pigs. Some vegetable crops were grown for stock feed. Before 1938 a Mulboard plough was used and later a disc plough. (Owen Mathias)

Ploughing the Paddock

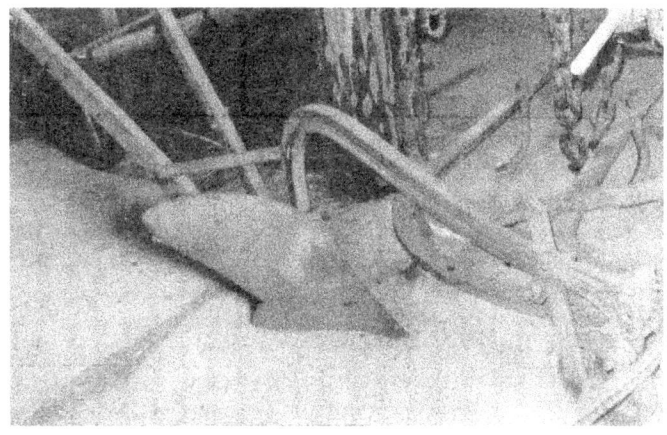

Meat Supplies

As was usual for the times, Lachlan Fraser was a subsistence farmer as well as a dairyman. In the event of him needing to supply his own meat, he built a post and rail holding yard with an adjacent slaughter area and butchery.

The butchery was situated behind the Green Point Gallery building. Unfortunately no evidence of this facility can be seen there today. Only the concrete pad remains which was situated beneath the two tall posts where the animals were butchered. It is obvious that shells from the nearby midden had been used in the concrete mix. (Dr. Margaret Gibbons and Lowell Reardon).

In order to have a selection of meat to eat, Lachlan Fraser, like most farmers, bred a few pigs. He kept one boar and two sows. The pig shelter was made from the trunks of strong Cabbage tree palms and the pen was situated down the hill below the dairy shed in the vicinity of what is now No.102 Seabreeze Parade.

Separated or skimmed milk formed the basis of the 'slops', which were fed to the pigs. Discarded vegetables, from the nearby market garden, were added to the feed.

When the pigs were slaughtered, selected cuts would be cooked and eaten, pickled in salted brine, or cured for bacon and ham at the Co-operative Bacon Factory at Wingham. Anything left over was sold or shared with friends.

Unwanted young vealers and yearling steers were either slaughtered for food, or sold to the butchery. Lachlan Fraser, like most of the early farmers, lived off the land. Some of his stock was selected for food and killed accordingly. Farmers of that era knew all about quartering their animals for meat and butchering them to get the best use from the carcasses. Lachlan would have fresh meat for 2 days and the rest would be salted. At times the larger animals would be shared with others.

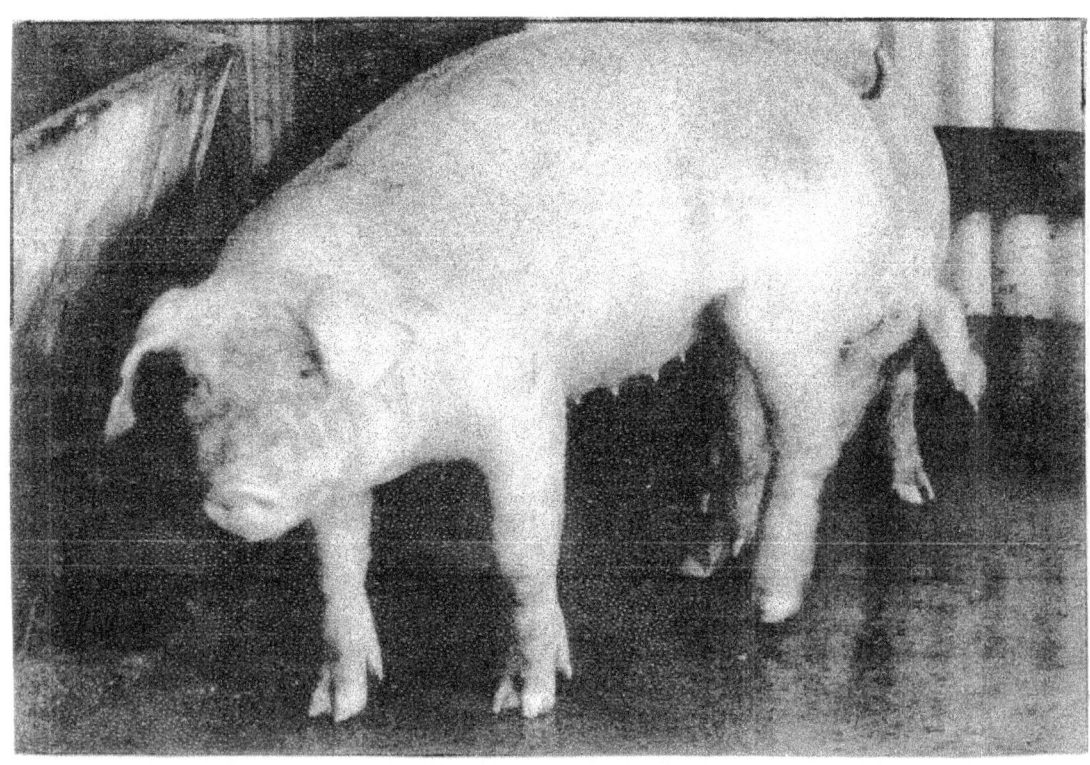

The Draft Horses, The Mare and the Gelding.

In early times the use of the draft horse was a necessary part of farming life. Lachlan Fraser used his team of two Clydesdale-cross draft horses to work on the farm as they are easier to manage.

They helped him to clear scrub, form roads from tracks, haul timber for fences, scoop out dams and batter the edges and pull the plough in the market garden.

Apart from all this work, they were necessary to pull the heavy wooden slide which carried the milk and cream cans from the dairy down to the jetty.

Lachlan's favourite was a lovely cream coloured mare who was harnessed up to a light sulky when needed. The sulky was driven into Forster each Friday, so that Lachlan could sell his farm eggs and other home-grown produce. When not working, all the horses congregated close to the side of the original small farm house building to shelter from the elements as there was no stable as such. (Owen Mathias)

In recent years, residents who lived close to this area, reported finding, when digging in their gardens, harness buckles, bits of bridles, stirrups and various sized horseshoes as evidence of this past activity. (Max Burroughs and Norman Moore).

Owen Mathias was only a lad when he first came over from this home farm in Piper's Bay to visit Lachlan Fraser. He would ride over on his chestnut gelding, called 'Joker'. Sometimes Joker would put the rails down and walk around to Green Hill farm just to enjoy the company of the other horses – mainly the little cream mare! Lachlan borrowed Joker a few times to work on the farm. Owen continued to visit Lachlan and a lasting friendship ensued. When Joker became old and felt his time had come, he left his home paddock for the last time and walked slowly from Pipers Bay towards Green Hill farm – finally passing away close to the other horses and his farmer friend. (Owen Mathias).

Water, Dams and Springs

As the property was used as a holding paddock for cattle in the past, we can presume that some form of water supply existed. Ross Kneebone advised that in the mid 1980's, there was evidence of an old dam out in the bush directly north from the end of what is now Bottlebrush Close. It may have been used by cattle in the 'bush paddocks' when Crown Land was leased by farmers, during lean times.

Lachlan Fraser had his rain-water tank beside his home for drinking water, but water was also needed for the horses, the dairy herd and to be used in mixing concrete. Fortunately, Lachlan was an accomplished water-diviner and used his skill on his own farm and for his fellow farmers by using a willow stick. This stick would twist or bend when he found water. He could not only tell the depth of the water, but also the way in which it flowed.

The larger of the two dams on the farm was located in the wetland out from what is presently Waratah Close. This earthen dam still collects seepage water. Owen went on to explain that it was general practice for draft horses to be used in the construction of dams. Using a horse-drawn scoop, the soil was dragged out and built up around the side edges. Later, a log would be dragged up and over the banks and together with the horses hooves, the dam wall would be packed down firmly. Once they had dug below the water table the water would seep up through the sand into the dam. As there was no fresh water creek running through the farm, other means of securing a water supply had to be found. The semicircular shape of the ridge, running through the property and the lowlands below, formed the perfect catchment area. The prevailing winds brought rain, which ran down the hillside and could be collected in dams.

Around 1990, when out walking, I noticed a dam site at what is now No. 42 Seabreeze Parade. It had become a boggy area filled with Bull-rushes, long grasses and She-oak saplings. Clearly rain water had been diverted into the dam from the steep hillside of what is now Frazer Avenue. A low rock wall ran across the property adjacent to No.40 Seabreeze Parade and an area of concrete, like an apron, adjoined it, presumably to allow the cattle to access the dam safely. It was evident at that time, that rocks had been dug out from the hillside opposite, to build the wall. A low corrugated iron shed was positioned on the flat area in front of where the rocks had been taken. Originally it may have housed a petrol-driven pump. Bill Deeley's home at 40 Seabreeze Parade, was built up on metal poles with a brick entrance room in the centre. Bill utilized the concrete area for an underneath space. Since then, the downstairs area has been closed in, a shed built and lawn grown over the backyard concrete. The land at No. 42 Seabreeze Parade was built up and well drained before the house was built.

Adjacent to Bill Legge's property at No. 20 Seabreeze Parade, there was a 6ft by 8ft concrete structure built around a spring-fed well. When the spare block was levelled and drained, equipment broke up the concrete structure so that it is no longer visible. Bill said the concrete wall would have kept the cattle away from the well. To this day that area remains soggy after heavy rain.

Natural springs occurred on the farm and were used to the best advantage. One was reported to be like a small fountain. It was situated where the Rural Fire Brigade grounds are today. John Mauger said that it was directly across the street from his home at No.107 Green Point Drive. When mowing the area in the early 1990's Bob Currans noticed that the ground around the Jacaranda tree was always damp. Later the tree was removed to make way for the Fire Hall driveway.

In recent times many residents have found evidence of springs on their properties. It was usually when they started to build their homes and cut into the hillside. It seemed that the underground water followed the rocky ridge and could be found leaking into under-house foundation areas, and as a result drainage being required to divert the water away. As some present day residents living on the flats have bore water to supply their gardens, we can expect that Lachlan had some bores installed. Even though the water would have been slightly brackish, it was deemed adequate for growing plants.

Charlie Bramble remembered a concrete edged tank being at the bottom of the hill behind No.98 Seabreeze Parade. Lowell Reardon said that there was a round tank positioned at the corner junction of four paddocks on the flats. An original corrugated iron water tank was cemented around the sides to make it more secure. Considering the scarcity of fresh running water Lachlan Fraser proved to be a very enterprising farmer indeed.

The First Jetty

The track to the jetty went along a similar route as Seabreeze Parade takes today, but a little higher up the hillside. Lachlan Fraser built the original jetty out from the little beach area at what is now known as the Foreshore Reserve. It went for about 75 yards out to the deeper channel, with a planked walkway about 3ft wide and piers cut from local timber. At the end of the jetty there were two tall posts for mooring visiting boats, and a small metal shed to shade the cream cans from the sun. (Owen Mathias) One could imagine that it was quite similar to the one in this photograph, with the walkway and his skiff tied up at the end

Second Farmhouse and Outbuildings

As time went by Lachlan was able to have his second dwelling built adjacent to his productive orchard. It was located further along the present day Seabreeze Parade at Lot No. 157 or Street No. 83. It would appear that Percy Myers, the Forster/Tuncurry joiner, built the dairy farm. The farmhouse was enclosed with a light wire fence. Lachlan was a rough and ready man with simple needs. He had two chairs inside his living room and didn't mind having fibro lining on the inside walls. Outside, there was an 8'x10' concreted area for the water tank, a wash stand and copper for doing the washing. The wood pile, for his fire, was further up the back because of the threat of white ants.

Lachlan's sister, Gladys, married David Pratt in 1933 and as the new farmhouse was now built, the first dwelling became available for them to live in. Dave worked as a labourer on the farm and Gladys helped out with the household chores. Some time later they left and went to live in Forster. The first dwelling then became the barn. The wooden floor kept the sacks of chicken food, grain, stock feed and farming equipment dry.

Across the road from the farmhouse was a lean-to utility shed. Lachlan was very inventive. He taught himself to weld and with Owen's help, made two forges out of bits of old farm machinery. One was made from an old milk separator and a handle from an Alfa Savel ploughshare. A twisted piece of metal was made into a fan blade and put onto the bowl-holder, forcing the air through the spout. When Owen was 16 years old, he was paid 20 shillings for shoeing a draft horse - a lot of backbreaking work for such little reward! (Owen Mathias)

The remains of an old post is the only evidence that I can find these days of the dairy being in the area of No,102 Seabreeze Parade. Around 1992 there was an old diesel engine block on this vacant land close to the street. Lowell Reardon remembered it and told me that as it appeared to be very old it was possibly part of the early farm machinery. Around 1992, another relic from farming days gone by is what appears to be a brake pad off an old dray - Bob Currans unearthed it whilst levelling and mowing the oval area at the Green Point Park.

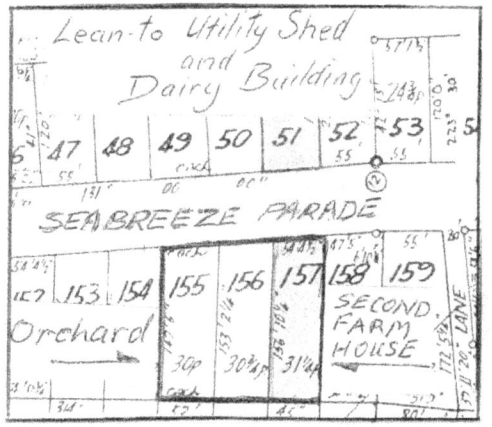

A Typical Farm Utility Shed

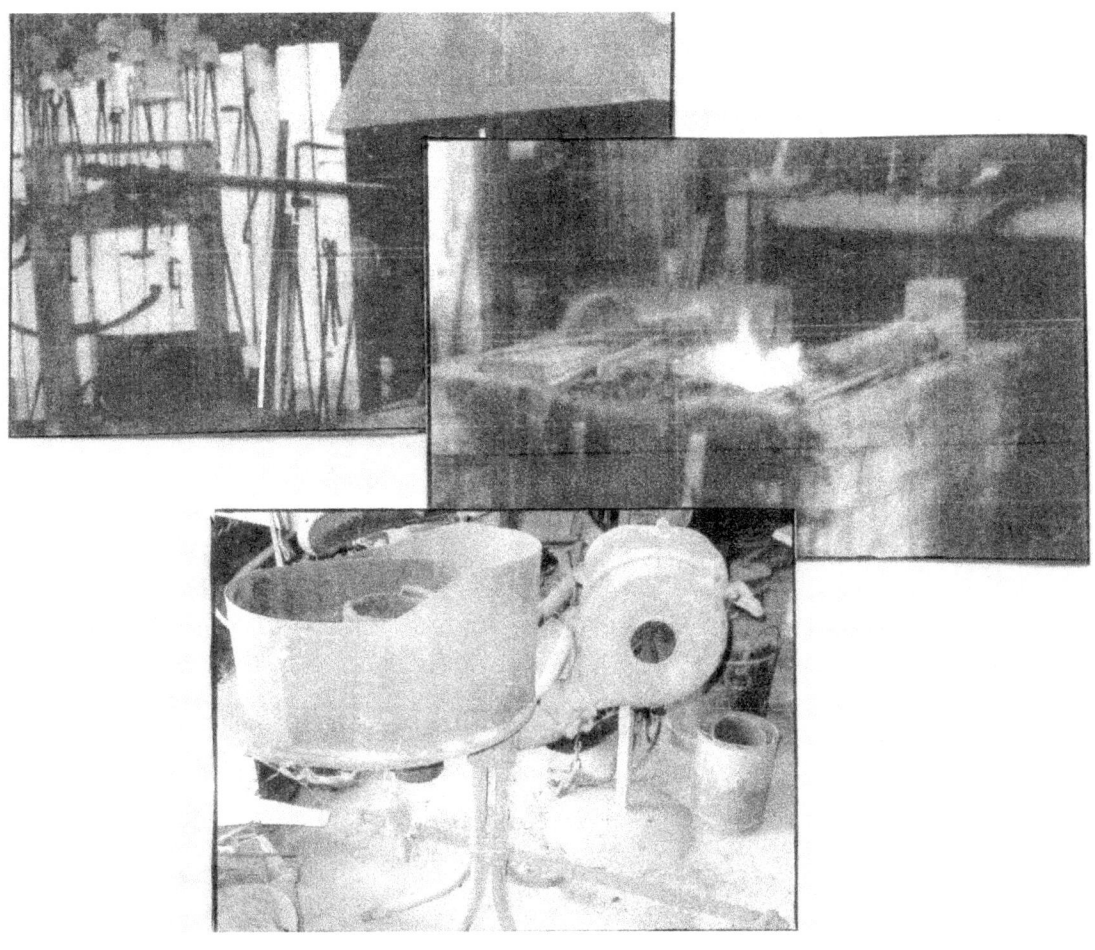

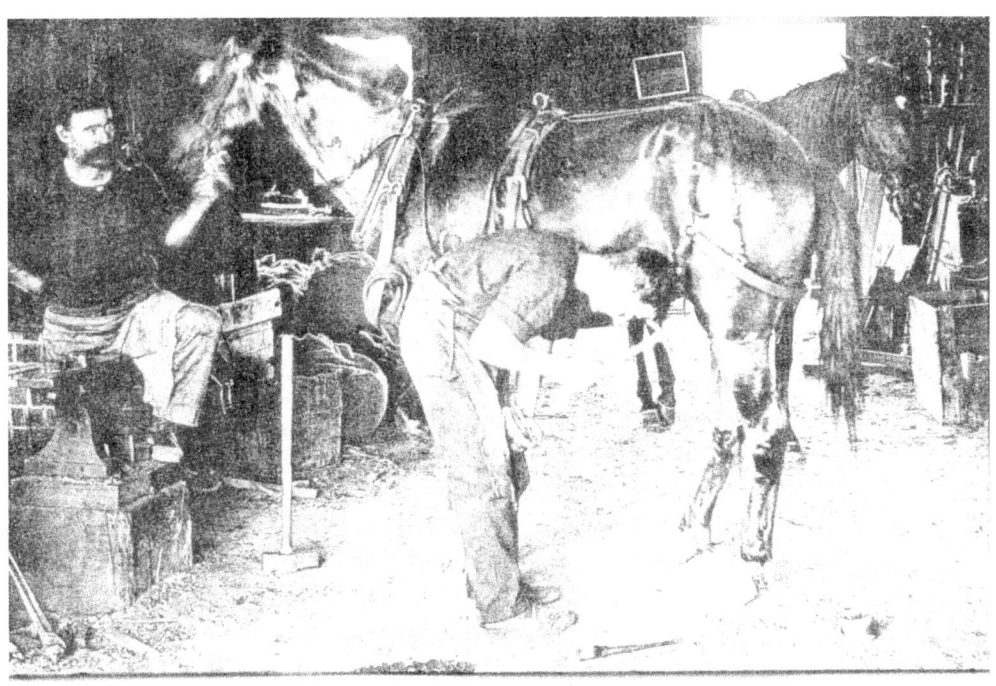

A History of Green Point
.... Horse Bridles & Collars

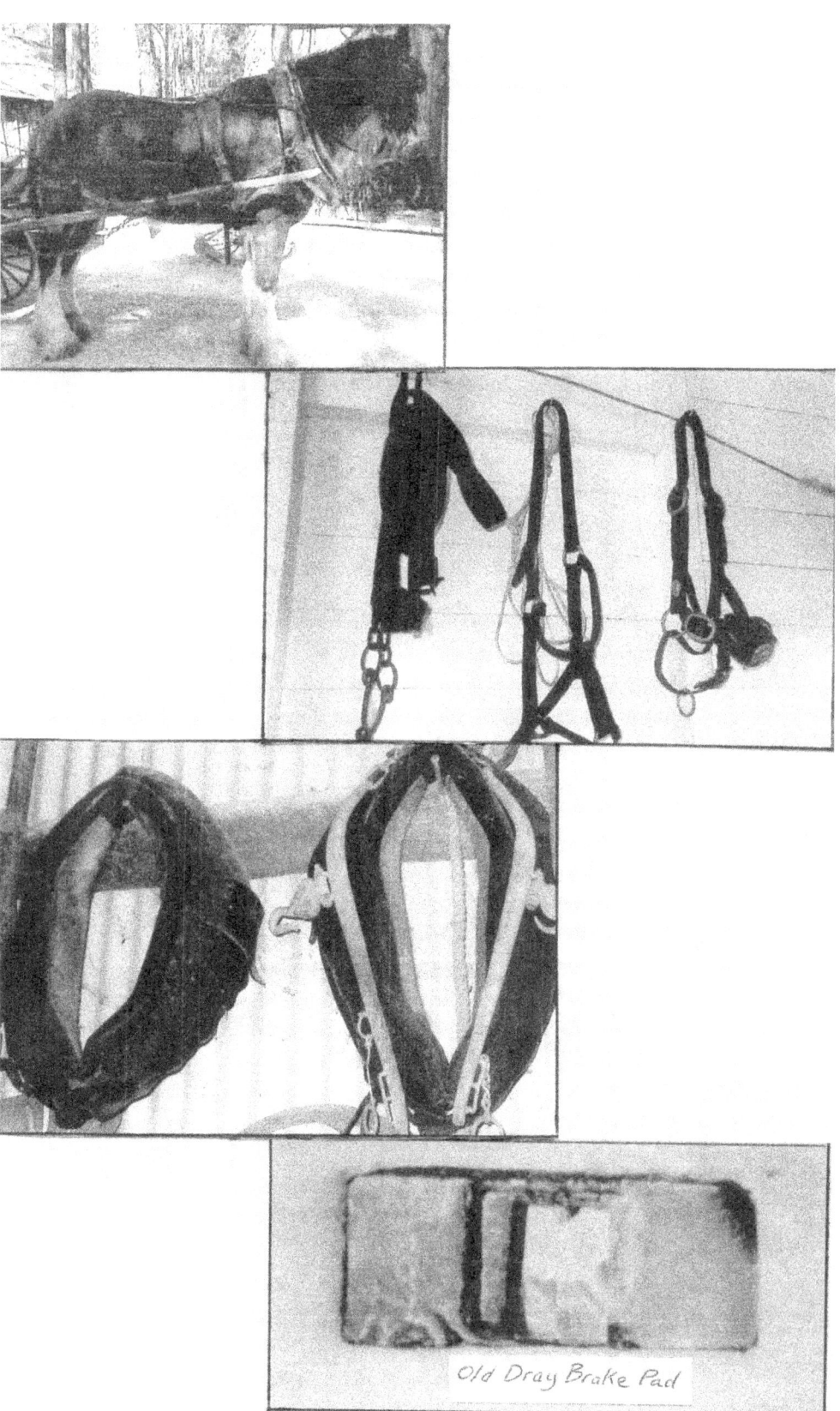

Old Dray Brake Pad

The Dairy

The dairy building was situated on the slope of the hill around No.102 Seabreeze Parade. It was a four cow plant. When milking, the rail was pushed up and two cows would walk through to be milked in turn. The cows were roped around the leg and after being prepared, were milked – one at a time. The milking equipment was taken from one cow to the other. When milked, these cows left for the paddock and the other two cows banked up would walk through to be milked (Owen Mathias) The creamery was separate from the milking bales and had gauze all round the top and bottom and weather-shield all around. (Chum Bramble).

I have taken these photographs of a dairy building, of similar age, to show what the dairy would have been like in Lachlan Fraser's time. Owen Mathias approved the pictures, with one exception, and that was that Lachlan didn't feed his cows when milking; so the feed bins wouldn't have been there. Owen went on to say that the dairy produced top quality cream. Lachlan built up a prime Jersey stud of 30-35 head of milking cows, 20 dry cows including calves and a Jersey bull. The cream was separated and the skimmed milk was fed to the poddy calves or put in with the slops for the pigs. Some milk was kept for personal use.

Originally, when Lachlan milked by hand, the cattle only had water troughs. Later, after the purchase of his milking machine around the 1930's, he installed a petrol motor to pump water to the dairy from the water storage tank below. A lot of water was used when working the dairy. The cow's udders had to be washed and the equipment and concrete floor had to be kept clean.

After the milking and separating, the cream had to be collected. Owen and Lachlan had made a sled out of a large piece of wood that had been discarded by road workers. The horses were harnessed and the cream cans were towed on the sled, from the dairy and down the rough track to where it is now known as the Foreshore Reserve. The heavy cans of cream were then carried by hand down to the little corrugated iron shed at the end of the jetty, where they were collected by Karl Emerson in his cream boat called the 'Wallis'. The cream was collected three mornings a week in the summer and two mornings a week in the winter. (Owen Mathias) It took 3½ hours to collect the cream from the dairy farms around the lake. The cream was then delivered to the Butter Factory at Tuncurry. (Chris Stein). Once there it was tested, and if it was not good, it was classed as dirty or second class cream. It would then go into other food products. Lachlan's Jersey herd produced first grade cream. On his return trip Karl Emerson would deliver any farm supplies needed: such as pollard, fencing wire, wheat and fertilizer and return the cream cans for reuse. The cream cans came in varying gallon sizes: 2, 5.and 10. The farmer could make up 12 gallons from one cream can of 10, plus one of 2 or 2 cans of 5 gallons each, plus one of two. (Owen Mathias).

Charlie's father, Rex Bramble, told a story of how Lachlan and Rex had differing opinions about Lachlan's newly acquired milking machine. Rex had experienced milking machines in the past and pointed out that it wouldn't remove all the milk from the cow. Lachlan, being proud of his new investment, argued that it would! They selected the best Jersey milking cow for the experiment. After it was milked with the machine, they 'stripped' the cow dry, collecting 1/3 pint of milk. Lachlan was flabbergasted and had to concede that he had been wrong. Disputes happened, but in the end, they remained great friends. It was very important to have the cow emptied as any remaining milk could cause problems for the cow. (Charlie Bramble).

.... *Approximate Position of Milking Shed*

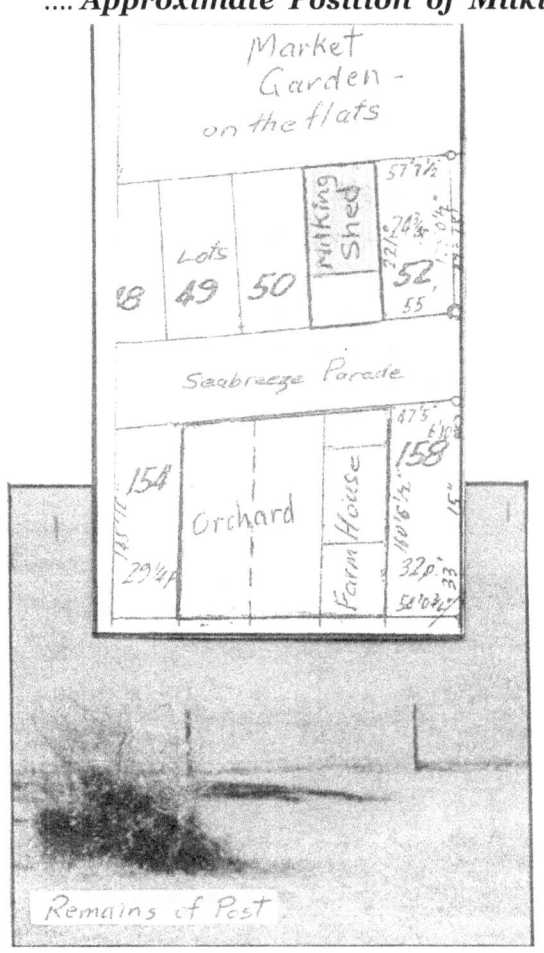

.... Old Milking Shed Machinery

A History of Green Point
.... *From Cream Boat to Butter Factory*

Cattle Grazing

To keep the Jersey herd well fed Lachlan cleared his land and periodically burnt the paddocks in rotation to encourage the new grass to grow. The improved pastures were spelled at times and in the winter months sorghum was given to the cattle. When the mosquitoes were bad, Lachlan would burn old logs in the paddocks. (Owen Mathias). Charlie Bramble remembered visiting with his father in the 1950's and seeing the cattle, all huddled together in the smoke, to get relief.

In times of drought and the grass in short supply, it was sometimes necessary to look further afield. The bush paddocks on Crown Land (Booti Booti area today) were leased and occasionally the islands on the lake were used. As with today, farmers helped each other out when needed. Lachlan had grown up on 'One Tree Hill' farm, which was close to the Underwood's 'Sea View' farm, in the Cape Hawke area. The call went out and Owen Mathias, Rex Bramble, Ron Underwood and his father, Henry, all came to help. A small group of driers (pregnant cows) and young heifers were selected to go over to Big Snake Island. Lachlan had built a low rock wall a short way into the lake and a chicken-wire and pole fence was erected. This helped corral the cattle. The men on horseback encouraged the cattle to walk across the shallows and then swim the channel. Owen Mathias remembers that, on one such occasion, after all their efforts, there wasn't much feed to be had there.

Around 1990, I remember seeing the remains of the corral fence, north of where Wharf Road is today, the existence of which was confirmed by Roger Schmakeit who was an early resident of Green Point. The remains of the fence would have been removed by volunteers as part of Clean Up Australia activities. Another time they tried putting 12 cattle on Yahoo Island, by swimming them over using a skiff or small boat. It wasn't a success as the grass proved to be of poor quality.

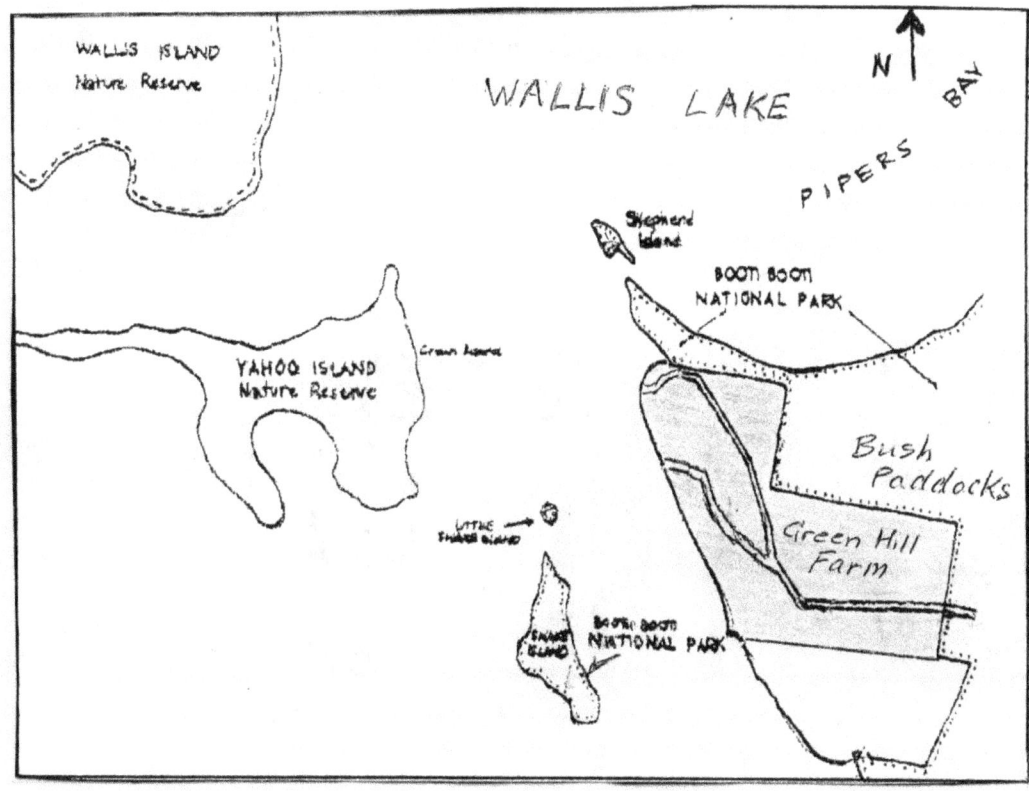

The Depression Years – 1929-1936

By 1929 Australia had joined the rest of the world in an economic slump. Prices of wool, wheat and butter were falling fast. The country was facing rising unemployment, a steep drop in the national income and investors abroad stopped placing money into Australian loans. The intricate system of credit and finance, by which nations exchanged their goods, was undergoing partial collapse.

Australia's economy, based on primary production, was particularly vulnerable to world panic. For tens of thousands of Australian of all classes, income was cut in half, but liabilities remained the same. It was the beginning of the Great Depression. Politicians of the day tried to stay the unemployment problem by introducing "Work for Sustenance" programs and by implementing food ration coupons.

By 1931, the States agreed to a plan by leading economists that all government salaries, rent and interest rates, were to be reduced and the internal public debt was converted to lower rates of interest, mostly on a voluntary basis. The Arbitration Court assisted by making a general 10% cut in wages.

These were desperate times as the farmers had to keep going, regardless, to help feed the nation. Work was in short supply and food very scarce, so people sourced their food the best way they could. Owen Mathias told me the story of how his older brothers heard of a rogue steer in the bush. They were expert horsemen and pursued the steer on horseback at break-neck speed, till they could eventually corner it. After shooting the beast, it was butchered for the much needed meat and brought back to the farm at Pipers Bay, to be shared around.

Owen continued that another source of food around the area were the wild birds. In season, flock birds were the mainstay in many a household. Topknot pigeons were between 40 and 42 cms. long and while sitting on top of the Cabbage tree palms eating the seeds, it was easy to shoot them. They were nomadic in habit and their movements coincided with the ripening of the native fruits and berries, especially the seeds of the Bangalow and Cabbage tree palms. White-headed pigeons were 38-42cms. long and also became nice eating. Pigeon pie, stew and soup, were on many a menu and wild ducks were also eaten.

Bullah Bramble said that the local grey teal ducks were shot when they landed on the little lagoons in the bush, south of Green Point. He added that "bush tucker like this helped a family through rough times."

(Cayley's classic guide to the birds of Australia)

Row, Row, Row the Boat!

In the 1930's some farms in the Cape Hawke area ran beef cattle. The steers sometimes had to wear baffles over their heads. These were made from a Kero tin, with one side cut out. The bottom part was hinged with two hooks that went over the horns. (Chum Bramble)

One of the most harrowing exploits that Owen Mathias related to me was when Lachlan asked him to go over to Yahoo Island to help him remove a 'wild' steer. It was imperative that the steer not venture over to Green Hill farm, as his prize dairy herd would be in jeopardy.

They rowed over to the island in Lachlan's small boat, where they constructed a yard from Tea- tree poles and managed to corral the large steer. After shooting and quartering the beast it was time to load the carcass into the boat and row back to the farm. All was progressing well until a strong northeast chop came on the water. This made it extremely difficult to row and manoeuvre with the huge weight on board. Owen recalled that it was a long exhausting journey back to the shores of Green Hill farm. The butchered animal was put on the slide and taken back to the farmhouse. It was usual in those days to share the meat with friends and any remaining meat would have been salted for later use.

Fun On The Farm

Owen Mathias used to visit Lachlan and work with him on the farm. He was about ten years younger than Lachlan, so was able to learn a lot about farming practices. It wasn't all work and no play – occasionally fun was to be had!

Lachlan was a practical joker with a great sense of humour. When needed, Owen and Lachlan cut each other's hair. Sometimes Lachlan's hair grew down to his shoulders and hair-cutting time became the case of lots of laughter.

Lachlan had a 'terrible laugh' – it was a deep loud and hearty 'Ho! Ho!' He often laughed at his own jokes and his friends couldn't help but laugh along with him, even when they weren't at all funny.

Lachlan knew that Owen loved custard and as he thought that he could do a good job of it he would make it on Sundays, in a billycan, and serve it with blackberries which grew in lots of places on the farm. (Owen Mathias)

Chum Bramble told me that Lachlan kept beehives and had a 44 gallon drum extractor, for the honey. He also made honey beer which was quite potent. A quart bottle from the hotel, with a crockery stopper, was used in the process. No one dared shake the bottle, as in the past, the stopper had blown off and it all exploded! Bits of the container, honey, beeswax, young bees and the brew went floating everywhere. He also recalled an egg eating competition - to see who could eat the most eggs.

Lachlan had lots of friends and when Melbourne Cup Day came along each year, all the local fishermen pulled in at Green Hill to spend time with him. They brought prawns that they had caught in the lake and then cooked at Smokehouse beach. Apart from enjoying his company they all came because Lachlan was the only one around who had a battery-operated radio for them to listen to the famous race. All work stopped, just as it does today!

The Lakes Way....*in the early days*

In the early days The Lakes Way was just a sandy track. Strong winds from the ocean blew sand constantly over the area and signs were put up at each end of the dunes to indicate whether or not the route was passable. The track south from Forster seemed to be ever changing, as people kept making their own way across the heath. The road was reasonable from Bulahdelah to Tiona, but from Tiona to Forster was a real mess.

On one occasion Selwyn Mathias had to use his drafthorse to pull a bogged car out of the sand. Luckily for Lachlan Fraser, the track from Forster to where the turn off across the wetland area is today, was firm enough for his horse and sulky to manage safely. (Chum Bramble)

Around 1938, when the Government Relief Scheme came in, it was proposed that The Lakes Way be constructed into a gravel road. Owen's father and his two older brothers worked with their three draft horses as part of the workforce of two dozen men, who worked on the project. As Owen's father's farm at Pipers Bay had a shale quarry, he negotiated a deal. They would blast, then remove the shale at "three pence per yard", on the condition that the contractors dig a much needed water dam on his property. Owen's mother ran a farm guesthouse and took in three boarders who worked on the road works project.

Shortly afterwards, in 1938, Owen joined the Army. He returned home and then followed his older brothers into the Australian Infantry Forces.

Wartime Struggle

September 1939 brought the outbreak of 2nd World War. Many young Australians joined the Forces and fought overseas whilst at home, people rallied to help in any way they could. By 1940, the crisis in Europe brought about a sudden speed up. Munitions and aircraft manufacture accelerated. During 1942-44 food, clothes and petrol were rationed. Women entered the factories and joined the Services. In September 1942, after America entered the war, Australia agreed to aid America to the limit of her resources – as America had agreed to help Australia. As the American production lines began to turn out war goods in astronomical quantities, Australia received her store of aircraft, vehicles, petrol, earth-moving machinery and machine tools. For Australia's part, she fed and clothed a great proportion of the Americans in the Pacific.

By 1943 there were 700,000 men and women engaged in some kind of war production. On the agricultural front, performance by farmers and their families and that of the women of the Land Army, resulted in Australia becoming the larder for millions of the fighting troops in Great Britain and at home. The years of 1944/45 brought drought and bush fires, but no one dependent on Australia's food went short. Handicapped by lack of fertilizer and petrol, the farmers overcame their difficulties by co-operation.

In New South Wales, District War Agricultural Committees persuaded farmers to pool their resources of men, machines, horses, seed and transport. Harvest times were cut down and production targets excelled. Some townspeople shut their shops for a few days a week and went to work in the fields. The overworked people on the land were no less heroic than the men who worked machines or furnaces in the cities.

After 1945, when the Japanese surrendered, the country went into transition - from war to peace Many were retrained or went into pre-war occupations. (The Great Jubilee Book, The Story of the Australian Nation in Pictures – Jules Feldmann – 1951) After the Second World War transport via the lakes and rivers gradually gave way to vehicles. When Owen came back home from service overseas he trained as a mechanic and started his own business called Gilmat Motors at Tuncurry where he worked until retirement. Housing was in short supply and the country had to regenerate by increasing employment. This was done by the building of large public works.

**The Fig Tree On The Hill
(105 Green Point Drive)**

Between 1953 and 1955 both Ron and Ted Underwood remembered visiting Green Hill Farm with their father Harry. As young lads at the time, they were particularly taken with the sight of a small tree sapling growing out of the centre of a large old tree stump.

Possibly a bird had deposited a seed in the fertile centre of the decaying stump. Over the years the Port Jackson fig has developed into the grand old tree it is today. It was identified by Wal Attard (Great Lakes Council) in mid-2014 As a Rusty Fig or Port Jackson Fig – Ficus rubiginosa.

As you can see from this photo the base of the tree is quite unusual. Instead of having a buttressed trunk it seems to have grown straight downwards, as if covering the old tree stump.

A New Neighbour

Early residents had told me of the existence of another market garden prior to the subdivision being developed.

In the 1950's Robert and May Aitken built their home on just under 50 acres of land, south of Green Hill farm. They grew corn, pumpkins, squash and other vine vegetables for sauces. They also reared chickens. Needing water for the farm work and garden Robert dug a well at the lower corner of the land down near the lake, but unfortunately the sand kept filling it in. After 5 years of hard toil they gave up farming and moved back to Forster. (Chum Bramble)

This property was probably where Turtle Crossing is today at No.161 Green Point Drive.

EVER WONDERED ABOUT "SANTA BARBARA"?

- on The Lakes Way, south of Green Point

In the mid 1950's it was a caravan park. Back then The Lakes Way terrain was at a much lower level. To keep the area safe from the effects of the strong winds and rough seas, the ground level had to be built up by approximately 6 metres. Many trucks dumped huge loads of heavy boulders and land-fill. The proprietor, Bill Hoile, his wife and his son Bill Jnr., used to run the Caravan Park and shop. The supplies were collected from the cream-boat when it called at the large jetty at Tiona. Remains of the jetty's piers were evident for many years, running out into the lake not far from the Green Cathedral. The boat-run also included a stop at the Creek Depot near Pacific Palms and one at Coomba Bay. (Ann Bramble) Tom Ryan remembered seeing the Caravan Park when passing on his way to Forster for holidays. It was quite hilly and the caravans were nestled under the Norfolk Island pine trees. Norfolk Island pines were usually planted along the coastline as navigational markers for the fishermen to find their way back to shore.

> BOOTI BOOTI: X ★ Santa Barbara Cabins & Caravan Park: 8m. from Forster P.O., Tel. Booti Booti 5. C, ES, HS, TS, LIM, KS, BG (nearby), ice, tradesmen, tents, pets on lead, swimming. Fees: Van & Tent sites D— 6/6 p.s., 6d p.p., 3/- power, W— 35/- p.s., 3/6 p.p., 20/- power. Vans W— 147/- to 210/-. Cabins W— 168/- to 264/-. Shell Service: As above.

Thanks to Mick Perry for this entry from an old Shell Tourist Information Guide, we are now able to envisage the early caravan park with its camping fees and services provided.

1985   2011

The Second Jetty and Inclinator

Over the years the old jetty became more rickety. Owen Mathias and Chum Bramble had seen bits of the metal sheeting, from the cream-can shelter, fly off into the lake during strong winds. It was time to build a second jetty.

Around the 1950's, Lachlan Fraser, Chum Bramble and Archie Thompson built the new jetty, just south of the present day pump station at the end of Wharf Road, It went out into the lake for about 70 feet to the deeper channel. (Chum Bramble) In December 2007, just a couple of the original piers of the jetty and a row of rocks with cockle weed attached could be seen from a boat at low tide.

The access track from the dairy to the jetty went behind where the houses are today, on the high side of what is now Seabreeze Parade. It ran north of the farmhouse at No. 83 and followed the ridge up and over the slope of the hill and northwest towards the lake. (Bill Legge)

Both Greg Golby and Dave Martin thought that part of the old track had run across their backyards, at No.79 and No.81 Seabreeze Parade, as the ground appeared hardened after many years of use. The track continued along the more level ground of the western hillside parallel to the lake and about half way down the slope. (Joyce Bushnell)

In order to be able to use the jetty and to transport his produce to and from the Butter Factory, Lachlan had to build an inclinator. Allan Steed, an early resident who lived opposite at the present day No.38 Green Point Drive, described it to me as a 'flying fox', probably because he had seen cables strung between the trees at the time.

Joyce Bushnell remembered that when she came here to buy land in the 1960's, she saw an inclinator which was built to transport heavy materials up and down the hillside. She also remembered a motor on a concrete slab, which powered a winch to hoist or let down the platform. Joyce went on to say that it was a flying-fox arrangement with heavy wires running down from the steep hill to the jetty.

Ann Bramble confirmed that it was an inclinator used for carrying supplies. She had seen it in action around 1953 when the cream boat called in at Green Hill farm on her way to school from Charlotte Bay. Ann remembered the flying-fox system which took the cream cans up and down from the jetty landing. It definitely worked on a 'cable system' and was to handle supplies, not people. Ann added that meat from the butcher, bread from the baker and the mail, were delivered via the cream boat three times a week.

When David Buchanan was building his home (very close to the site at No.1 Wharf Road and cnr. of Green Point Drive), I asked him if he had found any evidence of an inclinator on or near his property. He was able to show me the remains of a concreted area about 2-2½ metres square, half way down the block on his southern boundary line. The concrete slab extended onto the adjacent block of land at No. 31 Green Point Drive.

Presumably, after years of use, the inclinator hollowed out the hillside on its way to the jetty. To overcome the problem building site, David's home was built over the top of the deep hollow. In 1985 I remember seeing a low corrugated iron shed in the vicinity of the concrete slab, which may have housed the motor to power the winch for the inclinator.

.... Jetty Via Hillside Inclinator

The Legend of Fraser's Bull

Rex Bramble passed on many stories to his son Charlie about the exploits at Green Hill farm, and in particular, those pertaining to "Fraser's Bull". Over the years these stories have become part of folk lore. When asked about the temperament of Jersey cattle, Owen Mathias explained that although the cows were reasonably docile, Jersey bulls actually grew very big and indeed Lachlan's bull was extremely large and could be cantankerous, unpredictable, dangerous and fiercely aggressive!

From time to time, Lachlan's friends Rex Bramble, Chum Bramble and Keith McBride, would help him out by working in his market garden. In normal circumstances this would have been no problem, but here at Green Hill farm the bull pen was positioned opposite the market garden. It was a tense time for the men planting the cucumbers between the rows of corn – always checking to see that Lachlan was patrolling the fence line and had the huge bull under control. Lachlan was always at the ready, with a pitchfork in his hand, so dangerous was the cunning beast.

Another story was when Rex Bramble and the other fishermen who had fished the lake through the night, came to shore at Smokehouse beach for a well earned morning 'cuppa'. The youngest and fastest runner was selected to venture up the bank. His job was to start the fire and boil the billy. Mostly all went to plan, but they never quite knew where Fraser's bull would be lurking. It was 'his' territory and he didn't like intruders. The men kept a constant look out, always on the ready to run like the wind to the safety of their moored boats.

Rex Bramble and Chum Bramble related this story: "Imagine Lachlan sitting in the farmhouse relaxing in front of the fire – enjoying a well earned rest after a long day's work. Meanwhile, in town at the hotel, things were brewing. Some of Lachlan's 'merry' friends had decided to surprise Lachlan for his birthday. They drove their cars via the bush track across the wetland area to avoid detection then parked in the dark bush outside the property. Sneaking through the fences, and crossing two paddocks, they felt confident and didn't worry about the occasional giggle and loud whisper to each other. They crept up to the house, bottles of beer in hand, around to the back door and ready to shout out in full voice, 'SURPRISE'! Old Lach got a big surprise, but when the friends turned around to see the angry bull standing just behind them in the doorway, they got an even BIGGER SURPRISE! Someone had left a gate open and the bull had followed them all the way."

Sand Mining

As mentioned previously, The Lakes Way in the 1950's used to be a very rough road indeed and often was closed because loose sand blown across the road made travel impossible.

When Mineral Deposits Sand Mines and R2 Mines commenced operations in our area in the 1960's The Lakes Way was improved and made suitable for their heavy trucks to transport the sand to be processed for the extraction of rutile and other minerals. Significant areas of the Aeolian landscapes were mined for heavy minerals, such as rutile and zircon. They were used in white paint manufacture, air and spacecraft parts and nuclear reactors and other highly technical applications. Black grains in the sand can be seen on many beaches in the area. Mining of the rutile was economically important and profitable and brought work to hundreds of unemployed men in the region.

Sand mining meant clearing all the vegetation on the eastern side of The Lakes Way. The paperbark trees along the roadway died because of wind burn from the ocean. Later, when the sand dunes were regenerated, the vegetation provided shelter from the ocean winds and the paperbark trees returned. The entrance to the sand mining machinery yard and rig was about 1½ klms south of Green Point turn off.

Apart from the sand mining adjacent to Seven Mile beach, there were other sand mining deposits at Black Head, Tuncurry, Janies Corner, Elizabeth Beach and Sand Bar. Some areas were mined for only a couple of years and others for up to 5 years at a time. Operations closed down around 1980. In the 1960's the coastline around Myall Lakes became the focus of one of the great conservation battles in Australian history. Sand mining and potential development of large coastal areas of private land threatened to reshape the coastline of NSW. Conservationists called for the protection of the entire lake's system and associated Tcatchments. Things came to a head in the mid 1970's when a string of high coastal dunes south of Smiths Lake were threatened with mining. Extensive conservation gains continued in the 1970's and early 1980's with nature reserves gazetted for the Wallis Lake area.

Sand mining, Bluey's Beach, 1970s *Regeneration of the sand dunes at Seven Mile Beach - 1986*

The End of an Era

According to Charlie Bramble the farm in the early 1960's was really lovely.

Because of new dairy regulations, requiring the purchase of expensive stainless steel vats and cooling systems, many dairy farmers were selling up their properties. Lachlan Fraser followed suit and sold his 'Green Hill' farm. C.H. Degotardi (Sales) Pty. Limited had previously been involved with land sales in a subdivision at Smiths Lake and then took on Green Hill farm as their next project. Lachlan worked the farm right up to the time of sale in 1960.

Later, Lachlan moved to Forster to live on a 40 acre property in an area that the locals called 'Frog Hollow'. (Owen Mathias) His home was on the hill by The Lakes Way, just north of where the entrance to The Lakes Estate is today. (Annette Bramble)

As he got older and needed help his friends Chum and Barbara Bramble visited more regularly. Chum drove Lachlan to and from Newcastle, for his special boot-fitting appointments and Barbara helped out with his washing and did some cooking.

Over time, it became apparent that Old Lach was ill and he had to go to Cape Hawke Memorial Hospital to be treated. Whilst there he had a very important visitor, Sir Arthur Roden Cutler, the then Governor of the State of NSW who was in Forster/Tuncurry at that time to officiate at the Centenary Celebrations of October 1975 and was able to make a goodwill visit to see patients at the hospital.

Thanks to Chum and Barbara Bramble and this photograph, we can now see what Old Lach Fraser looked like. It wasn't long after it was taken, that sadly, he passed away from the effects of a stroke.

Through the memories of his many friends, I feel privileged to have had an insight into the life of 'our farmer', Lachlan Fraser. Like many in our region he was a typical hard working dairyman, much appreciated by all, and I'm sure will be remembered by the residents who now live in the area which was once his 'Green Hill' farm.

Lachlan Fraser
1898-1976

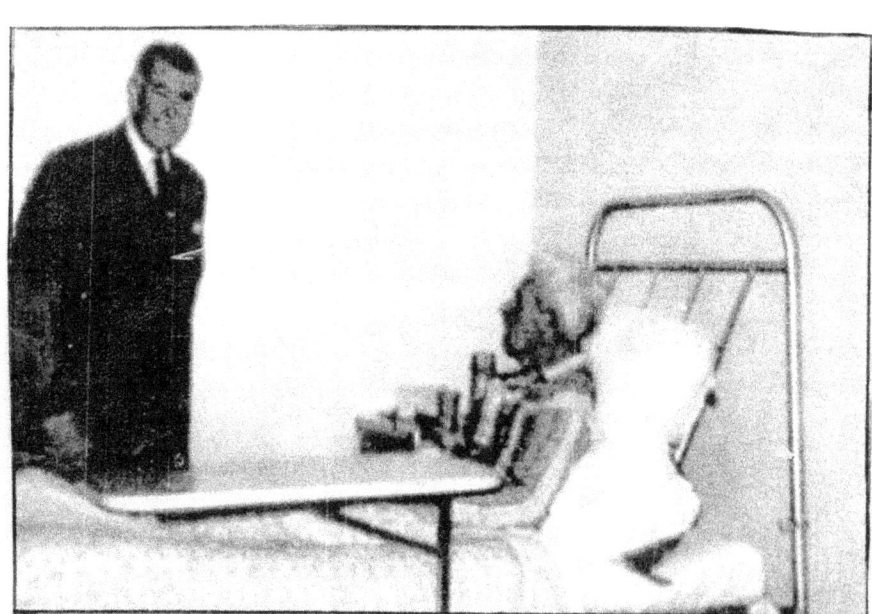

Change On the Way

As some dairy farmers in our region were selling off their properties around the late 1950's and early 1960's, C.H. Degotardi (a successful residential land developer from Sydney) took up the opportunity and soon became involved. In conjunction with Lucas Campbell Estates Pty. Limited, his estate agent firm of C.H. Degotardi (Sales) Pty. Ltd. went about selling the acquired farmland at Smiths Lake and Green Point for the proposed new housing estates. The Deposited Plan for the Smiths Lake subdivision was registered with Great Lakes Shire Council on 17/10/1960 and the Deposited Plan for Green Point was registered on 14/11/1960. Coomba Park was developed in a similar way two years later. (Lidbury, Summers & Whiteman-Surveyors).

In order to introduce prospective buyers to our region, newspaper advertisements were put in place and on the main radio stations. Smooth talking radio announcers spoke about these pristine areas, with their beautiful lake views, tropical palms and close proximity to many wonderful beaches and only 5 minutes from Forster. They advertised that for a full holding deposit of ten pounds, the prospective buyers could buy a block of land with INTEREST FREE term payments and "not to delay – the sooner you start, the sooner you'll be having fun in the sun!" It was a place to retire to, or invest in the future.

In those days the distance from Sydney could be a problem for prospective buyers. The old Pacific Highway was narrow and winding with only one lane each way. The train ride to Taree and then bus to Forster and beyond would be just as frustrating for prospective buyers. What they needed was an exciting mode of transport that left the people refreshed on arrival, expecting a bargain, and feeling very pleased with the outcome. The answer came in the form of a 'free flight' in a Sunderland seaplane from Rose Bay in Sydney to the Mid North Coast They would land on the water nearby the destination and be ferried by launch to the proposed subdivision site. Early Green Point resident Tom Ryan, reported the only proviso was, "that you were obliged to buy land!"

Between 1920 and 1930 Stan Gyler built the boathouse at Smiths Lake. This was spruced up to look inviting when C.H. Degotardi developed the area in the 1960's. The seaplane flew passengers up from Sydney and after landing on the lake they were ferried over, for refreshments, to the boathouse, which is now known as the Frothy Coffee Café. (Betty Bramble) Similar arrangements were in place regarding the Green Point subdivision. After landing on Wallis Lake, the prospective land owners were ferried by launch to the newly erected weather-shed on the lakeshore for refreshments. They were then able to walk around the subdivision to inspect the blocks for sale.

Some of the very early residents however, reported coming up from Sydney by East West Airlines to the Wallis Island runway then across by launch to Green Point. When asked about this Boyne Corrigan (Bud) Degotardi said "that the DC3 was owned by the Degotardies and as well as used for real estate purposes was chartered for trips around Australia. It was not a financial success and was kept for only a few years."

Left – Sunderland Flying Boat

Right – Douglas DC-3

The Big Sell

Old Lach's jetty at the end of present day Wharf Road, was repaired and finished off with a coat of white paint. As you can see from this photograph the jetty looked very inviting. The Sunderland seaplane would land out in the channel, not far from Yahoo Island and a launch would bring the prospective buyers into the jetty.

Chum Bramble explained that the seaplane couldn't land close to the jetty as the lake nearby was too shallow and there were many obstructions. It is presumed that the flagpoles at the end of the jetty were used for semaphore flags, which provided information about the weather and the state of the channels and bars across the rivers.

To entice the people to buy land the would-be buyers congregated at C.H. Degotardi's purpose built weather-shed with its large table and bench seats. For atmosphere, the shelter was decorated with brightly coloured flags. Finger food and refreshments of beer and soft drinks were brought in by plane and made available. After the agent had said his spiel the people were invited to walk around the area to choose their blocks. Over the next few years many people bought land and they, in turn, told their friends resulting in even more sales.

The weather-shed was positioned on the lakeside of the track, about 200 metres north of the jetty. (Bud Degotardi) Annette Bramble remembers there being a Norfolk Pine not far away, a high hill in the background and tall reedy grass growing by the lakeside. We can estimate that it was situated by the lake at the bottom of where No. 23 Green Point Drive is today.

By the early 1970's the jetty piers were the only things standing, as the railings had fallen off and the boards rotted away. (Andrew Schmakeit) The weather-shed was also in disrepair, deemed to be dangerous and so was dismantled.

The fibro-clad 'hole-in-the-ground' toilets were built a further 200 metres or so north of the weather-shed and about 3 metres up the hillside. (Bud Degotardi) By the mid 1970's they were covered in blackberry bushes and you wouldn't go near them in case of snakes. (Charlie Bramble) Around 2002, Coastcare workers found the buildings roughly behind No. 11 and 13 Green Point Drive. The 3-10 cm thick trunks of Lantana bushes had wound their way in and out of the structures breaking up the fibro walls and white ants had eaten into the woodwork.

Advertising and Transport

Sunderland seaplane

Smith's Lake

Bargain Sales

One of the first couples to buy land here was Joyce Bushnell and her husband, Denis. Joyce remembered climbing about half way up the steep hillside track, then veering south and over the ridge towards where they selected their land. They chose at least three blocks of land, as did many other early buyers. As a long term investment the blocks proved their worth. This copy receipt dated 21-2-1960 from C.H. Degotardi (Sales) Pty. Ltd. shows that they paid £251/8/9 with a purchase price of £275 less 10% Contract Deposit. Stamp Duty being £3/18/9.

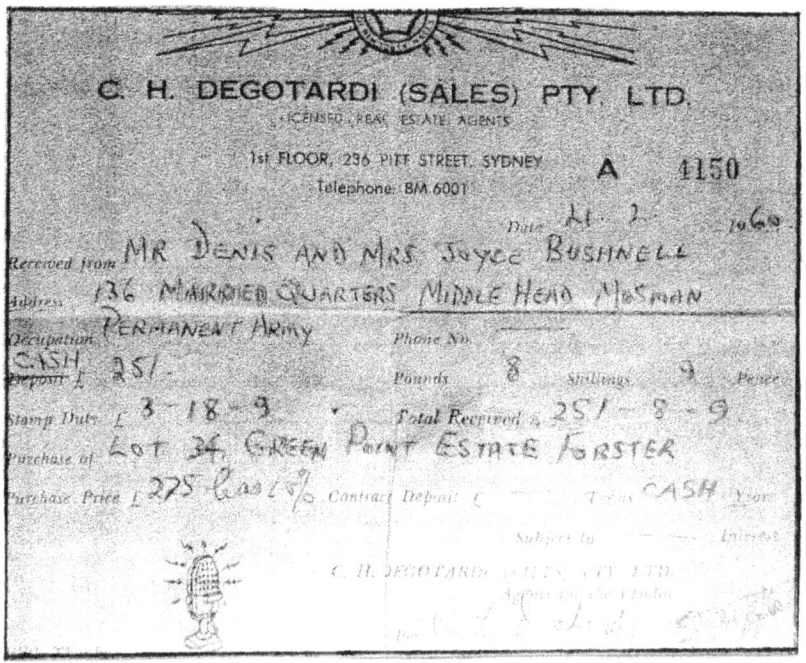

Presumably arrangements were made, that when enough capital from land sales came to hand, the subdivision would be developed. The D.P. No. 31825 was signed off at Great Lakes Shire Council on 6/2/1960 and registered in Sydney on 27/6/1961, which was extremely quick for those times according to the surveyors at Lidbury, Summers & Whiteman. Bud Degotardi, nephew of Charles Degotardi, surveyed Green Hill farm. According to long term fisherman Greg Golby, the local fishermen, in the early days, referred to our area as Green Hill Point. Later, developers shortened the name to Green Point. Our thanks to the Degotardi family for the photograph of Bud surveying at the corner of The Lakes Way and Green Point Drive.

Unlike today, the Certificates of Title were very ornate documents, with the names of the previous landowners written on the back of the very large certificates. Our area in the 1960's came under the Shire of Stroud Parish of Forster and County of Gloucester. Sample documents supplied courtesy of Norah Greenwood.)

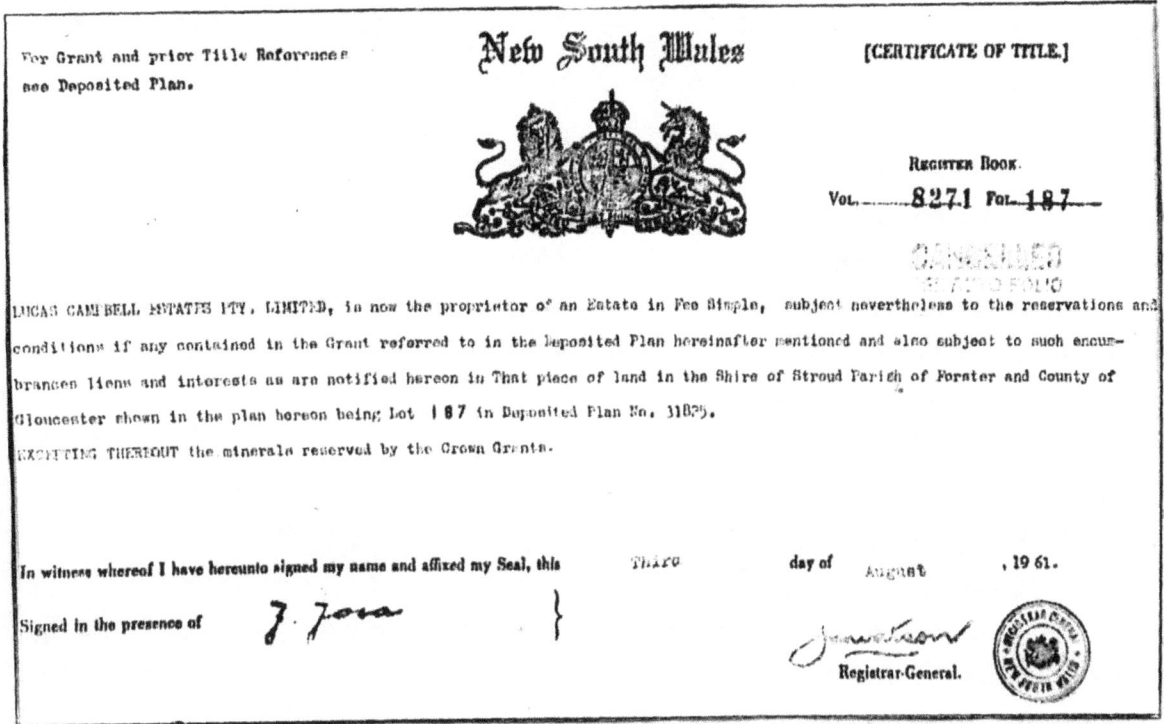

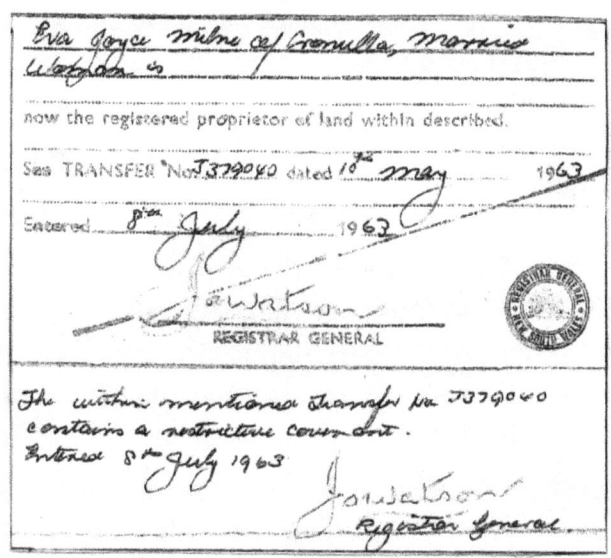

As a point of interest The Great Lakes Shire was constituted and came into being in 1980. The organization was an amalgam of what had been Stroud, then Great Lakes Shire and part of Manning Shire. The Hon. H.F. Jensen MP, Minister for Local Government officially opened the new Council Chambers and Administrative Headquarters at Breese Parade, Forster on 22/8/1981. In the early 1990's, the previously known Great Lakes Shire Council became the Great Lakes Council. In 2006 the combined Council celebrated 100 years of Local Government.

Green Point Subdivision

Looking at the subdivision plan, we can see that the lots were divided up into house blocks, small acreages and Public Garden Recreation Spaces. However, at the corner of Green Point Drive and the high side of Seabreeze Parade, you may note there were originally 6 tiny lots. These lots were proposed for a group of shops, having access at the rear via Green Point Lane. We can assume that later the community was deemed to be too small to support the shopping centre. These 6 lots, namely lots 311-316 inclusively, became 3 house blocks.

Lot 318 which runs behind the lakeside houses in Green Point Drive and Lot 309 behind Seabreeze Parade are both classed as Public Garden and Recreation Space. There are 2 areas for Lot 317 – one down towards to the point classed as Public Garden and Recreation Space and the other being the Public Reserve where the Community Hall and Green Point Park are located.

Section R 72773 was upgraded to Booti Booti National Park in 1992 and Lot 316 continues to be held by Council pending discussions with National Park authorities.

When the subdivision was first developed the access road from The Lakes Way was unsealed and very rough indeed. In the mid 1970's residents often preferred to drive to Forster via the wetland track, rather than experience the sharp rocks and sandy patches of the road out. (Olive Steel) However, the wetland track was sandy and wet in places. Being narrow, it was perilous when another car came at speed from the opposite direction. (Annette and Charlie Bramble)

The subdivision roads generally followed the contours of the land and would have been reasonably easy to construct; with the exception of the high ridge section of Green Point Drive between Lucas and Campbell Avenues. This apparently had to be blasted to make way for the roadway. The rocky hillside had to be cut away on the high side of the road, as seen by the steep footpath areas and the long drops on the opposite side of the road.

In the early stages, the subdivision roads were crudely formed. (Joyce Bushnell) The bitumen topping was thin and roads very narrow. Over time the topping was redone and the roads became a little wider. Green Point Drive became the main road and the less used roads like Frazer Avenue seemed to be neglected and potholed for many years. Waratah Close, Camellia Place and Bottle Brush Close were the last roads to have bitumen topping.

As we can imagine Wharf Road would have been named after the jetty that was there at the time of the development of the subdivision, also Seabreeze Parade named after the sea breezes that are experienced there. We can assume that Frazer Avenue was originally misspelt and should have been Fraser, after Lachlan Fraser. Lucas Avenue was named after Ralf Lucas who was one of the directors of Lucas Campbell Estates Pty. Limited. Campbell Avenue was named after C.H. Degotardi's first wife's family. (Bud Degotardi)

I was intrigued by the notation on the subdivision map about the "remains of a burnt stump" at the bottom of Wharf Road. After asking Andrew Schmakeit whether he remembered it, he remarked that indeed he did and that it was a huge wide post near where the jetty landing area would have been. Looking at the map it appears to have been a reference point for survey measurements. The stump has since been removed to be featured in a resident's garden

Subdivision Survey Map

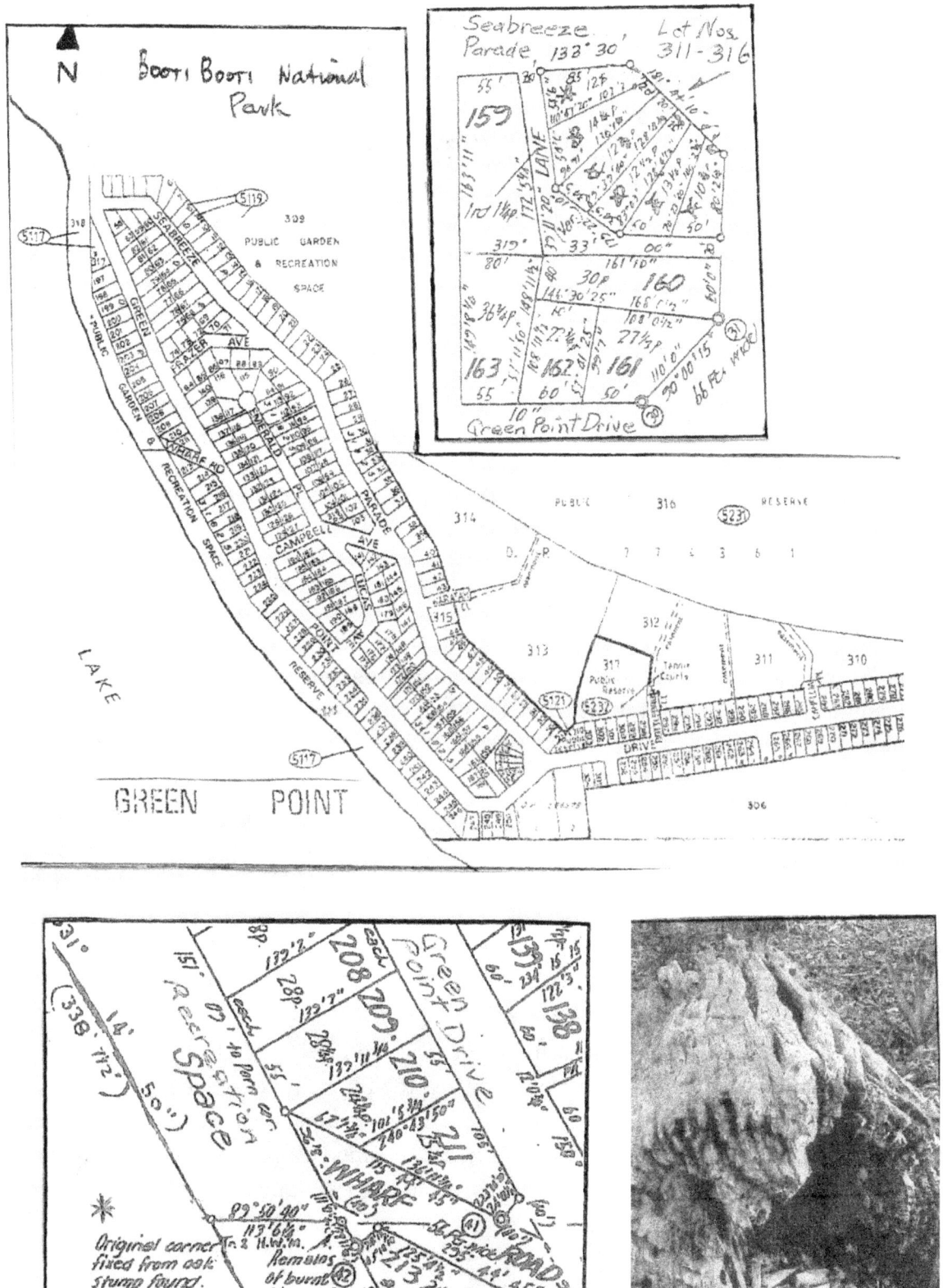

In the early 1990s it was envisaged that Lot 309 Seabreeze Parade could be made into an oval and No.20 Seabreeze Parade would have been the access road. Like the shopping centre, the community wasn't large enough to sustain the venture. Unfortunately the open space at Green Point Park was deemed to be too small in area for a soccer field but it still affords the room for children to freely kick a football around.

The area between Lot No.'s 21 and 22 in Seabreeze Parade is the access to the sewerage pump station. Other sewerage pump stations are situated at the bottom of the hill between No.103 and No.105 Green Point Drive and at the end of Wharf Road beside the lake.

There are a number of easements between blocks, which generally allow for natural drainage. In some cases Council has put in drainage and spillways to protect the environment. There is a walkway between Lot No.'s 247 and 248 Green Point Drive, to allow residents to enjoy the Smokehouse area by the lake.

Lot No. 306 has two access areas, one beside where the shop used to be located and the other beside the bus stop in Green Point Drive. Presumably this Lot has been held for future development, if and when it becomes necessary.

Holiday Friends

Whether it was because of the need for a new home, the promise of fantastic fishing, a place of peace and tranquility, the beautiful bushland and the native wildlife, the marvelous sunsets, or just the freedom to roam and explore, some new landowners were drawn to Green Point and took the opportunity to camp on their land for holidays. In those days families didn't worry about roughing it. It was all part of the fun!

One family in particular was the Schmakeit's. From around 1965 Renata and Bill and their four children camped on their block at No,7 Green Point Drive. They slept in the trailer and a small tent. The children virtually had all of the subdivision area to roam free and explore.

Bill loved his fishing and Renata enjoyed her early morning swim each day in the lake channel below their block. Over time, they erected a small fibro shed at the front of the block, as the new house would eventually be built further down towards the lake. Many years later when the house was completed, Renata had a pottery kiln installed and the building became her pottery shed. Renata's pottery work was well sought after and sold in many specialty shops.

By chance, Renata had met Margaret Mueller at a Villawood pottery class in Sydney. When Margaret and her husband Richard bought their land at No. 71 Green Point Drive in 1969, they became close friends and met up whenever their holidays coincided.

Bit by bit, perched on the steep hillside, Margaret and Richard built their tiny cabin/dwelling containing four bunk beds. They had a camp light and collected their water in large containers. They always enjoyed the bushland surroundings and especially eating meals outside under the stars. (Margaret Meuller)

Building Problems - Lack Of Electricity

Lisa and Stephen Seadon were both school teachers. Lisa had put in for a transfer to Forster School, which came through much quicker than expected.

They loved the area and wanted to settle as soon as possible. At the time some blocks at Green Point apparently were being sold for the value of unpaid Council rates. Fortunately, the couple was lucky enough to acquire a lovely block overlooking the lake at No.3 Green Point Drive.

Building a home without electricity and water was the next problem! They bought a large water tank and a heavy-duty generator and then started to work on the dwelling.

Although the home was completed in 1972, they were still without electricity. Living with a generator for power was a problem, as in the evening, if they wanted to use the shower, all the lights had to be turned off and someone had to watch the generator because it caused too many sparks. (Lisa Seadon-Hall)

The loud noise of the generator echoed around the area and could be heard at night as far down the road as No.71 Green Point Drive. (Margaret Mueller)

Families like the Schmakeit's, who were intending to build soon, were quite annoyed by the delay and pushed with other landowners to get the electricity connected as soon as possible (Andrew Schmakeit)

As early as 8/1/1972 Mr. W. J. Seadon (known as Stephen) had applied for the extension of electricity to Green Point subdivision. He requested the service be put on to his proposed residence in particular and Shortland County Council replied that they would investigate the development within two months.

The SCC required a minimum of ten residents who intended to be permanent, in order for the extension of the electricity to proceed. A circular letter went out to all landowners and a copy forwarded to the Ratepayers Association on 25/9/1972. Eleven landowners replied to show that they were nearing completion of their homes or intended to build in early 1973, and not later than October 1973.

On 25/1/1973 the SCC advised that the survey was complete and construction of power poles would commence later in 1974. The electricity was connected by 20/6/1974. (P.A. records)

The electricity was brought up via Bulahdelah. During severe storms in 1990's, the electricity supply was often cut off due to damage caused by fallen trees. Blackouts occurred over many years, usually without warning, and the interruptions often lasted up to 6 hours as the damaged lines had to be located. To stop this inconvenience from happening in the future, arrangements were made to enable the electricity supply to be switched over to Forster's power grid.

A Difficult Delivery

In 1972 Lisa and Stephen Seadon of No. 3 Green Point Drive were the first residents to build a new home at Green Point. The day the incinerator was due to be delivered no one could be there to take delivery. The fibro home was not quite up to lock-up stage and the front door had been positioned sideways across the opening, with a chair behind it to hold it in place.

The truck driver had found his way from Taree out to Lisa's home in the subdivision and took her delivery item off the truck, putting it down on the ground out the front. Suddenly, there was a menacingly loud growl and rather shocked he looked up to see the huge hairy head of a large German Shepherd dog. Not too keen on big dogs he jumped quickly into his truck and sped away. The driver had been spooked by the apparent height of the ferocious looking animal. The dog had stood up on the chair and leant over the door which made him look larger than his actual size. In reality, the pet was quite friendly, but the truck driver didn't wait to find out! (Lisa Seadon-Hall)

Water Tanks

In the early days of the subdivision, there was no town water so householders had to put in large water tanks, some of which were located under their houses to collect their own rain water. In the late 1970's, in times of severe drought, Olive and Ernie Steel used to collect town water in containers from a tap in a park at Forster Keys, to top up their dwindling water supply.

Sometime in 1983 a water reservoir was proposed for the village of Green Point – positioned in the vicinity of No. 54 Green Point Drive – being the highest point in the area. (Jenny Klinkhamer) Records show that Great Lakes Shire Council decided to proceed with the acquisition of the suitable reservoir site in order that it would provide an available water supply for Green Point at some future date should it become necessary. When it was found that Town Water was proposed for Green Point within 8 years the idea was cancelled.

Blasting

Another problem associated with building in the late 1970's early 80's was the need of blasting to remove unwanted rock from the lower side of some blocks in Green Point Drive. Damage had occurred resulting in a nearby resident's brick water tank leaking most of its stored water. The Progress Association requested that Council endorse all building applications to the effect that blasting was not permitted under Ordinance No. 43 of the Local Government Act. However, should blasting be necessary, any work must be carried out by experienced personnel and under the supervision of a Council engineer.

Working Together

As most residents belonged to the Progress Association and the Volunteer Bush Fire Brigade and both organizations operated simultaneously the following groups have been dealt with separately for ease of understanding.

Early Progress Association

In the early years, Green Point ratepayers who regularly visited for holidays or to work on their house blocks, met up informally with the more permanent residents – later to form the Ratepayers Association.

The lack of an electricity supply was their main concern. As early January 1972, W.J. Seadon had written to the Shortland County Council applying for electricity to be connected to the subdivision. By January 1973 an additional eleven proposed permanent resident's names and addresses were also submitted.

By September 1973, when the number of permanent residents had increased the Green Point Progress Association was formed. Being the first permanent residents, Lisa and Stephen Seadon were very active in the organization. Although small in number, the group was strong minded and tackled problems head on. With the expertise of W.J. Seadon and Dr. Margaret Gibbons, plus the statesmanship and wisdom of the older Jim Markey, they battled for progress for the area and as a result, by 20/6/1974, the electricity supply was connected.

Jim Markey was affectionately called the 'Mayor of Green Point' and was considered "a friend to everybody and always ready to help." (Annette Bramble)

The Association worked hard to protect the environment and Dr. Margaret and her husband Laurie Kilham were volunteer rangers.

Ron Mitchell drew the original 'tree logo' for the letterhead which represented the Port Jackson fig growing at No.105 Green Point Drive.

Apart from the lack of electricity other issues to be dealt with included the urgent need for telephone services, proper mail deliveries, a school bus service and the collection of household garbage instead of villagers having to use the bulk bins positioned at the end of Green Point Drive near the intersection of The Lakes Way.

Correspondence and consultation with Council went on for many, many years because of the terrible state of the Green Point roads, the lack of street lights and traffic signs - all based on safety issues of the residents and children.

At that time Progress Association meetings were usually held in resident's homes as they were more conducive to families with young children.

Struggle For Services –

Imagine life:

Without A Telephone – No Homeline – No Mobile

Well, that's what it was like in the early years of the Green Point subdivision.

Tom Ryan recalled how he was lined up in the Chemist at Forster and he overheard the attendant asking Bill Schmakeit for his PHONE NUMBER. "What phone number?" he loudly replied. "We haven't even got the water on!" Bill's response was only voicing what other Green Point residents felt. He was a builder by trade and felt frustrated by the lack of telephone services. It made his business negotiations very difficult, especially when building supplies had to come all the way from Taree.

As far back as March 1973, Mr. W.J. Seadon had been writing on behalf of the Progress Association to the Australian Post Office requesting the telephone be installed in his home. At that stage the application was kept under review until cables could be installed.

In April 1974, the then President of the Association, Perce Adams, sent a letter expressing concerns about the high fire risk and the fact that it was a popular place for tourists. By then eight homes had been built and six more were under construction. Accidents had occurred and a recent fire was stopped only feet from one of the homes. The nearest telephone was at Santa Barbara, over 4 miles away; therefore help was difficult to obtain and often delayed in arriving.

In June 1974, the Post Master General's Department, explained that major works estimated at $78,000 were required to lay cables from Forster Exchange to about 60 waiting applicants, a new industrial development and a new housing subdivision. Extension to this cable for another four miles to serve a few applicants at Green Point was estimated to cost a further $22,000. It was hoped that cable could be laid as far as Forster Keys where 300 building blocks were being developed during 1974/75.

The Postmaster General, Mr. R. Bishop, explained in his letter that the cable carries the junction lines between Taree and the Pacific Palms Automatic Exchange. It contained no wires, which could be used for subscriber services.

By October 1974 Great Lakes Shire Council had joined the fight for telephone services. In November 1974 they asked the PMG to urgently consider Green Point's need and wanted the problem reviewed for the 1974/75 financial budget.

By January 1975 there were 20 dwellings erected or in the course of being built, so the Association requested twenty application forms for home telephones from the District Telephone Manager at Newcastle. On 6th February the application forms were sent out.

Advice on 4th June 1976 from the Minister for Post and Telecommunications stated that telephone services at Green Point were dependant upon the completion of a multi-stage major cable project, designed to service the southern part of Forster and ultimately Green Point. The final stage was scheduled for completion by June 1976 and services to the twenty applicants would be installed shortly after the cable was completed.

No Mail Service – Only Telegrams

The lack of telephones in the early days of Green Point was further exacerbated by the fact that there were no mail deliveries.

There was no ordinary mail delivery service.......only telegrams!

The Post Office seemed indifferent to the fate of 'urgent telegrams'. Instead, they were handed to the first resident from Green Point who happened to go into the Post Office after that office received the telegram. If it didn't happen that day then it was just 'too bad!'

One case concerned a seriously ill relative of a Green Point resident who eventually died before the family member could reach her. The telegram arrived 'too late!' Progress Association letters of request for urgent telegrams to be delivered to Green Point went out to Mr. P.E. Lucock MP at Wingham and Mr. H. Mason who was a member of the National Country Party in Forster.

On 4/6/1976 Mr. Eric L. Robinson, the Minister for Post and Telecommunications, wrote to say that Green Point was beyond the free delivery zone as far as telegrams being received at Forster Post Office. However, as there are no telephone facilities provided to Green Point, telegram deliveries are made only on the payment of a $5 portage fee. In each case the sender of the telegram is advised of this.

After interviews with a senior Australian Post representative who called at Green Point, Association members were assured that when the contents of the telegram are of sufficient importance to warrant immediate delivery, delivery would be made with portage charges to be collected from the addressee.

Contract Mail

As there was already a Green Point in the Gosford area residents were concerned about the misdirection of mail. It was suggested that it be called 'Green Hill Point' instead. However, on 12/9/1975 the Geographical Names board assigned it as its local name, Green Point. The Association continued to negotiate and discuss the difficulties associated with no mail deliveries and by 1/11/1977 they were successful when contract mail deliveries came into being.

Garbage Service

Initially, the residents had to burn their rubbish in their incinerators or bury it. In 1980, after lobbying Council, the Association was able to obtain 3 bulk bins for Green Point. They were situated on the northern side of Green Point Drive close to the corner of The Lakes Way and emptied every three weeks. On 16/10/1980 a bi-weekly garbage collection service was commenced. In April 1981 a resident's survey was done to see if they wanted an individual collection. As it was to cost permanent residents $36.16 p.a., it was decided to continue with the bulk bins for the time being and request Council for an extra bulk bin at holiday times as the overflow was an eyesore. Once a week household garbage collection commenced on 1/1/1983. (P.A. records).

Caravans To Houses

In the early 1970's to early 1980's many families struggled to build their new homes. Times were difficult as building supplies often had to come all the way from Taree. It often took years, not months to build. For convenience, some had caravans on their blocks whilst building their homes.

When Dave Martin settled in Green Point in 1973 there were only 5 houses in the subdivision. A tiny population indeed! At first, he lived in a shed and caravan, until his home at No. 81 Seabreeze Parade was completed in 1978. (Dave Martin)

Dr. Margaret Gibbons and her husband Laurie Kilham arrived in Green Point on 6/8/1975. The family home in Darwin was literally 'blown away' during the onslaught of Cyclone Tracy in December 1974. They settled at No. 70 Green Point Drive – at first living in their small Bongo van until they built the shed. The house was built later, followed by the births of their children. (Dr. Margaret Gibbons).

Others, like Eleanor and Bryce Wickham, who bought their land at No. 2 Green Point Drive in 1978, stayed in a caravan park for 2 years until their home was built, moving in on 31/5/1980. (Eleanor Wickham).

In 1978, Beryl and George Schoonhaven moved to No. 8 Emerald Place. Whilst they built their home they lived in their caravan. Due to the steepness of the block the caravan had to be positioned close to road level. (Tom Ryan)

Col and Val McPherson also stayed in a caravan park whilst they built their home at No. 12 Frazer Avenue. They came and worked each weekend, clearing the land and then building their home. They bought their block on 7/7/1980 but it took until December 1982 to be completed. (Col McPherson)

Charlie and Annette Bramble moved to the old farm house block at No. 83 Seabreeze Parade around 1980-81. The story goes that two escaped prisoners from Brisbane's Boggo Road Gaol had camped in the old house and unfortunately it was burnt down in the late 1960's. This was confirmed by Donald Oakes who was holidaying with his family in Emerald Place at the time. He recalled being stopped by police on the rough road into Green Point in 1968 and warned of the escaped prisoner at large who had burnt down the old farmhouse. (Bill Raward)

It took a long time to clear away the remaining rubble. There was half a brick chimney left standing and old bottles and spoons were unearthed around the foundations and out the back the remains of a path and the old tank and tank stand. Whilst building their new home they lived in a caravan on the land and to help them out, Jim Markey, who lived behind their block at 86 Green Point Drive kindly allowed them to use his shower and toilet facilities.

(Charlie and Annette Bramble)

Around 1980, building supplies became more readily available as hardware stores were established at Forster and Tuncurry resulting in more homes being built. (Col McPherson)

Fishing Holidays

During the 1950's and 1960's Forster and the surrounding areas were famous for recreational fishing. Many families traveled up from Sydney for their annual holidays – 'just to catch fish'!

Some landowners at Green Point took the opportunity to visit for holidayis. One of the earliest holiday places was Chapman's cottage situated at No. 4 Emerald Place and lovingly called 'The Shack".

I understand that later the family built another dwelling at No. 26 green Point Drive, which was aptly named 'Little Calmer'. Until around the mid 1990's this small fibro building, which over looked the lake, was nestled under a large and beautiful gum tree.

The One That Got Away

Ernie and Olive Steel came to live at Green Point in 1977, building their home at No.15 Green Point Drive. In the past, they had spent many happy times on holidays at Forster. The main attraction was 'the fishing' and now that they had an opportunity to live by the lake, they spent lots of time fishing from their boat just off shore.

One day they caught an enormous crab and excitedly hurried up their steep stone steps, placing the bucket with the crab near the back of the house. They then ran to alert their neighbours to come and see their bounty. In haste, they hadn't covered the bucket and unfortunately their 'super catch' had made its escape, all they way back down to the lake! (Ernie Steel)

Exploring Green Point

In the early years of the subdivision Deborah and Dave Martin, a young couple who settled at No. 81 Seabreeze Parade, both enjoyed bushwalking around the area in their free time. Especially memorable for them was walking the bush track, in springtime, at the end of what is now Bottlebrush Close, with the groves of beautiful wattle trees in full bloom and other native wild flowers and trees.

For exercise Dave used to ride his bike around the area enjoying the scenery. He remembered clearly how rutted and bumpy the track used to be by the lakeside. It wasn't the most comfortable of rides!

Early residents had their own names for the sandy beaches around Wallis Lake. Smokehouse for instance was called 'Sandy Beach' by the Schmakeit family and Lisa Seadon referred to the area as 'Silvery Sands'.

Fire Brigade Formed

Originally the fire brigade at Green Point was a 'self help' organization with two young chaps taking it on (Oscar Bowden) - Fire Control Officer for the area from 1970-1991. Lowell Reardon explained that they were actually Roy Harden as Captain and Ron Mitchell as Deputy Captain.

Because of the remoteness of the area and the ever threat of bush fires, the community decided to form an official Bush Fire Brigade. On 25/5/74, guest speaker Gordon Birchell, came to see about the formation of the brigade.

In early 1974 there were two bush fires on the headland at Lot 309 – behind Seabreeze Parade. As the Bush Fire Brigade 'just' managed to save the headland on both occasions the

Progress Association wrote to Great Lakes Shire Council asking for access to the eastern side of the lake so that it could be used, when needed, for a fire break.

On 30/1/1975 the Bushfire Fighting Unit approached Council for more equipment as a disturbed person had recently lit four fires. Fortunately winds were light at the time or the result could have been disastrous. It wasn't until 24/9/76 that the Brigade was presented with an 'old' trailer-tanker. (P.A. records)

By around 1978 there were approximately 15 permanent households in the subdivision (Tom Ryan). This meant that more residents were able to join the ranks of the volunteer bush fire fighters, as indicated by the Honour Board from the early days of the Brigade. The Honour Board was painted by a local resident, Brian Gordon. Most able-bodied male residents were members of the Brigade and were often members of the Progress Assoc. as well. (Olive Steel)

George Schoonhoven became Fire Captain and later, Group Captain. Early in 1980 he arranged for Oscar Bowden to come from Newcastle to talk to the young recruits and training and practice fire drills were held. Landowners, in order to keep their land clear of high grass and bush, allowed the Brigade volunteers to do periodical burn offs for fire practice, and the small donations towards their funds were greatly appreciated. (Beryl Schoonhoven)

When patrolling the edge of grass fires the firemen wore heavy uncomfortable metal knapsack water containers, with pump or lever action pumps. Originally they used pieces of a wet hessian bag on the end of a long handle, and if not available at the time, a broken branch would do. In later years McCloud Tools, consisting of a rake/hoe implement, were introduced, as there was less risk of spreading the embers. It was dangerous work as our area had a lot of long dry native grass, which when burnt, could travel extremely fast. (Lowell Reardon).

A History of Green Point
Green Point Bush Fire Brigade

PROPOSED CONSTITUTION

1. The name of the organization shall be Green Point Volunteer Bush Fire Brigade hereinafter referred to as 'The Brigade'.
2. Objects: The brigade shall come together and maintain an efficient bush fire fighting unit such as to be ready and equipped to:
   - Organize preventive measures to control fires.
   - Check and extinguish bush fires
   - Assist in general emergencies as required
   - Train members in the effective use of equipment.
3. Membership: All local residents are entitled to become members. A register of members shall be kept showing in respect of each member: his/her name, address, date of commencement of membership.
4. Funds: The funds of the brigade shall be used for the purpose of purchasing equipment or public relations with members or as directed so on a meeting by members and properly approved. Members will have the right to query any financial transactions by the secretary.
5. Office bearers: The office bearers shall be : Fire Captain, Senior Deputy Captain, Deputy Captains, Secretary/treasurer – in this case the captain will chair the meetings.
6. Disruptive members can be dismissed by a majority vote at a meeting and can be reinstated by the same means if this is necessary.
7. Members are obliged to follow instructions given by senior officers either on exercise or active firefighting.
8. Officers are obliged to put the welfare and safety of members as first priority.
9. It is the obligation of each member to report any damage to station or equipment.
10. An Annual General Meeting is to be held once a year to elect officers and a general meeting to be held at least every two months.

Early Fundraising for Fire Hall

From 1973 until 1978 fundraising amounted to Progress Association fees of $2 and later on in 1983 to $3 per family. This covered the cost of postage and stationery as the Association at the time was mainly working to establish community services. By 1978 it was recognized that a Fire Hall was needed to house firefighting equipment and could be used as a community meeting place. Times were hard as most residents battled to save to build their homes. Many had a builder erect their house to lock-up stage, then did all the inside work themselves; so it was not surprising that the Fire Hall took quite a while to construct.

Firstly there were negotiations with Council as to where the building could be constructed. Lot 309, an area behind Seabreeze Parade in the Public Recreation Space, was suggested. It wasn't until 30/9/81 that a decision was made. The newly proposed Fire Hall would go on the only Council owned reserve available at the corner of Green Point Drive and Seabreeze Parade, in the children's park area.

In the meantime, George Schoonhoven had a plan. He had a Pest Control business and sprayed new homes against white ants. He negotiated with his builder friends in the Forster area to collect any rejected and damaged bricks from building sites and bring them back to Green Point to help build the proposed Bush Fire Brigade Hall. Plans for the building were drawn up by Allan Dunn and submitted to Council. Later, around June 1982, Allan Dunn and Dave Lux (who also built the roof and timber work) – left their names in the newly poured concrete floor as seen below. A local 'brickie' did the brickwork using the damaged bricks. Allan Dunn remarked that the bricks, concrete and roof trusses were all donated and most of the work was voluntary. To cover the variation in the colour and type of bricks used, the outside of the building was painted a tan-red colour. The Bush Fire Council donated the front roller-door worth $600 and the Great Lakes Shire Council provided gravel for the driveway.

The building, with water tank on the tank stand and outside toilet, was completed around 1982. Brian Gordon painted the Bush Fire Brigade sign which was attached to the front of the building. When town water became available, Tom Ryan donated his labour and the materials needed to do the necessary plumbing. In the early 1990's, under the Community Employment Programme, it was arranged to have the hall painted a pale green. Later, Phil McAsey and his helpers, painted the building a cream colour and had the Bush Fire Brigade emblem on the front wall. With hard working and dedicated people like Lisa Seadon, Renata Schmakeit and Beryl Schoonhoven at the helm, the community ladies worked tirelessly to raise funds for more bush firefighting equipment and future community projects anticipated by the Progress Association.

Residents enjoyed the community party and dance at the Fire Hall and the raffle and sausage sizzle brought in much needed funds. Cake stalls were held out the front of the hall and when white elephant stalls for bric-a-brac were held, they were advertised in the Advocate Newspaper.   Besides working very hard they enjoyed the camaraderie and friendships were formed.

Fire Hall Colour Changes.....from tan-red, to pale green, then cream.

Fire Brigade Vehicles

Early equipment was quite basic, to say the least. Originally brigade volunteers were only given a free helmet and a pair of goggles. They had to buy their own overalls, woolen socks and heavy duty boots. (Oscar Bowden) It was a very welcome addition, when the Great Lakes Shire Council issued the Brigade with some much needed equipment. It came in the form of a 'trailer and pump', which were delivered on 24/9/1976. (P.A. records)

Oscar Bowden explained that it held about 100 gallons or more of water with a petrol-driven Briggs & Stratton engine pump. The trailer and pump were stored beside Dave Luks's home where the Fire Brigade building stands today. Charlie Bramble explained that when in use it was Dave Luks who mainly towed it around with his vehicle.

As there was no mains-water supply in Green Point at that time the tanker was slowly filled from the spear-point bores and when things were really bad, water was taken from house water tanks. (Lowell Reardon) Having to use their own vehicles in a fire to tow the trailer-tanker was a concern. Later, George Schoonhoven found a lady in Forster who wanted to donate her '67 Ford Zephyr station wagon. It hadn't been used for years and when they took it out of the garage it wouldn't go.

Lowell Reardon renewed the motor and gear box as the motor had seized up. It was later 'hand-painted' red.

The next acquisition for the Fire Brigade was an old Bedford 2 W.D. Cat 3 Tanker. (Oscar Bowden) It was a 'big day' to remember when the little group received their 'first genuine Fire Truck.' A picnic celebration was held at the Sailing Club and a large symbolic key was presented for the occasion. (John Amato) Later, Oscar Bowden applied for the purchase of a new Toyota Landcruiser 4WD for the Brigade, through the Fire Dept. Funding Scheme. (Lowell Reardon)

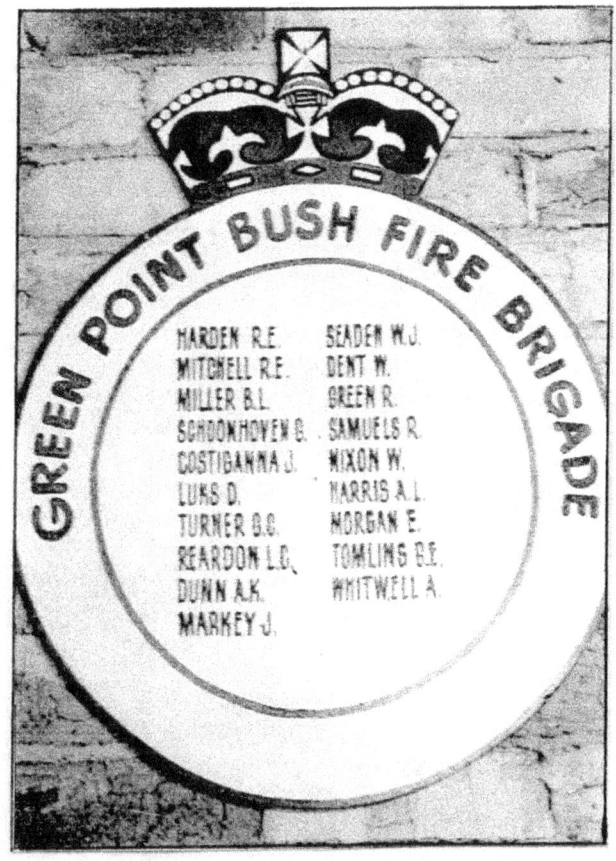

Oscar wanted a short wheelbase vehicle which could quickly be driven to the fire source, pulling the trailer-tanker instead of waiting for the larger fire truck and driver to arrive. The Toyota 4WD was also to be used as a transport vehicle to take brigade members to other fire locations.

The old Bedford Tanker held 200 litres of petrol for its motor. As the petrol fumes from the truck could blow up with the excess heat in a big fire, moves were made to acquire a safer vehicle.

Picnics At Green Point

In the 1950's Tom Ryan's parents, like other tourists at that time, arranged to take boat trips with one of the boat operators who worked on Wallis Lake. They would visit farms and pull in for a picnic where possible.

By the late 1960's and early 1970's when C.H. Degotardi rejuvenated the jetty at the end of Wharf Road, holiday makers started to arrive here for their picnics at the weather-shed. Thanks to Sonya Jordan we have photos of this memorable occasion.

Tony Amato was a fisherman who worked from Tuncurry. His launch, seen in one of the photographs was named 'Rose' after his wife. When his friends from Sydney came up to Forster on holidays, he took them on boat trips around the lake. Older residents may recognize some of the other people - Rex Bramble (Charlie's dad), is paddling his family into shore in the dingy and Tony Amato (John's dad), has his fishing boat moored at the end of the jetty. In the weather-shed's photograph, Tony Amato (wearing the cap) is with Jim Markey in the foreground. It appeared to be a meeting place for all the locals at that time.

Problem Driveway

We have all had them, but when George and Francis Linnerer put in their driveway at No.58 Green Point Drive, they had a really BIG problem. Their very steep access up the hillside, was blocked by a huge boulder. Francis decided to attack the 'floater' rock with her tiny pot-plant gardening tools. Bit by bit, soil was removed from around the large rock and eventually it was left standing alone.

Fortunately, at the time, the land across the road was vacant. When they levered the boulder it gathered speed, crossed the road, rolled down the hillside and stopped at the lake shore; where it still resides to this day. Job done! It could be said that 'from little things, BIG things Go!'

The Forest Garden ...'Memories of the past – shape our future!'

They say that gardens often reflect the gardener. In the early 1960's Renata Schmakeit missed the pine forests of her homeland in Germany so much that she planted 'lots' of pine trees on their block at No. 7 Green Point Drive. The fragrance of the pines, as they rustled in the wind, was what she needed. As seen in this photograph taken from No.9 next door there really were a 'lot' of Norfolk Island pines planted in the garden.

ost of the pines were removed later when the house was being built. However, in 2007 two very tall Norfolk Island pines still remained on the southern boundary line. Unfortunately, in October 2006, the trees were struck by lightning and started slowly dying from the tops down. Being close to adjacent buildings they were deemed unsafe and had to be removed in 2007.

Early 1980's　　　　　　　　　　1990's　　　　　　　　　　Mid 2006

Noises In the Night

In the late 1970's and in the 1980's Olive Steel of No.15 Green Point Drive remembered the rhythmic putt-putt noise of the inboard motor of Bill Deeley's fishing boat as it went along the channel in the early hours of the morning. A sound that she enjoyed! Interestingly, Bill mainly fished for food for his cat. (Eleanor Wickham)

I remember being delighted by the varied calls of the night birds near our home at No.14 Green Point Drive . Most unusual was the Coucal Pheasant with its coop-coop call repeated a number of times as if going up and down the scale of notes and increasing in speed as it went. Other favourites were the Tawny Frogmouth with its deep continuous humming sound of oom-oom-oom and the Southern Boobook owl with its repeated, mo-poke, mo-poke call. .

Another noise experienced by the early residents was the gentle lowing of the cows coming from the farm at Pipers Bay. Eleanor Wickham of No. 2 Green Point Drive remarked that the noise had a comforting effect and brought a sense of calm to the evening.

However, not all evenings were restful. On the contrary, one evening in the late 1970's Lisa Seadon who lived at No. 3 Green Point Drive was unexpectedly woken by a terrible blood-curdling sound. The 'loud raucous growling', accompanied by banging, was enough to scare anyone.

Movement outside the house in the dead of night, when living a distance from neighbours, was alarming. Later, it was realized, the noise was caused by an overly amorous male Koala, pursuing his female mate in a nearby gum tree in the garden.

Koalas were also sighted by Vera Lynn in the gum trees behind her home at No, 89 Green Point Drive in the 1970's. The last Koalas were observed in trees at No. 70 Green Point Drive on 10/11/1979 by Dr. Margaret Gibbons. As urban developments encroach on their territory, it is no wonder that in some areas the Koala is on the threatened species list.

Lights On the Hill

When there were only around six or so homes along the ridge of the subdivision and another six or so down on the flats, the lights from homes on the hill afforded a feeling of safety - a neighbour within reach!

When out night-fishing on the lake residents calculated their position in the channel by the light shining from 'the house on the hill'.

By the early 1990's, residents on Green Point Drive with water views, were noticing the first twinkling lights across the lake from Coomba Park. Those with a view over Pipers Bay to Cape Hawke, soon found that they too could watch the lights turn on across the lake. Reflections on the water – a delight to watch!

Taree Shopping

Early residents found shopping for all of their necessities quite difficult. Forster had only one general store which didn't always have essential goods in stock and at times was quite expensive.

However, Taree had a large store called 'The Barn' which was where Olive Steel and her neighbours went to shop once a fortnight. With a pencil in hand they would write the price of the goods purchased on a brown paper bag , then take it to the check-out to be added up.

By banding together they were able to share transport to Taree and by buying in bulk and dividing the goods up later they were able to save on bargains.

Travelling To School

The Schmakeit family moved to Green Point to live in January 1975. Tania Schmakeit fondly remembered walking with her brothers, whilst pushing a bike loaded down with school bags, out to the Green Point turn off, where they caught the Adam's family Bulahdelah bus.

Thelma Gordon recalled how her school children had to be driven to Forster Keys area where they caught the bus to Forster. A connecting bus took their eldest child to Taree where he attended college. After much lobbying by the Progress Association a school bus service was established, in the early 1980's, for Green Point.

Wayward Wanderers

From time to time cows from the Pipers Bay farm used to take the track around the lake's shore, following the feed.

Lisa Seadon-Hall recalled how she had a visit from one of the wandering cows. As yet, the steps up to the front door of their home at No.3 Green Point Drive hadn't been built and instead two wide planks of wood made a handy ramp. Being curious, the cow took up the invitation and walked right up the ramp to the front doorway and started bellowing for food - it just goes to show what length cows will go for a feed!

Wandering cows visited Green Point and later, after they had moved on, it was time to collect the dry cow pats to use as fertilizer for the garden. (Ernie Steel)

Weather Patterns

Over the years we seem to experience a cycle of weather patterns – floods, droughts and fire.

In the mid 1960's large areas around Forster experienced flooding. Charlie Bramble recalled that due to extreme flooding around that time, his father had to moor his fishing boat close to where the Forster Keys roundabout is situated today. The flood problem was ultimately solved when in the mid 1970's the Forster Keys Development allowed for flood mitigation to be taken into consideration. The whole region was affected when the Manning area received 13" of rain between 19th and 20th of March 1978. About 7,000 acres of land in the Manning Shire alone were inundated. The rapidity of the rise in the river was also unprecedented and the loss in terms of stock, equipment and communication lines more catastrophic. (Manning River Times)

As a result of the northern rivers flooding, large amounts of debris moved down the coastline and some washed up on Seven Mile Beach, including pieces of timber, trees and broken vegetation and even a dead sheep. (Olive Steel)

At that time heavy rain fell in our area also. The lake's water level rose and the islands went under water. Chris Sutton, an early resident, remembered seeing the wildlife animals swim away from the islands towards the safety of Green Point. A heavy log at the bottom of Schmakeit's block at No.7 Green Point Drive was driven up onto the shore by the storm and flood. Bill Schmakeit cut a section out of the log to use for cleaning his fish catch. (Andrew Schmakeit). It created the perfect place to sit at low tide and listen to the gentle lapping of the waves and watch the sunlight make dappled shadows on the sand below.

Such was the extent of the rising flood waters from the lake, that the vacant block at No. 1 Seabreeze Parade, was completely submerged. (Olive Steel) The fishermen had to leave their vehicles up on the roadway as they couldn't drive down to their moorings. (Charlie Bramble)

A time of drought followed and residents Eleanor and Bryce Wickham were forced to buy in water as levels in their water tank became very low - inevitably, fire followed in early 1981.

The Fury of the 1981 Bushfire

Starting in the bushland on the southern side of Green Point Drive, about half way between The Lakes Way and the present day chicane, the fire raged towards the village and the homes on the southern side of Green Point Drive. Thick black smoke heralded the blaze and it wasn't long before the police were involved, closing off the road into the village. The bush fire volunteers were on the move and George Schoonhoven (the Bush Fire Brigade Captain) was directing people away from the fire. In his haste he tore the hamstrings in both his legs. Being unable to run he crawled towards the roadway. Two young police officers, one male and one female, noticed him and ran to his aid then threw him into the back of the police van. He shouted to them to "shut the windows, don't touch anything and keep your heads down." The flames went over the top of the vehicle and crossed to the other side of the road. He had badly burnt his hands and needed treatment. After that close shave he retired from the Brigade, but continued his interest in local activities being the first aid man for the Green Point Soccer Team in the 1980's. (Beryl Schoonhoven)

Death of the Trailer-Tanker!

In the meantime Dave Luks, Charlie Bramble and Laurie Killham were trapped in the area we now know as Turtle Crossing. There had been a period of drought and even the swamp had dried up. Dave had the trailer-tanker attached to his ute and they all went out to fight the fire. Suddenly, the dry reeds of the big swamp caught alight. Dave couldn't turn in the small area that he was in at the time, so they disconnected the trailer and went to turn the ute around before reconnecting the trailer. Whilst they were preoccupied with the trailer the fire surrounded them and they were forced to flee for their lives. Laurie stayed as long as possible before leaving but the smoke and flames became too dangerous to stay any longer. He ran for his life and left the tanker pumping away. Charlie recalled how funny it seemed to hear the brr- brr- brr- brr-brr- of the tanker - "it was as if it had died!" he said. Later on the tanker was reclaimed. Lowell Reardon replaced the melted hoses and repaired the pump motor. The tanker went on to live another day. (Charlie Bramble) Beryl Schoonhoven later said that George had remarked "that they hadn't lost one back fence!"

Terrifying Experience

The fire continued to follow the bushland towards Thelma and Brian Gordon's home at No. 129 Green Point Drive. They chose their property because of their love of the Australian bush. Most appreciated was 'the view' of the magnificent gum trees at the back of the block. Now the scene had changed! Their favourite trees and surrounding bushland, up to the back fence, had become like a red hot furnace. Thelma, who had not experienced a bush fire before, was terrified. The tall gum trees looked like flaming torches with burning embers flying around in all directions and Coast Banksia seed pods exploding like fire crackers. The extreme heat and the roar of the wind made it a frightening time because of the close proximity to their home. Over time the bushland recovered – for all to enjoy.

Mercy Dash!

All residents start to worry when seeing dark clouds of smoke billowing from the Green Point area. Lowell Reardon was at work in Forster when he noticed the fire on the horizon. The electricity had been cut off which meant that his dad, Theo, didn't have power for his oxygen machine. The fire had moved further up behind the houses in Green Point Drive, and thick smoke was being driven by the wind towards Theo's home at No. 78 Green Point Drive. Lowell had to move fast as his father was finding it very hard to breathe. He raced into the next door premises of AIM Hire and collected four tanks of compressed oxygen, promising to supply doctor's certificates as soon as possible. In the meantime, it was a real emergency, as his dad could die from his emphysema. Loaded up, he drove as far as Forster Keys where he was stopped by the fire brigade and the police. He put his case to the Tuncurry Brigade Fire Captain, Noel Gogerly, who said that he could try to get through. He was told to wind up the windows and keep to the centre of the road, but he was stopped again at the corner of The Lakes Way and Green Point Drive. Leaving his car there he negotiated again with the fire brigade members. With the cylinders safely on board and being a brigade member himself, he knew the risks when he jumped onto the back of the fire truck. It was a matter of running the gauntlet, as the truck sped through the walls of flames each side of the road. They delivered the oxygen in time and Lowell returned to the fire area to help the other volunteer firefighters. A bulldozer was brought from Forster to cut the needed firebreaks in the bushland surrounding the village. Burning embers ignited a fire on Yahoo Island which exposed the old cattle yards.

Mining Rig Destroyed - Mineral Deposits Limited had a Special Lease No. 462 which allowed the sand mining company to do test drilling for rutile deposits. The area covered parts of the moors, south of Forster on both sides of The Lakes Way. The test rig and machinery yard were situated close to the big swamp on the southern side of Green Point Drive and operated day and night. Such was the ferocity of the bush fire that when it went through the area, the company rig and truck were destroyed. On 1/7/1981 Mineral Deposits Limited advised that drilling was suspended due to a shortage of drilling rigs. A decision, when and if to mine in the future, would depend on mining costs and market conditions. (P.A. records) After the fire, remains of the melted aluminium alloy from the truck's motor, was collected by the Fire Brigade as a souvenir. (Lowell Reardon)

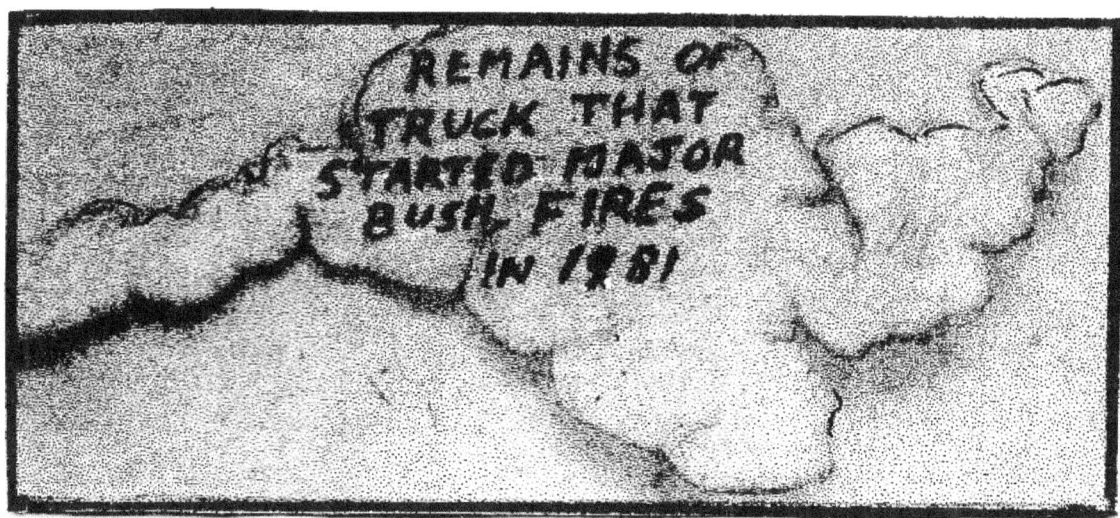

Green Point Craft Gallery and Restaurant

The population of Green Point was rising steadily and there was potential for business investment.

Dr. Margaret Gibbons with her husband Laurie Kilham and their family moved from No.70 Green Point Drive to develop the property at No.105 Green Point Drive. A shop was built, then, by 28/8/1982, a native plant nursery. The nursery plants were all spread out in the front area under the shade of the large Port Jackson fig tree and many home owners bought plants for their new gardens.

Then in 1983 the 'Long Sands Tea House' was built. The Gallery shop had a diverse number of arts and crafts, including paintings, sculptures, pottery, woodwork and glassware. Renata Schmakeit displayed her pottery and local artists their paintings and woodwork. The delicately coloured glassware pieces were set up near the window to allow the light to shine through the vases and plates. A potter named Ruth Coghlan started pottery workshops in the little shed to the east of the shop and students could fire their pottery in a big drum utilized as a kiln.

By 1985 Michael took over the shop area and supplied morning teas and lunches. Tourist buses, for a short time, brought customers for the delicious Devonshire Teas.

Pam and Graham Williams, who used to run an art gallery in Adelaide, were the next people to take over the Gallery. They brought a new energy and knowledge about the artwork displayed. Indian cuisine was introduced with meals being served in the evening, in addition to the usual morning teas.

In 1998 Col Race and his partner Anne Pratt took over the running of the Gallery Restaurant. In winter, the open fire made dining there feel cosy, and combined with the friendly atmosphere and wonderfully prepared food it made for an enjoyable night out. As the award winning business grew, to accommodate the extra clientele, the outdoor area was enhanced and heating installed.

No matter what changes were made in the management of the restaurant the merchandise available at the Gallery was always of high quality, diverse in nature, and became well known in the district.

The Gallery restaurant was refurbished and reopened on 16/4/2010 as The Gallery Function Centre. On the menu was 'Smokehouse Woodfired Pizza' together with home made bread. Lena and Norman Moore managed the business and arranged musical entertainment on the weekends. Weddings and parties were also catered for.

The house band was called 'Gallari'. Feature bands were offered accommodation in their home as an incentive to call in and play at Green Point on their way up the coast to the popular music festivals. 'Hat Fitz and Cara' and 'The Preatures' were the most famous bands to perform at the venue.

Unfortunately, the population pool in the local area was not big enough to justify continuing the business and the venue closed in August 2011.

Gallery & Restaurant

GALLERY & RESTAURANT

Visit us and be intrigued by
our unique and varied display.
Devonshire Teas, Light
Lunches and snacks.

FINE INDIAN CUISINE
B.Y.O

Lunch Daily - 7 Days a week

Dinner - Reservations Essential

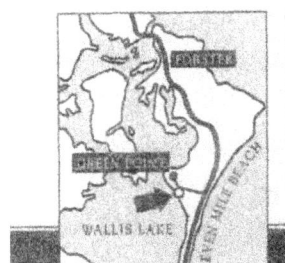

Green Point Drive,
GREEN POINT,
FORSTER
NSW, 2428
Telephone
(065) 54 5816

(8kms from Forster)

The Gallery Function Centre
SMOKEHOUSE WOODFIRED PIZZA & BAKERY
65575444 Bookings FULLY LICENCED

The First Children's Playground

In August 1981 there were 50-60 children living in the area, split evenly into under 5 years and 5 to 12 year olds. By 1982 two thirds of the residents of Green Point were young people with young families. It was acknowledged that there was an urgent need for a safe place for the children to play instead of having to play on the roads. The Progress Association wrote to the Department of Sport and Recreation for assistance in designing an adventure playground. Their thoughts were to build a pine log construction, to provide at least four swings and a piece of rocking equipment, like a swinging log (in preference to a seesaw), also a fort with a ladder and slippery dip. The Great Lakes Shire Council allowed $1,000 towards establishing the playground and they hoped to put all of this money into materials with volunteers providing the labour.

The reserve area next to the Bush Fire Brigade hall was approved by Council for the children's park and the Association set about making it happen. By November 1982, the pine log fort and the swing set were erected at the western end of the block. Later, Dave Luks donated his children's old cubbyhouse, which was relocated to behind the BFB hall. Council agreed to mow the reserve.

(See slippery dip in centre of photograph)

Children's Playgroup

In September 1983, the Green Point Playgroup was formed and mothers participated with their children two days a week for play activities. A cake stall raised $85 to be used to buy paint brushes, glue and several large toys. Working bees kept the area tidy.

Expecting the population to grow in the future and the number of children to increase, the Association requested Council to allow provision for playground and sporting facilities in any future subdivision requirements.

A History of Green Point
People Power - *A United Stand By Residents*

In November 1983 the Progress Association was alerted to a proposed Commercial Development for Green Point, of which there had been no community consultation! The Development Application was to go to Great Lakes Shire Council on 6/12/1983, which meant that action had to be taken as soon as possible.

The proposed DA was to establish a sailboat hiring facility on Reserve No. 1114 at Green Point. In other words, a boatshed and kiosk were to be erected in the area that we now know as Booti Booti National Park at the northern end of the subdivision. Booti Booti State Recreation Area Trust was to lodge the application on behalf of the Developer with provisions for a boatshed, food outlet, amenities block and access road.

The Association quickly arranged for a 'Special Meeting' of residents on the 10/11/1983 at 8pm at the 'Long Sands Tea House' at the Green Point Gallery to discuss the situation. Residents were encouraged to write letters of protest if they weren't able to attend.

Leila and Theo Reardon wrote that "It would ruin the natural character of the area and lead to more traffic on our already overburdened and unsafe roads. Also, that the waterfront was fast disappearing and that we must hold desperately to the family picnic and leisure area." They preferred to see it stay in its natural state, as a development would leave it open to vandalism. B. Coxon wrote that "The Booti Booti area should be kept intact for future generations and not cut up and subdivided in the name of tourism."

Representatives from the Council and Booti Booti SRA Trust were invited to attend the Special Meeting. The President of the Trust Mr. Geoff Edenborough, outlined the proposal and endeavoured to answer the barrage of questions put to him by the residents. Almost 80 angry residents were present and the meeting lasted over 3 hours. They resolved to write to Council stating their objections and to send a delegation of Committee members to meet the Shire representatives as soon as possible to request Council to 'reject the proposal.'

Residents were genuinely concerned about the state of the roads. They felt that the roads would become more degraded and therefore interrupt the flow of traffic. The safety of the children - with increased traffic, the narrow roads and speeding tourists was also a concern. The development would not benefit Green Point; instead, would be a disadvantage to residents. Not having the water or sewerage connected at the time, water and septic tanks would have needed to be installed and pollution of the pristine environment was a concern. If the venue was not a success long-term, the natural beauty of the area would be compromised with structures and could lead to vandalism. In short, the development was NOT WANTED!

It was said that the people of Green Point village had chosen to live in harmony with their surroundings. With the help of residents like Dr. Margaret Gibbons and Brian Semple, the pipe-dream was 'nipped in the bud'. (Eleanor Wickham)

Although Council refused to approve the DA on 20/12/1983, it wasn't all plain sailing! At that time, Booti Booti SRA Trust had the legal right to develop their land without Council's consent. It was necessary for Council to prove their objections and show that it didn't benefit the area at large and was detrimental to the community.

After an appeal by Booti Booti SRA Trust around 26/3/1984, followed by a Draft Management Plan done around 4/6/1985, the Association had no alternative but to ask, on the 12/6/1985, the then Minister Planning and Environment the Hon. R.E. Carr MP to intervene on behalf of the Green Point Community. The development didn't proceed which finalized the situation.

The Community Planning For the Future

A Special Meeting was held on 15/9/1983 to discuss the need for recreation/sporting facilities for Green Point and the availability of funds for the type of project under the Community Employment Programme (CEP). It would be labour intensive and usually funded $1 for $1. Suggestions offered at the meeting were: Tennis Court, Playing Field and a Community Hall.

On 27/10/1983, the Shire President at the time, Bruce Parsons, came to the Progress Association meeting at the Bush Fire Brigade hall to discuss the viability of the sporting complex/facility at Green Point. It was pointed out that they were going to need something for their growing community in just a few short years

.... Fundraising

In the meantime, the Green Point BFB was also fundraising for more firefighting equipment and facilities for their new Fire Brigade hall. As the fundraising was usually done jointly, by the same few residents, the proceeds from the fundraising activities were often shared.

With goals set, the community started fundraising with a 'purpose', starting with a Market Day held at the 'Long Sands Teahouse' carpark (Green Point Gallery) on 14/1/1984 at 4pm. There was a large variety of market stalls, a chocolate wheel and a merry-go-round acquired from the Nabiac Apex Club. Everyone had a very enjoyable time and it was a great success, with many donations from local business houses.

The next fundraiser was a fete held on 10/10/1987, where proceeds amounted to $1,095, with a clear profit of $480 being shared equally between the two groups. An amount of $62 donated on 9/3/1988 was also shared as was the amount of $161 being the proceeds of a sausage sizzle at Santa Barbara on the 4/9/1989. On 17/2/1990, a cake stall with homemade cakes, biscuits and sweets, was held at the Fire Brigade hall. Renata Schmakeit donated one her handmade stoneware pottery canisters and George Schoonhoven donated a bottle of good wine for the raffle: resulting in $68 for the Association and Bush Fire Brigade. (P.A. records)

Earlier, in September 1983 the local Community Radio Station, 101.5 – 2GLAFM, commenced broadcasting and Beryl Schoonhoven became the Marketing and Promotions Manager. George Schoonhoven helped build the booster station near the Telstra Tower on a mountain near Bulahdelah and he used to advertise the radio station on the side of his Pest Control work van. (Beryl Schoonhoven)

Beryl used her expertise to organize many fundraising activities to benefit the BFB. One such example was when in March 1990, Beryl advertised the event on the radio station and over 100 bikers turned up at The Ruins camping area for a weekend barbecue. Beryl was in charge of the catering and when they ran out of food had to go and buy more. They sold drinks and cooked meals on their mobile barbecue equipment – made especially by a resident from Coomba Park. They had to stay in tents themselves, on site, as the demand was so great for their services. The raffle alone raised $80. As many of the helpers came from the Progress Association, a donation of $100 was given to the Association from the funds raised. A Mother's Day cake stall and raffle at the Fire Brigade hall on 12/5/1990 made $158. (P.A. records)

A Community Remembers

Errol (Jim) Markey was a much appreciated, community spirited, early resident of our area. (John Mauger) As a leader and founding member of the Progress Association and Vice cPresident for a two year period (1981-1982) he strived to achieve 'progress' for Green Point and was also stationmaster of the volunteer Bush Fire Brigade for many years. Sadly, in 1983 he passed away and his ashes were scattered in the reserve area next to the BFB hall in 1984. In recognition of his tireless work the members of both groups joined as one to erect a plaque in his memory. Later, in May 1988 the area became known as 'Jim Markey Park.'

The plaque was mounted on a concrete plinth close to a gum tree planted in his memory. The tree had large stones placed either side to protect it from damage. Unfortunately, the tree later died and Renata Schmakeit planted a Bunya pine in its place on 21/2/1993. Over time Renata planted a variety of trees to enhance the reserve. In 1997 the area was no longer needed for a children's park as new playground equipment was made available nearby.

When the original Bush Fire Brigade hall was being demolished to make way for the construction of the new Rural Fire Service shed in August 2009, the front post and rail structure and 'Jim Markey Park' sign were removed. The memorial plaque was also removed and set aside. Later it was repositioned closer to the road on the eastern side of the property. Due to deterioration over the years the old memorial plaque was refurbished in 2010 by the Community Association. In early 2016, Great Lakes Council removed most of the tall trees on the property to enable the RFS members to better utilize the space.

In August 2016, when work commenced on the extension to the Fire Brigade shed, the memorial plaque had to again be put to one side until work was completed. On 6/9/2017 the plaque was finally repositioned close to the Brigade building between the two driveways and soon afterwards, the original 'Jim Markey Park' sign was refurbished and placed at the back of the reserve area.

Too Close For Comfort.......

Sonya and Bob Jordan of No. 17 Green Point Drive had gone away for a few weeks and when they returned home they were greeted by a 'disgusting smell', coming from somewhere in the 'garage'. It wasn't until they looked underneath the parked car that they found the culprit. Apparently a Red-bellied Black snake had found its way into the garage and couldn't get out. It had curled up under the car and unfortunately died there – probably from lack of water, as it was hot weather at the time. It took many days to get rid of the horrible smell.

Being surrounded by native bushland it is to be expected that at sometime we would come in contact with the native wildlife. Red-bellied Black snakes are still sighted in the village but not as frequently as in the early days. If not provoked, they move slowly and most residents don't mind them. Generally, the Eastern Brown snakes have relocated into the bush and wetlands and are seldom seen around homes these days. The long Diamond pythons and the thin green and brown Tree snakes are still around but with the continued urbanization of our village, there have been fewer sightings

It wasn't only snakes that came too close for comfort – Monitors could also be a nuisance.

When Paul and Jenny Klinkhamer came to live at No. 13 Green Point Drive around the mid 1980's, they had a visit from a nearly 2 metre long Monitor lizard which came up to their back door. As they had spent many years living in Indonesia and experienced Komodo dragons in their travels, their reaction was to just 'shoo' the reptile away.

In contrast to this story, we have a tale from Barry Dunn, whose residence was only a few blocks away at No. 21 Green Point Drive. Barry had invited his city slicker friend, Henry Morris, who was the President of South Sydney Junior Leagues Club at the time, to come to Green Point for a holiday. Henry had gone down to the lake for a swim, but ran back – screaming in full voice – "there's a crocodile chasing me"! By the time Barry arrived at the scene the Monitor lizard had climbed a tree in fright. Barry went on to say that "his friend didn't have any idea of what our wildlife looked like."

A History of Green Point
Puppy Dog 'Tales'

There once was a story about two intelligent dogs that lived at Green Point in the mid 1970's. One wanted to 'help out' and the other wanted a 'help up'!

The first was a short-haired German retriever named Darby owned by Charlie Bramble. Charlie would take the dog down to the lakeside when he pulled in his fishing nets. After watching intently how Charlie sorted the fish into two piles for the boxes, the dog thought that he'd 'help out'. He would go to the net and gently lift the fish out and bring them up to the shore. He had a pile for the small fish and a pile for the large fish and never made a mistake!

The second dog was an old basset hound named Amanda which was owned by Betty and Perce Adams, who lived at No. 2 Frazer Avenue on top of the steep hill in Green Point Drive. In contrast to the first dog this one was very large, very long and very heavy. She also loved to visit the lakeside and would waddle down the hill on her short stumpy legs with her tummy nearly touching the ground. It was great fun going down, but on the way up it was another thing altogether. She would go as far as she could and end up sitting in the middle of the road, half-way up the hill. There she sat, ready to be 'helped up' the rest of the way – waiting until a resident driver came along. They all knew to watch out for the basset and would stop and open the car door and she would climb in - ready to be dropped off at her home.

Memorable Occasions

Blackberry Picking -

Just as Lachlan Fraser and Owen Mathias enjoyed their 'blackberries and custard', many early residents also recalled enjoying picking 'nature's bounty'. In the 1970's and 80's there were quite a number of favourite blackberry patches around the area. Armed with billycans and other containers and wearing old clothes, to avoid being stained, and heavy shoes or Wellington boots for protection from the sharp thorns, the residents would go out to collect the ripe juicy fruit. Sometimes, a sheet of tin was used to press forward into the thicket and later used to stand on for reaching up to pick the most succulent looking berries. Most of the time one was eaten and the other dropped into the billycan. Some were eaten with ice-cream or custard and the rest made into jam or pies to be eaten later. Wild blackberries are classified as a weed these days and have almost been eradicated by spraying, so unfortunately the joys of family blackberry picking have become a fading memory.

Weddings - Past and Present

The most unusual wedding was when, in around 1992, early resident Tania Schmakeit was married at 'dawn' on Seven Mile Beach., The wedding party and close neighbours found their way down to the beach in darkness. With bare feet they all waited on the sand for the dawn-sunrise. It was the beginning of a 'new day' and a 'new way of life'!

A more recent wedding was held on 9/9/2017. Laura Murrell, another past local resident, returned to Green Point to celebrate her marriage. After the ceremony, beside the lake, the celebrations continued with a joyous reception held at the Community Hall. The experience and appreciation of living in such a beautiful lakeside environment brought both of these young brides-to-be 'back home', to make new memories to cherish.

The Saga Of The 'Escaped Goat'!

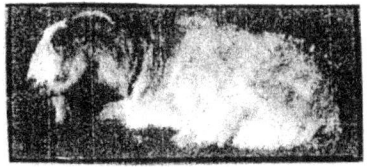

Being a semi-rural village, earlier residents took the opportunity to keep horses, chickens, ducks and other animals. In recent years there seems to be a resurgence of interest in keeping chickens as residents appreciate the benefit of fresh eggs and involvement for the children.

When a neighbour left the area Paul Dougherty adopted a goat named 'Molly'. It was usually tethered on the vacant sloping block at No, 6 Lucas Avenue, from around 1985-1995.

Later, in 1998, Wally Paszyn brought four orphan baby goats back from Goodooga – west of Lightning Ridge and, naturally, for a little while they had to be bottle fed.

When Baa-baa-ra the sheep was, sadly, no longer with us, 'Billy' the goat was introduced to the vacant block at No. 1 Seabreeze Parade. He then became the 'community goat' as residents would occasionally leave food scraps out for him.

One day, whilst out walking, I was surprised to see two visiting Japanese tourists creeping warily up to our friend Billy to take photos of him. Perhaps for them he was an unusual sight to see and the close encounter was worthy of remembering.

Later, in 2007, Cathy Oldfied from the coffee shop, was walking one evening with a friend when Billy got loose. Her friend grabbed the rope to capture the animal – BIG MISTAKE! Being very annoyed, Billy tried to butt her and proceeded to chase her.

As her friend held tightly to the rope Cathy shouted loudly – "Let go – LET GO THE ROPE!"

Lake Views Go – As Trees Grow

Early 1970's resident Bill Deeley, who lived at No.40 Seabreeze Parade, recalled that he could see across the swamp from his home to the edge of the water in Pipers Bay.

Lowell Reardon used to walk from his home near the present day chicane in Green Point Drive, straight across the paddock to Seabreeze Parade to milk his cow twice a day. As there were few tall trees to block the view Pipers Bay was clearly visible. (Phil McAsey)

Around the same time Perce and Betty Adams built on the corner of Green Point Drive at No. 2 Frazer Avenue. They had 360 degrees of uninterrupted views of the lake from their 'home on the hill.'

Tom Ryan's photographs, taken around 1977, show different views of the lake - Pipers Bay from No. 9 Emerald Place, Big Snake Island from Green Point Drive and Yahoo Island from the hill in Green Point Drive.

Col McPherson of No. 12 Frazer Avenue took the photograph of the view of Pipers Bay and Forster from the roof-top of his home around 1981.

The photograph of the view from up the hill on Green Point Drive was taken in 1984. Lisa Seaden-Hall, who was the first permanent resident, had her home at No. 3 Green Point Drive next door to the log cabin house. At that time both homes had expansive views of the lake.

The scene at the end of Green Point Drive, approaching what is now the carpark area for the Foreshore Reserve, appears vastly different today. The tall trees having grown over the years, now block out the view of the lake beyond.

The views from our block at No. 14 Green Point Drive, photographed between 1985-1990, show how we could see right to the edge of Pipers Bay, with Cape Hawke in the background. Early residents may recognize some of the older dwellings in Seabreeze Parade.

A common feature of the landscape was the tall ribbon grass growing on the vacant blocks. In times of drought the dry grass posed a definite fire risk.

Other photographs show that the salty marshes of the swamp area were clearly visible during that time. When the wetlands flooded, it looked like an extension of the lake.

....1977 – 1981 Lake Views

.... 1984 – 1989 Lake Views

.... 1990 Views from Green Point Drive

.... Lake Views 'Go'

This early 1990's aerial view of Green Point, by courtesy of Leanne Legge, shows the many vacant blocks of land available at that time. Also, the sandy swimming area beside the lake that was known as the 'Silvery Sands'.

Water views **go** as the surrounding trees **grow.** Our area is fast becoming true to its name -

Green Point !

Community Land Made Available

When Ross Kneebone cleared his property at the end of Bottlebrush Close, around the early 1980's, the land was covered in dense scrub and low trees. He recalled that when sitting on his tractor he was unable to be seen from the road as the foliage had grown so tall.

In September 1985 the land was subdivided into 5 lots. Later, around 1988, the Great Lakes Shire Council acquired approximately 2 acres or 0.9 hectares of this land for 'Public Reserve'.

This area became another Lot 317 and was designated for a 'future community building and children's park.'

By September 1990, the Green Point Progress Association and the Green Point Bush Fire Brigade had become separate entities, each able to better pursue their separate fundraising agendas. It was then envisaged that a Community Hall could be built on the site and future sport and recreational facilities be constructed

Legal Preparations Made

Local resident, Tom Shepherd, helped draw up the rules for the new Progress Association Constitution, which was lodged with the Business and Consumer Affairs Office in August 1990. William Heague, a local solicitor, arranged for the Certificate of Incorporation, which was received by the Association on 6th September 1990.

By having the Certificate of Incorporation it meant that the Progress Association Inc. was recognized as a legal entity, the importance of which is that members are protected against Public Liability claims (e.g. accidents) because in case of litigation, the liability lies with the legal entity and not with the individual members. From then on the group became known as the Green Point Progress Association Inc., thus making it possible to arrange insurance cover and apply for Council and Government grants in the future.

Aims and Objectives

In October 1990 the objectives of the Association were set down in the rules below:

a) To promote and foster community awareness and co-operation amongst the residents of Green Point.

b) To maintain and develop the natural environment of Green Point.

c) To maintain, improve and/or develop the public facilities of Green Pont for the benefit of the residents.

d) To advise the residents of the rulings and decisions of Local, State and Federal Government Bodies in as much as they affect Green Point or the local community.

e) To otherwise represent the residents of Green Point when and where it may be deemed
appropriate.

Sporting Complex Planned

As previously mentioned, a 'special meeting' was held on 15/9/1983 regarding the need for sporting facilities and a future Community Hall. At the AGM on 27/10/1983 Bruce Parsons, the then President of the Great Lakes Shire Council, was invited to discuss the viability of a sporting complex/facility. Fundraising started in earnest in 1984. More discussions were held in May 1987 and in April 1988 working bees were organized to clear the rocks from the newly acquired Reserve area, prior to the grass being mown by Ross Kneebone.

In August 1988, the Progress Association received $100 from Council's Community Service Fund to help with the proposed development. By December 1989, a survey showed that the population of Green Point had grown to 240 adults and 110 children. The small children's play area at Jim Markey Park was no longer adequate and a new larger area for sporting activities for the children was definitely needed.

A Public Meeting, attended by 26 local residents was held on 8/4/1990. It was explained to the group that it was not a Progress Association meeting, but a 'Public Meeting' to discuss the proposed Plan of Development for Green Point Reserve. A brief reference to the background and present status of the project was given and finance and funding discussed.

When avid tennis players, Lana and Bill Raward settled in Green Point, they envisaged having a tennis court – not only so that they and others could enjoy playing the sport, but also for the social interaction of the community. It was thought that court rentals would bring in funds for maintenance and for other proposed building projects. The 'tentative' Draft Plan was circulated and the meeting voted unanimously to carry on with the project without delay. For convenience, it was decided that it would be best to allow the Progress Association to manage any necessary arrangements with the different authorities.

In June 1990, the Association's Sport and Recreation Committee made a submission for funding through the Hunter Area Assistance Scheme, so that they could commence preparation of the sporting area. Council discussed the project in July and then in December 1990 the Proposed Development Plan was 'approved in principle'. Unfortunately, on 22/7/1991 Council confirmed that the HAAS funding had been temporarily suspended due to insufficient funds and that the Association should apply again next year.

It was decided at the Association meeting on 27/8/1991, that a 'subcommittee' be established and charged with the initial planning and to consult with Council. The following residents were elected – Lana Raward, Greg Wilcox, Terry Wright, Helen Walsh, Alan Robinson and Vera Bendixen. (P.A. records)

A History of Green Point
PROPOSED DEVELOPMENT PLAN

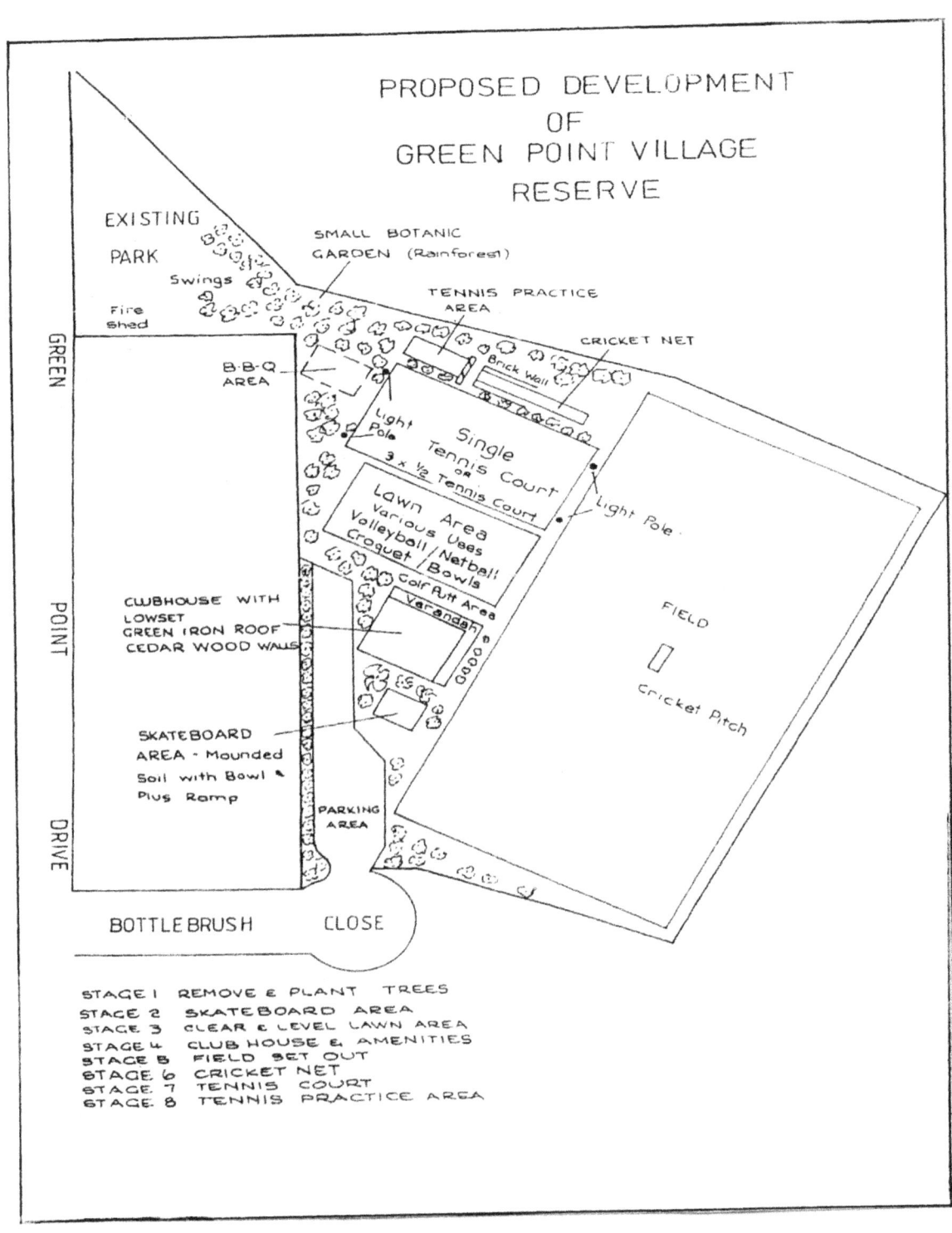

Telephone Booth –

The Progress Association was instrumental in acquiring a telephone booth for Green Point. As early as July 1974 the Association applied for a public phone box. Being a small isolated community at the time, it was needed for public safety. In February 1975 the request was denied again as it wasn't classed as financially viable, due to the fact that the initial capital outlay, annual operating and maintenance costs, wouldn't be covered by the revenue returned. On 24/8/1978 another request to Telecom Australia was made, arguing that the population had increased by 150% and there were more recreational visitors to the area. In September 1978 the reply was the same, as a public phone box was still not viable at that stage.

On 7/11/1986 a letter from Bruce Cowan MP, member for Lyne, explained that Telecom had strict guidelines regarding public telephones in outlying areas because of vandalism. Nevertheless, he agreed to make a representation to the District Telecommunications Manager in Kempsey. On 21/11/1986 the reply from the Manager was that our area didn't meet the criteria for the installation of a public telephone as their survey showed that 75% of Green Point residents had a phone connected.

On 24/4/1991 a request was made to the Public Phone Installations section of Telecom Aust. at West Kempsey. As a result, the Manager visited Green Point and discussions took place with the shop owner Carol Deeney, who explained that the nearest public phones were at Tiona Caravan Park and Forster Keys – each about 7 kms away. Many people had asked for the use of her phone at the shop – builders and tradesmen engaged on constructions at Green Point, tourists, local residents and holiday home owners and that all would appreciate the installation of a public phone. It would also be useful in the event of bush fires and accidents. Later, in May 1991, Telecom's Area Manager agreed in principle to the installation of a public payphone facility for Green Point. This depended upon access to cabling, permanent 240V power, reasonable supervision and safety for vehicles parking and payphone users. Later in the year a public payphone was installed, on the footpath, outside the shop in Green Point Drive.

Post Box – In August 1995 the Association argued that there were now around 500 residents in the area and although Green Point was serviced by a mail contractor, we were still lacking a proper facility for posting mail. It was not acceptable that residents leave their mail at the shop for collection by the mail contractor on his rounds and that it was a careless and unreliable way for Australia Post to provide service. This last correspondence was successful, as on 6/10/1995, when it advised that a post box would be installed in the November.
(P.A. records)

The Convenience Store

The Green Point store (known then as The Trading Post) has had many proprietors over the years. Each new owner provided essentials and expanded customer service in different ways. As time went by a residence was built on top of the shop, a carpark constructed and customer seating provided outside. The petrol pump facility became available and a liquor licence obtained.

A building application for the shop went to Council on 27/6/1990 and by December 1990 Carol and Terry Deeney established the 'Green Point Trading Post.' In October 1991, Carol was elected as a councillor in the Great Lakes Council. Deeney's owned the shop for about 4½ yrs. Robyn and Athol Gale bought the business around 1994 and built the residence above in the following year.

Ram Raid After hours one evening, a ram raid occurred at the shop. Athol rang the police as soon as he heard the crashing noise of the glass shop doors being smashed. Armed with a baseball bat he then made his way downstairs to ward off the intruders, most of whom had, by then, run to their vehicle. One of the men however, was intent on taking alcohol from the cool room, so Athol quickly shut the cool room door, trapping the would be robber inside. In order to stop the vehicle from escaping the police parked across Green Point Drive and arrested the occupants then drove down to the shop to collect the other man from the cool room. (Rob Dunsterville).

In October 1998, the new shop owners, Jane and Lee Adams and their two daughters Elyse and Kasey were welcomed by the community. In the year 2000, Tom and Cathy Sneddon and thir daughter Alyssia took over the running of the shop.

Then in August 2002 Roger Paterson and Sharon Hug took ownership and were there until they sold the shop to James and Brendan Murphy who bought it from them in May 2007. The name was then changed from The Trading Post to The Green Point General Store.

Break-In...Not everything always ran smoothly with their new venture. One evening in 2008, James decided to have a one-off outing to the movies. Whilst he was away a neighbour, on seeing a man climb up onto a large pot plant outside the shop and enter through a window, rang the police. The cigarette section had a security grill so was safe from the thieves but the five men were still able to take some alcohol before they made off. Suddenly, the neighbour noticed one of the men was back making a phone call. She rang the police again and cried – "they're back, they're back"! Apparently, their getaway vehicle had broken down at the corner of The Lakes Way and Green Point Drive and the man had walked back to ring for help. The police arrived soon after and arrested the men but as they had hidden the alcohol somewhere in the bushes James wasn't able to recover his goods.

Unfortunately, as the venture was no longer a profitable concern, the business was put up for sale on 15/4/2013. Old stock was sold off on a weekend in the May and the premises were completely closed in June 2013. (James Murphy) The property was eventually sold in February, 2015. The various owners of the shop have all provided the community with good customer service – at times taking bookings for the Community Hall and tennis courts. Their presence and contribution to our community are sorely missed.

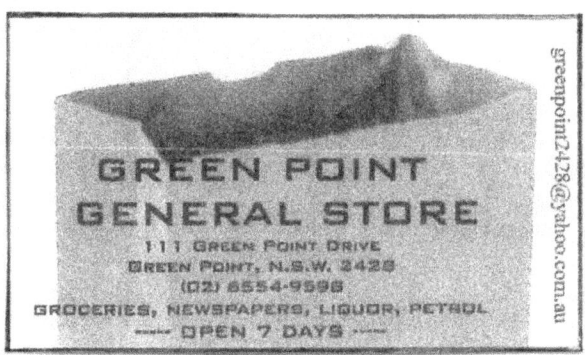

Gallery And Coffee Shop

In 1990, Cathy and Ken Oldfield moved up from Sydney to settle at 44 Green Point Drive. Later in 1993, they opened their 'Country Palings – Petals and Pots' business.

Cathy's gallery is so named because her father made interesting recycled items from hardwood fencing palings. When Cathy first opened, she had many of his well crafted creations for sale. Even though these items are a thing of the past the name has remained.

Apart from the wonderful coffee, teas and delicious treats on sale at the coffee shop other items available include artistically arranged floral displays, handmade handbags and silk scarves, jewellery, and home decorating items.

It is a popular meeting place for friends and tourists to relax and enjoy a delicious morning or afternoon tea whilst sitting on the attractive deck overlooking our beautiful corner of Wallis Lake. Originally, they helped to put Green Point 'on the map', and continue to attract locals, holiday makers and tourists alike.

Country Palings – Petals & Pots

Town Water

As far back as 1977 residents were enquiring when the water would be connected to Green Point, but at that time it was considered uneconomical. By mid 1978 the Great Lakes Shire Council had requested that the Public Works Dept. do a separate feasibility study as they were concerned about the health of the young families. The Dept. advised on 24/6/1980 that a pipeline was currently being installed and would 'ultimately' be extended to Green Point. Pacific Palms and Smiths Lake ratepayers also wanted the scheme implemented and had previously written to authorities on many occasions.

In 1980, the Health Commission of NSW carried out water testing of private supplies and bores in the Pacific Palms area. They found that samples of private, semi-private and commercial water supplies revealed that the water was unfit for human consumption. Also, in 1985, water from the underground bores in the Boomerang Beach aquifer was found to be unsatisfactory and that residents should boil their water for drinking and domestic purposes.

In February 1982 the cost of the water connection work was estimated at $770,000 and it was predicted that it could go as high as $1,000,000 by 1984-1985. In June 1988 some Green Point residents had objected to the proposed water scheme based on the grounds that excellent water was available in their rainwater tanks. Later, when GLSC was offered a 50% subsidy from the State Government via the Public Works Dept. to help with the project, they decided to use the grant as soon as possible – or the funds would be channelled elsewhere and in the meantime costs would continue to escalate.

On 23/10/1990 Richard Powell, Water and Sewerage Engineer for GLSC and Mike Schoevers, Project Engineer for the Public Works Dept. came to Green Point to attend a community meeting outside the Fire Hall. The forty residents at the meeting had details of the water scheme explained and their questions answered. (P.A. records)

The water to be supplied would be pumped from the Manning River into off-creek storage at Bootawa Dam. Here, the water settles out in the dam, and the only treatment required is the addition of chlorine to kill any bacteria. Very small amounts of fluoride were also added for the protection of teeth. The service connections would be without cost to existing houses on the understanding that they would be carried out shortly after the pipe laying was completed. The total cost was ultimately estimated at $6.6M and Council's share would be $3.3M which was to be paid from loan funds –repayment of which would be paid from rates levied by the District Water Rate. All ratepayers levied a water rate within the Shire area would contribute to the cost of the water supply. Water rates and charges for Green Point would be the same as at Forster, Bulahdelah, Hawks Nest etc. As a guide, the likely costs of rates for 1990 were $320 for properties that are connected and/or built upon and $260 for unconnected vacant land. Rebates of up to $87.50 per annum applied to eligible pensioners. Residents later received a letter from Council enclosing an application for connection which was to be filled in and returned as soon as possible. Council did not require the removal of existing rainwater tanks. (GLSC)

By January 1991 the water was available to Green Point, (P.A. records) and to Pacific Palms area by 1992. (A & G McKay). During 1998 and 1999 numerous breakages occurred in the water mains along The Lakes Way between Forster and Tiona. (The Advocate 15.9.1999) In 2000 the pipes were replaced free of charge as the pipe manufacturer conceded responsibility for the quality of the pipe installed. (P.A. records)

Ironman Triathlon

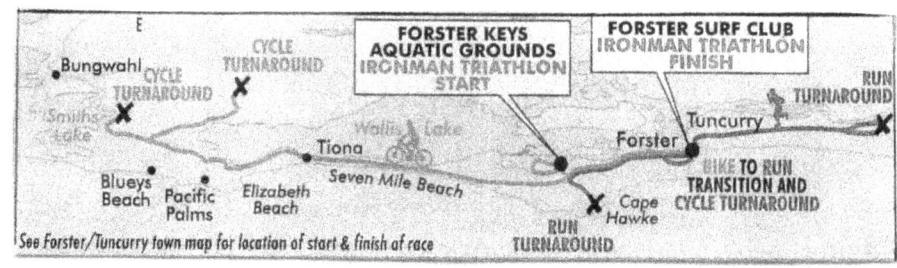

In the early years of the Ironman Australian Triathlon, members from the Green Point Progress Association volunteered to man road closure barriers at the junction of The Lakes Way and Green Point Drive. As marshals, they controlled the traffic going out from Green Point. In March 1991 Bob Currans and Bill Raward volunteered for duty for the first three hour shift and I decided to join them as company. Soon more residents arrived to form a very enthusiastic group. It wasn't long before the cyclists came into view and made their way towards us – up the long gradual hill from Forster. As each cyclist approached we all applauded loudly and shouted encouragement. It seemed to help as many competitors gave a wave of acknowledgement. We were privileged to barrack for a blind competitor and his wife who rode tandem. Later, we went into Forster to watch the run-leg of the race and again we were able to see the young couple being cheered on - this time running together joined by a length of red cord. It was very emotional to watch – a special moment to always be remembered.

Background...... In 1985, Australia's first 'full distance' Triathlon was held in Forster with a field of 165 competitors. In 1987, the field increased to 400 as it was also the National and State Championships. This bi-annual race continued to grow in popularity until the 20th Anniversary Triathlon in April 2005 when it attracted 1,619 men and women. The 3.8 km swim, 180.2km cycle and 42.2km marathon run, were deemed to be world class. Unfortunately, after 20 years in Forster, the organizers took the race to Port Macquarie. However, soon afterwards, Forster became involved with many new and adventurous sporting challenges, which continue to be enjoyed by competitors and spectators alike.

Keep Watch For Fires

By around 1985 the 'hot dry' weather pattern had returned. Eleanor Wickham recalled how Lisa Seadon at No 3 Green Point Drive was shocked to see smoke rising from the bush, near the lake, below her home. "It was very scary for Lisa at the time as no one was home in the log cabin house next door to her home - apparently children had a camp fire which got out of control." Luckily the fire was put out promptly before it could cause too much damage.

By 1991 the very hot dry weather was here again and ground fuel had dramatically increased since the last big fire of 1981. It was inevitable that another 'BIG FIRE' was due to happen!

Frightening News - On March 27th, 1991 my husband and I left for a short holiday away and en route stayed at Coonabarabran. On arrival at the accommodation we turned on the television for the Regional News programme just in time to see scenes of a raging bush fire and the announcer reporting "and the residents of Green Point are surrounded by fire." What a shock to hear! We just had to trust that all was going to be well on our return home.

The fire originated south of Green Point at Camp Elim and made its way up the middle of the bushland. (John Amato) At first, being affected by a south west wind, it drove towards Green Point. Suddenly, the wind changed to a south easterly direction. (Paul Murrell) As a crown fire it easily jumped across Green Point Drive between The Lakes Way and the village and then over the tops of the three houses near the chicane on the northern side of the road. (Lowell Reardon). The fire continued on to follow the tree line behind Camellia Place then burnt towards Pipers Bay until it came to the marshes. By then the fire was burning on three fronts and extended over a large area. Fire Brigade members and residents were able to beat out any spot fires in the low scrub behind Seabreeze Parade, caused by burning embers. (Paul Murrell) By 1991 the population had increased and it was a new experience for most residents. Some were nervous of the situation and prepared to go down to the lake's shore if needed. (Eleanor Wickham) John Amato recalled how worrying it was for him at work in Forster with his wife Jan at home in Green Point which was surrounded by fire. Luckily, his son Michael was collected from school by his grandparents and all they could do was to wait until authorities opened the access road.

We returned home to see blackened tree trunks in the Booti Booti area. Electricity poles on the Green Point Drive access road were badly burnt – many having to be replaced later on. Also, a large gum tree branch had fallen onto the roadway east of the chicane, and a native beehive was relocated by Lowell Reardon.

Lower Seabreeze Parade

Great Expectations For a Hall of Our Own

Around April 1990 Alan Robinson, who was Vice President of the Progress Association at the time, and also a local real estate agent, brought some heartening news to the next meeting. He had heard of an old disused tennis clubhouse on a block of land at Taree St., Tuncurry. The small building was 'available' if the Association approved: but first the committee members would have to view the building and agree to its suitability. As a result, Bill Raward, Ernie Steel, Bill Schmakeit, Roy Staddon and Allan Steed all went over to Tuncurry to check out the building. As a matter of interest the early Taree Street concrete tennis courts at Tuncurry were built around 1925 by Harry Wright, who also built the tennis clubhouse. (Wilma Shannon). Lana Raward, a local resident, mentioned that around 1941 when she was 15 years old, her mother used to play tennis on those courts.

.... Then Disappointment

Bill Schmakeit, the appointed local builder, had estimated the costs to dismantle the building, transport it to Green Point, then re-build, would cost between $800 and $1,000 and that the total cost including footings, new roof etc. could reach $3,000 or more. As this amount was clearly beyond their current means, the Association resolved, on 10/12/1990, that the offer of the building be declined in favour of the eventual construction of a new building. However, on 13/12/1990, at a Committee Meeting, the resolution was overturned in favour of dismantling the building then transporting it and stacking it on the reserve for future erection and refurbishing by voluntary labour. John Chadban, Shire Health Surveyor at the time, suggested that possibly the building could be transported wholly, by road, to Green Point. Alan Robinson made enquiries and costs were discussed again.

.... Final Resolution

Happily, this time the costs sounded affordable, and the decision was made to accept the offer of the building and arrangements were put in place to transport it to Green Point – everything was coming together. The land was available, Great Lakes Shire Council provided copies of the Development Plan P19/63, funds were raised, and NOW ..... a building supplied. Council had arranged for the fill to be cleared away from Bottlebrush Close to allow better access to the block and Association volunteers held working bees to clear the vacant land in preparation for the delivery of the building. Boundaries were pegged out on 7/1//1991.

Picture: Allan Steed and Bill Raward meeting with Council representatives.

Building Transported

In April 1991, arrangements were made to bring the small Tuncurry tennis clubhouse building over to the reserve land at Green Point. The following photographs show the low loader and crane from Hall's Crane Service at Taree being involved in the move.

Initially, the roof of the building had to be modified to enable safe travel over the Forster-Tuncurry bridge. After Bill Schmakeit, John Mauger and Bill Raward had done the work needed, the small building was lifted up onto the truck by the crane and the journey began. The road was closed whilst the building made the crossing over the bridge and the local police helped by directing the traffic.

Once at Green Point, the building was expertly lowered onto temporary brick piers. Bill Raward, a bricklayer by trade, had built the new brick foundations for the building ready for it to be permanently positioned nearby. Total transport costs amounted to around $1000 - for the large low loader $600 and the heavy duty crane approximately $400.

It was great to have the new building, but there was still plenty of work to be done in the future. Water and electricity had to be connected and the building painted inside and out. Also, the Association's insurances had to be paid and funds raised to cover building repair costs. (P.A. records)

The 'new building' was just the BEGINNING!

.... On the Move

A History of Green Point
.... Building Positioned on Foundations

.... Building Ready for Use

Members of the Lions Club helping out

Association Meeting Places

From September 1986 until June 1990, the Progress Association meetings were held in the Fire Hall. Then a letter, received by the Association on 20/6/1990 from the Green Point Bush Fire Brigade, advised, with regret, that it was not possible for them to continue holding their meetings in the Fire Hall. This was brought about by the fact that the roller door had fallen down and nearly hit Allan Steed. As an active member of the Fire Brigade he was covered by the Brigade's Accident Insurance. Obviously, if a non-member was injured in the Fire Hall they would not be covered. Consequently the building was to be used by registered members only and with permission by emergency services attended by George Schoonhoven or on his behalf. The Association sincerely thanked the Fire Brigade members for the use of their hall during the past years.

From then on Association meetings were held at the home of Dr. Margaret Gibbons until November 1990 and then at the home of Bill and Lana Raward until November 1991. By April 1991, the Association meetings were held monthly as there were many issues needing to be discussed. The community building had to be repaired after it was modified for transport and the roof rebuilt and sarked. Council required that the roof be reinforced and extra beams put across the ceiling. Bill Schmakeit became the builder in charge of the renovations. In order to be able to do all of the building work arrangements had to be made for Shortland County Council to supply electricity to the building. In the meantime, a generator was borrowed in May 1991, from Trevor White and a power pole erected in readiness for the electricity supply. Also town water needed to be connected to the property. Costs were estimated at $3,193.

By October 1991, the old tennis clubhouse became known as the 'Community Hall'. On 5/11/1991 a request was made to the Forster Lions Club for help to paint the building. Jack Hall, a retired house-painter, was a long term member of the Lions Club and arranged for some of the men to help members of the Association with the painting. Bob Jordan, a local resident, kindly donated all the paint for the job. To enable Association meetings to be held comfortably and to accommodate the number of members in attendance, low priced stackable chairs were bought from a secondhand dealer, the Tip Shop and other local organizations. Allan Steed made a number of trestle legs to support secondhand doors to be used as tables

The first Committee Meeting held in the new Community Hall building was on 2/12/1991. It was decided that there would be no meeting in January and that the February meetings would include the AGM with election of officers and yearly membership dues paid. Also, in December 1991, Great Lakes Council reimbursed the Association $1,495 towards the costs of the electrical installations. Grading and drainage of the Reserve was requested of Council in January 1992.

In April 1992, town water was connected to the property with a tap and water meter installed at the street. To save costs the Association resolved to do the plumbing themselves. By May 1992, the water was connected to the kitchen sink and by June the same year the hot water system, still being in good working order, was connected.

Ron Mitchell, resident, donated a kitchen divider bench, cupboards and a glass fronted notice board. Over time more tables were bought and some were donated by the Forster Bridge Club. Residents added various articles for use in the hall: an old photocopier, old ladder, crockery, glasses, cutlery, linen and curtains. Appliances included and old refrigerator, small oven, electric fans and jug and an old oil heater for winter night meetings. The required fire extinguisher and fire blanket were put in the hall by GLC. The Association arranged a postal box for correspondence on 7/9/1992 to ensure security for the organization. (P.A. records)

Christmas Celebrations

In the early 1970's Ron Mitchell, a retired farmer from Armidale, settled at No.90 Green Point Drive. He and his mate cleared a bush track through the scrub, from what is now known as the Foreshore Reserve, through the bushland towards Shepherd Island. (Bob Currans) Sheltered from the NE winds, the clearing at the end of the track became a picturesque picnic spot for the locals. Each year, from around 1979, the combined Bush Fire Brigade and Progress Association members met for their Christmas celebrations.

The picnic usually comprised of a sausage sizzle – sausages, onions and bread supplied. Residents were to bring their own salad, drinks and seating arrangements. In the years that followed Santa, played by Jim Markey, Jack Hall or Lyle Wrightson usually arrived by dingy with small Christmas gifts, introduced as a treat for the children. But, with no Santa Clause outfit being available at the time, it was decided that King Neptune, arriving in his boat, would be the next best alternative. These early 1980's photographs, courtesy of Lowell Reardon, show Laurie Kilham suitably dressed up for the occasion – distributing the small gifts to the village children. Beryl Schoonhoven recalled that at the 1989 Christmas celebrations she played 'Mary Christmas'. Wearing a red skirt with white cotton-wool hand sewn around the hemline, she joined Don Rutley who played Santa and added that they always had 'lots of fun'.

The area became Booti Booti State Recreation Park around 1977 and by 1985 the National Park's Authority had supplied the little picnic area with three long wooden tables with bench seats, and a small metal-edged fireplace complete with neatly stacked wood ready for use. For convenience, a garbage bin was erected on a post nearby. Later on, access was made easier as Council had graded the track in order that their rubbish truck could maintain the bin. Unfortunately, after 1992, when the picnic spot became part of Booti Booti National Park, the area was unable to be maintained due to lack of funds and staff. It wasn't long before the picnic facilities were destroyed and trees cut down for firewood.

The last combined Christmas Party at the picnic spot was on 9/12/1990. In 1991, A Christmas Party picnic with games and small presents for the children was planned at the Green Point Reserve; but because of the poor response it was cancelled. As an alternative and to bring custom to the local restaurant, members of the Association met at the Gallery Restaurant for a Christmas meal together. The children, however, were not forgotten. Instead, Santa drove around the streets of Green Point and when the small children heard his bell ringing they would run outside in their pajamas and dressing gowns, to wait patiently near their letter box until he came into view. Soon enough, Step Wilson, dressed as Santa, would come around the corner driving his trusty draft horse, whilst riding up on top of the dray. The dray was decorated like a chariot, with lots of ribbons, tinsel and balloons. Santa's helpers were sitting on the back ready to give out small bags of mixed lollies supplied by the Association

When Step Wilson had moved away, the Bush Fire Brigade took over the commitment. This time, the children waited to hear the 'siren' on the old Bedford fire truck before running out the front. By 1998 many of the little children had grown up and started to run behind the fire truck or chase after it on their bikes and scooters. It was found that this practice couldn't continue because of insurance complications so unfortunately, from then on, the little children missed out on this special activity. Sadly, as the populations increased, the initial uniqueness of the little village had changed. These days, to continue the tradition, residents can meet at the Community Hall for Christmas celebrations, where a greater number of people can be catered for comfortably or alternatively, down at the Foreshore Reserve. A Christmas Lights Competition, with prizes funded by the Association, is also held, in order to interact with the community. This activity has proven popular and many colourful and artistic displays have been seen around the village.

Residents Enjoy Christmas

Sporting Complex.......Fundraising

With the Sporting Complex in view, the Progress Association committee set about raising funds for the first stage of the project, namely the construction of a tennis court. Using their past experience in fundraising the ladies of the Association took up the challenge and came up with new and innovative ideas to raise money.

The following gives an idea to what extent the fundraising committee, and the community, worked to obtain funds for the future.

On 1/12/1990, a cake stall and white elephant stall were held as well as a Christmas hamper raffle. Later in the month, a premier film - Days of Thunder was shown, which raised $710. On 23/2/1991, Renata Schmakeit held a cake stall plus a trading table which, together, raised $278. Some of the Association members held fund raising events in their homes – the first being a 'lace party', held on 15/3/1991. In March, the raffle for a donated Easter cake raised $397 and the sale of buns raised $61. This was followed, in April, by a seafood raffle and a lamington drive which raised $448. A Tupperware party held on 30/4/1991 was followed by a Mother's Day stall on 10/5/1991 held in Wharf Street, Forster raising $102.

On 23/5/1991 the Association held their first bus trip excursion to Dingo Tops. It proved very popular as many of the residents who were able to attend brought their friends and family members along which helped make up the numbers for the large coach. Forty six people enjoyed the outing and it was decided to have more bus trips in the future. The raffle held on the coach proved to be a good fundraiser. The raffle for the ladies leather clutch purse was drawn on 8/6/1991.

On 4/8/1991 Renata Schmakeit started her monthly market stall at Pacific Palms market. Her stall sold second hand clothing, donated bric-a-brac, jams, pickles, cakes and biscuits and homemade crafts.

Bob Currans – a retired pastry cook and the dedicated group of fundraising ladies, came together on 22nd & 23rd August 1991 for 2 days of production line cooking of 'Green Point lamingtons' at Lana Raward's home. Orders were taken from local residents, their friends and relations as well as from members of Forster Bridge Club and Forster Arts and Crafts. The following month brought the next bus trip, on 24/9/1991, which was for morning tea at Barrington Tops, followed by a sausage sizzle lunch at Chichester dam. A Camelot Dinner-Ware Party was held on 10/10/1991 and a raffle for a tapestry was drawn in November 1991.

The market day at Pacific Palms on 1/3/1992 raised $118. Unfortunately, due to inclement weather, the market day in July raised only $50. However, the next one held on 2/8/1992 raised $60. The raffle for Morag and Scottie dolls raised $285. A Nutri-Metics make-up party was on 3/8/1992 and by then the Silver Circle fundraising group was operating. On 11/10/1992 there was another lamington drive followed by another Nutri-Metics party on 12/10/1992 and a street stall in Forster on 23/10/1992.

By this time the Community Hall was in reasonable working order with electricity and town water connected, a working hot water system, a kitchen sink, cupboards, and tables and chairs for seating. A 'Giant Garage Sale', held on 18/10/1992, proved a great success with many stalls outside in the grounds and Devonshire Teas served in the hall. This fundraising event bought the whole of the community together. Over the years donations from residents and businesses were always gratefully accepted.

Fundraising ... Bus Trip

Fundraising ... Fete

Tennis Court...... *Mounting Costs*

On 16/2/1992 Great Lakes Council indicated that one concrete tennis court could cost in the order of $16,000. In May 1992, a formal quote showed that the cost to construct ONE tennis court in concrete, complete with fencing, was estimated at $23,000 – plus contingencies making a total of $25,300.

It was a daunting task to raise funds considering the financial cost of the tennis court. Council had confirmed that it could not provide any funds; however, it advised the work done to obtain written quotes and survey results showing the number of tennis players in the village would be very useful to support application for funding.

In order to cover all available avenues for funding, the Progress Association applied for two similar State Government funding grants in June 1992 - one with the Hunter Area Assistance Scheme and the other with the NSW Department of Sport & Recreation. Each submission was for $12,000 on a dollar for dollar basis. To match the $12,000 grant, an Association bank loan for $6,000 was guaranteed by Council plus another $6,000 from Association fundraising. Work could then commence depending upon the outcome of receiving one of these funding grants.

On 3/8/1992 the DA was approved by Council and on 7/9/1992 the application for funding through the Sport & Recreation was passed by Council with 'top priority' and contact was made with three tennis court contractors to obtain updated quotes.

In October 1992, under the Capital Works Programme, a Federal Government grant was announced. In November, with the support of local resident and Council Member, Carol Deeney, the Association was able to apply for funding, when she managed to persuade Council to propose – not ONE – but TWO tennis courts for Green Point. As a Councillor, Carol continued to be an advocate for the Green Point community whenever problems occurred.

Council then made changes to the Proposed Development Plan for the sporting complex, requiring that two tennis courts were to be built at an estimated cost of $36,673. Council confirmed that the Federal grant of $36,670 had been approved with work to commence by 1/12/1992.

The Association arranged a special price of $110 per cubic metre for the concrete from Readymix, representing a saving of $3,000 on Council's tender. Council was then to update and follow up all quotes previously obtained by the Association and prepare final cost estimates.

On 1/2/1993 Council engineers reported on the final plan and estimates of costings. The total cost as 'revised' and including a 5% contingency figure was $46,670 which was $10,000 above the approved Federal grant of $36,670. Fortunately, the Dept. of Sport & Recreation's grant had been approved which covered the $10,000 shortfall for the construction of the courts.

Construction Of the Tennis Courts

Great Lakes Council could not contribute financially to the construction of the tennis courts, but helped out with the site preparation which was estimated at a cost of around $10,000.

Work commenced in December 1992 when Council removed several small trees from the tennis court's site and coffee rock soil was deposited, spread and levelled over the area.

Then in early 1993 the fencing contractor and his team concreted in the metal fence posts surrounding the courts and the tennis net posts. Next, Council workers poured the concrete slab in four sections over four days. To ensure that school children didn't deface the concrete slab, Bob Currans and Bill Raward stood guard each afternoon.

In April 1993 Snauwaert Australia surfaced the courts playing area in Synpave colours – grass green with tan surrounds and marked the lines in white. Next, the cyclone wire was attached to the metal fence posts and gates affixed. At lock-up stage the tennis nets were installed. An old disused umpire's seat was donated but was found to be unsuitable.

The rough coffee rock surrounding the courts had to be battered to a gentle slope and grass cuttings planted to stabilize the banks. Native trees and shrubs were planted in the garden at the southern end of the courts and shrubs planted on the slope at the northern end. The official opening was put off until the sewerage work and toilet block were completed.

Court Hiring

The courts were in use by July 1993 and hire rates were published in The Advocate newspaper on 28/7/1993. Arrangements were made with the Trading Post shop to handle bookings and collect hiring fees. In August, Sunday morning 'free open days' were introduced, but disappointingly, not many people took advantage of this privilege so by 4/10/1993 the idea was scrapped. Later, it was agreed that Progress Association members were able to hire the courts at a lower cost than non-members. Court hiring rates still remain very reasonable. (P.A. records)

Tennis Players

Local residents who were already playing tennis with a Tuncurry social group asked them if they wouldn't mind giving their support to Green Point by coming to play on our courts instead. By January 1994 this became the Wednesday morning social tennis group. Later, local residents who also played on Friday mornings were joined by other residents to form the Friday morning tennis group. Soon after, a number of local residents gathered together each Saturday for a barbecue and social tennis. When there was a shortage of courts available for the Forster Youth Tennis Competitions, Green Point courts were used for the preliminary knock-out matches. Jamie McDonagh, tennis coach from Forster, used to come out to coach some of the Green Point youngsters.

As playing tennis became more popular residents and holiday makers and their families took the opportunity to enjoy the game. Over the years court hiring fees have helped boost needed funds and brought the community together socially.

Tennis Courts .... Taking Shape

Tennis Players

Construction Of the Croquet Court

The croquet court was measured to size and heavy timber edges laid around two sides at the required level. The Progress Association was offered turf material from the coring of Forster Tuncurry Golf Club greens. This offer was gratefully accepted and many trailer loads were collected. The fill was spread by volunteers over the required area beside the Community Hall, levelled, and then rolled with a borrowed heavy hand-roller. The lawn area of the court was completed by April 1995.

In June 1995 it was suggested by Great Lakes Council that the croquet court be fenced to protect it from damage. Around the same time Council had removed old cyclone fencing from around an oval in Tuncurry and offered the posts to the Association - the proviso being that all the heavy concrete around the base of the posts had to be removed prior to being transported to Green Point. Bob Currans, Allan Steed, Bill Raward, Ron Mitchell and Paul Klinkhamer took up the challenge. The metal posts, were much appreciated and the Association approved $200 to cover the cost of the fencing including a gate into the area.

Trevor Buwalda supplied the wire fencing materials at a low price and Allan Cardwell, the tennis court fencing contractor, returned to donate his time and expertise to help and instruct the men on how to construct the fencing around the croquet court.

The Association bought an English style croquet set for $424 and a blackboard to be used for scoring. Residents of all ages came along to enjoy the gentle exercise and a player's contribution of 50 cents went towards expenses. By March 1996 a dozen enthusiastic residents played on the 3rd Sunday morning each month followed by a picnic lunch in the Reserve.

The photo below shows residents after playing a game of Pirate Croquet at a Community Fun Day held at the hall on 16/10/97. By November 2000 the Croquet Club had closed down due to a lack of interest.

Sporting Complex : Funding Pressures

Fundraising was a priority and every effort was made to raise Progress Association funds for the community project. The funds raised not only allowed for the finishing touches to the Community Hall and Reserve but it placed the Association in a stronger position when applying for funding from Government sources. At the Association's AGM, held on 21/2/1993, the balance in hand at 31/12/1992 was $6,523 of which to that date, $5,141 was from fund raising activities. A truly great achievement!

Fortunately, around March 1993, an 'earlier' application for a $12,000 State grant from the Dept. of Sport & Recreation was approved, but there was a proviso – it was dollar for dollar funding.

In order to fulfill the terms of the $12,000 grant, the Association made up their contribution with $6,000 from funds, plus an ANZ Bank loan 'guaranteed' by Council, for the remaining $6,000 needed. The loan was arranged over three years with repayments of $197 per month. To facilitate this transaction, Council required that a Committee be elected and registered to function under Section 530A of the Local Government Act. Accordingly, the meeting elected a committee to be known as the Green Point Sport and Recreation Committee.

Based on the successful grant, Shire Clerk and General Manager of Great Lakes Council, Mr Rex Mooney, advised the Association to present a 'revised' project costing, making use of the additional funds for any work related to the tennis courts.

The grant of $12,000 plus $6,000 from Association funds, plus the $6,000 bank loan amounted to $24,000. A balance of $10,000 was still owing from the cost of the construction of the tennis courts, leaving $14,000 available for 'work related' projects.

Fundraising continued at a pace as funds were needed to pay the monthly loan repayments as well as the ongoing costs of any necessary improvements.

The Associations aims were as listed below:

1. Finish the roof of the veranda

2. Relocate and improve the swings and other children's games which were removed from their previous site.

3. Clear and level the playing field at least enough to enable the younger members to make some use of it.

4. Construct the planned amenities block.

5. Plan the landscaping and proceed with planting.

6. Fence off and pave the parking area.

Sewerage Scheme – Meetings with Residents

Unlike the new subdivisions of today, developers at the time were not compelled to supply essential services to the landholders,

When the sewerage scheme became available to Green Point, Great Lakes Shire Council went to great lengths to liaise with residents and to involve them in the decision making, supplying them with questionnaires.

As with the introduction of town water, there were residents who also objected to the introduction of the sewerage scheme. Many meetings were scheduled with the authorities to promote better understanding and explain any future costs.

Green Point residents were invited to a meeting planned for 8/3/1979 at Pacific Palms where a spokesman from the State Pollution Control was to advise about the sewerage outfall north of Seven Mile Beach. By August 1980 the Public Works Dept. stated that town water was then supplied to the sewerage works in Forster.

At a meeting in June 1988, some Green Point residents were still objecting to the proposed sewerage scheme; as existing arrangements for sullage waste disposal were adequate as far as they were concerned and that the enormous expenditure required to implement the scheme, of which half would be passed on to the ratepayers, was not warranted.

At a further meeting held in November 1988, Tony Reed, the Water/Sewerage Engineer at GLSC discussed future plans and expected costs of the sewerage scheme. In September 1990 a Public Meeting was held at the GLSC followed by a number of meetings when finally, in 1991, Mr. Richard Powell, the then Water/Sewerage Engineer at GLSC, explained in some detail the functioning of the Forster Treatment Plant and its capacity for dealing with effluent from Green Point, an increase of only 2%. He went on to answer questions relating to the available options and concerns about the quality of the treated effluent being discharged through the ocean outfall. Residents were invited to visit the Treatment Plant on Open Day, which was to be held on 11/7/1991 and to also attend the Public Meeting at Council on Saturday 27/7/1991. There would be, in attendance, industrialists and marine biologists, also consultants specializing in the disposal of effluent, for which 17 options had been studied; with our area leading the State in this kind of work, (P.A. records)

Mr. Powell sent out a series of progress reports to all Green Point residents. On 9/9/1991 he advised that residents had stated a preference for option No. 1, which involved the collection of sewerage by a conventional gravity system and then pumping it to the Forster works for treatment and disposal. He also stated that Council would consider the augmentation, upgrading of treatment and effluent disposal options and that the Dept. of Public Works was soon to commence work on the design of Option No.1. (GLSC)

In June 1992 the Association members voiced their concern to Council about possible power cuts and how they could affect the sewerage system and possible overflow into the wetlands. (P.A. records) Another Progress Report dated 16/9/1992 from Mr. Powell explained that a Review of Environmental Factors had been completed with no significant associated environmental impacts. With the design work almost completed, contract documents for the supply of materials and construction to be finalized by October 1992, tenders would be called during November 1992. (GLSC)

Septic Tanks

In the past Green Point residents had to cope with using septic tanks. On the flat, where soil was sandy and easy to dig, construction would have been relatively easy, but on the ridge where it was mainly rocky outcrops, costly rock picking machines had to be used and in some cases controlled blasting was needed. Where reticulation systems, due to shortage of viable space couldn't be installed, an Envirocycle system had to be put in instead, at a cost of $5,000. When the sewerage system came along these septic tanks had to be emptied and filled with soil, or otherwise utilized for an alternative purpose.

Preparations For Sewerage Connections

In preparation for the sewerage scheme, Green Point landholders were obliged to pay a special levy for at least 2 years to help pay for the sewerage to be connected to 'new' areas. In October 1992, Council sent out a map to each householder showing the position of the proposed sewer pipe lines running through their property. It was then up to the resident to arrange for a licensed plumber to discuss the best position for the junction point in their garden. A 'Consent of Entry' form followed in December 1992, which had to be filled in and signed in order that the contractors, 'Eire Constructions Ltd.', could commence their work.

In March 1993 the contractors prepared their depot site and storage area on the northern side of the Green Point reserve. At that time the area was a vacant paddock with a few scattered trees. Portable buildings for the company office and amenities block were delivered to the site. Company vehicles, large dump trucks and different types of excavation machinery followed. Large white plastic pipes were stockpiled ready for the job in hand. Council advised residents by mail that work was to commence soon.

Work Starts

The sewerage pipe lines were dependent upon the terrain of the area as they had to allow for the fall of the land down to the four Pump Stations situated around the area. Arrangements were later made for the surrounds of these buildings to be camouflaged by native plants. Some residents were lucky as the pipes were laid behind their blocks, but others had to have the pipes running through their established gardens. Even though the contractors made every effort not to inconvenience residents it came as a bit of a shock to find a noisy excavator in their back yards at 7a.m. in the morning! Trees, shrubs and garden beds all had to be dug out before a trench was dug across the lawn and the pipes put in. Once across, the neighbour's side fence had to have panels removed for the machine to continue its work.

Clean Up

Rock and rubble had accumulated in the depot area and when Bill Schmakeit approached the contractors in May 1993, they agreed to deposit some of the fill on his block at Lot 38, Seabreeze Parade, to help build up the ground level. When the sewerage works were completed in January 1994 a huge hole was dug at the depot area. All leftover rubbish, including bits of broken pipe, large pieces of concrete, lengths of timber and remains of trees, were all deposited in the hole then buried and the land levelled.

A History of Green Point
From Septic Tank To Sewerage System

A History of Green Point
Official Opening of Green Point Sewerage Scheme

On 22/3/1994, the General Manager of Great Lakes Council, J.C. Fitzpatrick wrote on behalf of the Mayor, Sandra Machin, extending an invitation to all Green Point residents to attend the Official Opening of the Green Point Sewerage Scheme, to be held at the Community Centre at 10am on Friday 15/4/1994. In readiness for the occasion a commemorative brass plaque was attached to the side wall of the amenities block.

The Green Point Sewerage Scheme was officially opened by The Hon. Ian Armstrong, Deputy Premier and Minister of Public Works. The Government dignitaries addressed the crowd of residents from the veranda and after the official speeches and formalities concluded, the ladies of the Association supplied a morning tea of sandwiches and a variety of delicious cakes.

Forster sewerage works was upgraded in 1995 for full tertiary level, to be reused in Forster or discharged through the existing outfall at Janies Corner. Work on the construction of the sewerage scheme for Pacific Palms started in 1994 and was completed in 1997.

Community Hall – Building Extensions

.... Concreting of Hall Veranda Floor

When building the foundations for the Community Hall, Bill Raward allowed for a veranda to be built on the western side to overlook the tennis courts. The brickwork surrounding the area was later filled with soil and rubble.

The tennis courts had been in use since July 1993 and tennis players still had to walk along wooden planks from the back door of the hall, across the fill and down to the courts. At a Progress Association meeting on 7/12/1992, $400 was approved to concrete the floor of the veranda. By February 1993, when the fill in the veranda settled, Bill Raward and Bob Currans made up the form work for the concrete floor and George Cavalletto did the concreting. Soon afterwards brick steps were built.

.... Amenities Block Built

As the old pit toilet behind the Fire Brigade hall was the only amenity at that time, and with the sewerage connection soon to be available, it was imperative that a new toilet block be constructed as soon as possible. In the meantime, the Fire Brigade toilet was improved as a temporary measure. The Association meeting on 4/5/1993 agreed that the first priority was to build a toilet block and storage room as per the rough sketch prepared by Bill Raward, with final plans and costings to be prepared at a later date and submitted to Council. The budget for the building was $11,000. On 8/6/1993 the Association went ahead with the bank loan.

The construction of the amenities building was proceeding satisfactorily so a payment of $6,000 was made, on 6/7/1993, to the builder Todd Haddon. On 3/8/1993 his final invoice for $4,927 (including a $70 refund for the building application fee) was received and paid. The floor tiles for the toilets were discounted as they were left over from another job. To further keep costs down Association members bought second hand toilets and hand basins from the Tuncurry Tip Shop at bargain prices. The sewerage was connected to the amenities block by December 1993 and inspected by March 1994.

The Association funds were made up of a $12,000 NSW Sport & Recreation grant, plus $6,000 bank loan and $6,000 of fundraising totalling $24,000 - LESS the $10,000 shortfall due to the construction of the tennis courts. The balance of $14,000 covered the final cost of $13,650 for the completed amenities block – meaning that through fundraising by the community it contributed most of the cost of building the facility.

.... Construction of Hall Veranda Roof

On 1/11/1993 the Association Committee received and approved a quote from local builder, Allan Dunn, to construct the veranda roof for around $700. The work started shortly afterwards.

As the toilet block had already been built, allowing for a breezeway area, the veranda had to join up with the existing roofline. To save costs the builder used donated secondhand clip-lock roofing supplied by Bill Schmakeit.

The new veranda roof not only made the little box-shaped hall building look better in appearance but it allowed for much more usable space as well as shelter. In February 1994, for convenience and safety, a light was installed outside the amenities block.

.... Construction of Hall Front Steps

In order that the hall building complied with Council's safety regulations, the Association was required to update the entrance to the building. The original set of four small wooden steps up to the front door were deemed to be unsafe and the construction of a landing and wider steps with handrails were required. In March 1996, Roy Staddon, Bill Raward and Bob Currans undertook the building work necessary, together with a porch roof over the landing area. A Booral district timber mill merchant, Peter Gray, kindly donated the spotted gum hardwood for the job – saving the Association $250 towards the quoted cost of $332. With the paint being supplied by Council, the guttering and woodwork (except for the steps), were painted with heritage dark green and cream to match the rest of the building. To complete the work, the volunteers constructed a concrete slab at the approach to the steps. Around the same time the workmen erected a bollard fence to define the boundary of the carpark – koppers logs being supplied by Council.

Fundraising and Repaying the Loan

On the completion of the tennis courts around July 1993, a bank loan of $6,000 was taken out by the Progress Association, in accordance with the Government grant. It was anticipated that the hiring fees from the court use would cover the $196 monthly repayments. Generally, these payments were able to be paid but on some occasions, due to wet weather, there was a shortfall. In order to ensure the payments, fundraising activities had to be held.

Day coach trips were enjoyed by residents and their friends. On 16/5/93 a trip to Kendall Markets, was followed by a barbecue lunch at Swans Crossing. On 17/9/94, a garage sale and market day was held at the Community Hall. Then, on 24/10/1994 a day trip to Myall Lakes was held, with morning tea at Tea Gardens, lunch at Leggey's restaurant at Myall Shores and home via Seal Rocks. The Association ladies catered for the premiere showing of the film 'First Knight' at the Tuncurry cinema on 3/8/1995. A day trip to Maitland markets was held on 7/7/1996. At convenient intervals between other fundraising events large scale lamington drives were held which proved to be the best fundraising activity. Because bank loan interest rates during the year had increased from an initial rate of 9.75% to 12.0%, the payout time had to be extended by one month and therefore would now be finalized in August 1996.

Celebration Fete

A large celebration fete and garage sale was held on 15/9/1996 to celebrate the final payment of the Association's bank loan towards the tennis courts and amenities block. The event was widely published in the local media and on the day was well attended. Now that the Community Hall was fully operational morning teas with cakes and scones could be catered for inside the hall or on the veranda. Barbecue food was on sale and the many and varied market stalls were spread around the grounds. The local fishermen donated a huge seafood basket for the raffle. Gift vouchers were donated for the tombola by local businesses and residents supplied the food gifts and wine. Apart from going towards any shortfall in court hire fees needed to re-pay the bank loan some of these funds paid for hall improvements and running costs.

Ongoing Hall Improvements

In the years that followed and as funds and materials became available – either by donation, fundraising, Council or Governments grants, necessary repairs and improvements were able to be made to the Community Hall and surrounds. As a means of cutting costs, Association working bees were employed where possible. Eager volunteers laid sections of concrete paving near the hall, and installed the two picnic bench/tables on cemented slabs beside the tennis courts. Also, the existing bollard fence was repositioned further away from the large trees and low bollard fencing was constructed along the northern side of the carpark. To enhance the area, many native trees were planted around the perimeter of the park area. When general maintenance repairs to the hall became necessary, the men were able to carry out the work needed. They repaired and repainted dry rot areas in the old building and replaced wooden window sills, prior to helping with the installation of the five new aluminium windows (complete with security grill fly screens) When it came to painting the interior of the hall and repairing and painting the little cubbyhouse/shed both men and women were involved. Later, a number of appliances, including a refrigerator, microwave oven and a photocopier, were purchased to use by the Association. New lino floor tiles were laid, a number of second hand chairs and tables were acquired, a screen door fitted and an outsides light installed. Apart from approximately $1,000 p.a. towards maintenance of the hall, Council repaired a broken fibro wall, installed a light on a pole in the carpark, extended the front pathway and attended to drainage problems surrounding the hall building.

Community Involvement

Fun for All

Second Children's Playgroup - Green Point Grubs

In September 1993, when Eire Constructions Ltd. workers were using a fork-lift to clear their depot area on the reserve paddock, Bill Raward and Bob Currans asked if they could assist them to move the little 'cubbyhouse' from behind the Fire Brigade building. The 'cubby' was then repositioned between the Community Hall toilet block and the tennis court fence – later to be used by the Progress Association for storage purposes.

In mid 1995 enquiries were being made about the possibility of a children's play group being formed, but for this to happen an area near the Community Hall would have to be fenced. By 7/8/1995 Bob Currans and Bill Raward had enclosed the area with cyclone fencing, from the corner of the toilet block to the tennis court fence at one end and from the tennis court to the croquet court fence at the other. With the help of Athol Gale and Roy Staddon three gates were erected for access – one each end and an old heavy wooden gate at the entrance to the breezeway.

Now that the children could be enclosed safely, Gayle Redman started up the little children's playgroup called 'THE GRUBS'. The group was a registered member of the Playgroup Association of NSW. Playgroup fundraising helped buy play equipment and mothers came along to help out with craftwork and playtime. It was decided that the cubbyhouse would be best located down towards the croquet court. Howard Redman and some of the dads, used round logs as rollers to push it into position, where Bill Raward and Bob Currans had formed brick piers to support the little building. The next job was to clean it up and secure the window in readiness to store equipment and toys.

Four kinder sized tables were bought for $5 each from surplus stock at the Forster Education Dept. Office and two blackboards were made and painted by Howard Redman. (P.A. records) Gayle Redman related "that for approximately four years 15-20 pre-school children attended the group at the hall each Tuesday between 9.30am and 11.30am. Many happy hours were shared by parents and children, including the day Santa came to visit in December 1996. Ross Presgrave kindly played Santa each year arriving at the hall in the 'big red fire truck' which was always a hit with the young children." In April 1997, with safety in mind, timber uprights were painted and attached to the veranda railings by volunteers, John Cavanagh and Howard Redman. The cost of materials ($160) was shared equally by the Playgroup and the Progress Association.

The Rubbish Collectors

When Bob and I came to live at Green Point in 1990 we fell in love with the natural beauty of the area. We'd walk down to the Booti Booti area at the point (opposite Shepherd Island) each day to sit and enjoy the sound of the wind in the She-oaks, look out over the waters of Pipers Bay, and watch the black swans feeding on the glistening lake. It all appeared perfect until on closer inspection we realized that the area was littered with long-necked beer bottles. There must have been 25 years of discarded bottles hidden in the long grass by the lakeside or thrown into the nearby bushland.

We decided there and then that on future walks we would go armed with plastic shopping bags to collect some of the bottles and take them home to be deposited in our garbage bin. When the weight became too heavy to carry without splitting the plastic bags, Bob took down an old army kitbag which was soon filled. After clearing the area at the very point we systematically worked our way around the bush area beside the lake – often having to crawl around under the thick bushes to retrieve the cache of bottles.

Circuit Streets

During 1991, when walking the circuit each week day (weather permitting), we found that the village streets were also in need of a clean up. It was apparent that, over the years, the throwing of rubbish into the deep overgrown gutters was the norm. To make rubbish collection safer the stem of an old umbrella was sharpened to a point to make it easier to stab papers and the handle used to pull bottles out from hard to reach places. Residents became accustomed to seeing 'the rubbish collectors' walking the roadside on a regular basis. It was nice to receive a friendly 'good on you' or wave and a beep from their car horn in recognition.

Over the years, as more houses were built on the vacant blocks and new owners took pride in their gardens (including their gutters and verges), we found that the amount of discarded rubbish greatly reduced. Walks became shorter and more varied to include the cross streets and the park area by the foreshore. Later, as residents became more aware of the problem noticeable improvements were evident. John Hughes (a past resident of Green Point) for example, was also a familiar figure carrying a plastic bag and collecting discarded litter on his morning walks when going to the General Store for his daily newspaper.

Adopt a Road

By 1994, when I found that I was unable to continue playing tennis with the local group, I decided to go walking for exercise instead. It was quite evident that there was a build up of rubbish by the roadside from the Community Hall out to the junction at The Lakes Way. Whilst the tennis group played on I set off, once a week, with a supply of plastic shopping bags and my umbrella spike to clean up the roadside.

The bags, when filled, were far too heavy to carry back to the hall garbage bin so I piled them up at a number of locations ready to be collected by car later. On average, I would collect at least twelve bags of litter each week plus a variety of articles such as broken pieces of building materials, car parts, books, smelly fish and prawn heads, old clothing and dirty disposable nappies. Happily; over the years, the amount of litter collected on this stretch of road has reduced to around two full plastic bags each week, and with the help of other residents and the 'Clean Up Australia Campaign', the amount of larger dumped articles has been kept to a minimum. After walking back to the Community Hall, the park area was next to be cleaned. Then, after collecting the bags from the roadside, rubbish was recovered from the access track to Seven Mile Beach and the area around the bus shelter.

In June 1996, 'Keep Australia Beautiful' had an initiative through contact with local Councils, to introduce an 'Adopt a Road Scheme' to reduce roadside litter. As Great Lakes Council was becoming more environmentally conscious, John Cavanagh approached the Progress Association in July 1996 for volunteers to take on the length of Green Point Drive from The Lakes Way turnoff to the entrance of the village. As I was already cleaning this area regularly, I naturally became involved. To make it an official project, an 'Adopt a Road' sign was erected near the turnoff. After the area was scrutinized by the judges, I was thrilled to find that we had done well and that the 'Keep Australia Beautiful' Council (NSW) had awarded us a Certificate of Recognition for actively undertaking to improve our town and its environment through participation in the 1996 Tidy Towns Program. Later, at the awards ceremony, I had the honour of collecting the Award Certificate on behalf of the community.

Over the next 20 years, the work continued with Bob and I working together as a team, walking and using the car. When unable to clean the road, due to bad weather or illness, other caring 'Green Pointers' helped out as part of our team effort – a ritual that continues to this day.

Clean Up Australia Day

This organization was founded by Ian Kiernan in 1990, but it wasn't until 1995, when Great Lakes Council contacted the Progress Association, that Green Point became involved and Don Craig offered to organize a group to participate. Don continued as co-ordinator until Ron Davis took over around 1999. Terry Rolfe became co-ordinator in 2000, followed by Les Hardacre who took his place until Ron returned and continued the job until 2015 when he moved from the village. Fortunately, long time participants Gayle and Howard Redman, then became the co-ordinators for the next three years, followed by Gaye Tindall in 2019 and Margaret Blackwood in 2020.

The event is held on the first Sunday in March each year. After 'signing on', for insurance purposes, resident volunteers receive large bags for the collection of rubbish and a pair of sturdy gloves. When they have finished their designated area and the bags of rubbish left at roadside collection points, they return to the hall for a welcome cup of tea and sandwiches. The piles of rubbish distributed around the village are later collected by trailer or truck and taken back to the Community Hall carpark – ultimately ending up at the Tuncurry Waste Management Facility.

Generally, over the years, it has been a matter of 'out of sight – out of mind' as volunteers collect hidden articles from the bushland areas adjacent to the roadside. Mainly the collection is made up of left-over building materials such as lattice work, broken bricks, lumps of cement, pavers and tiles. General household rubbish includes old lounge chairs and other broken furniture, mattresses, television sets and other electrical items, broken bikes and toys. Rolls of wire and old crab traps, car tyres and batteries add to the list and there's always drink bottles of all descriptions, drink cans, cigarette butts and packets, plus confectionary and fast-food wrappers. Thankfully, the situation now appears to be much improved. In recent years a number of concerned residents have included the collection of roadside rubbish as part of their morning walk. Other factors which have helped reduce roadside litter are the phasing out of plastic shopping bags from department stores and the introduction of the 'Return & Earn' scheme. Members of the Green Point community continue to attend this activity each year and gladly volunteer their services. New volunteers are made most welcome, as over the years numbers have fluctuated.

Ian Kiernan AO, Chairman and Founder

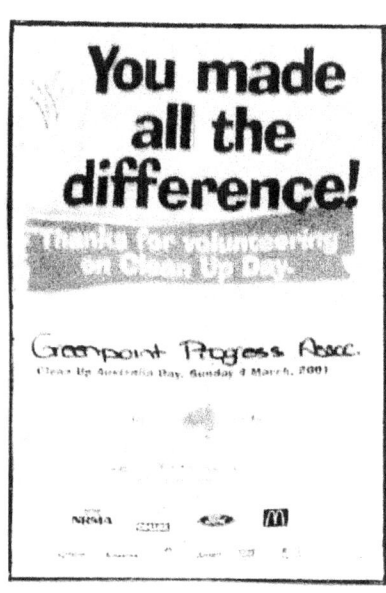

Volunteers Signing On

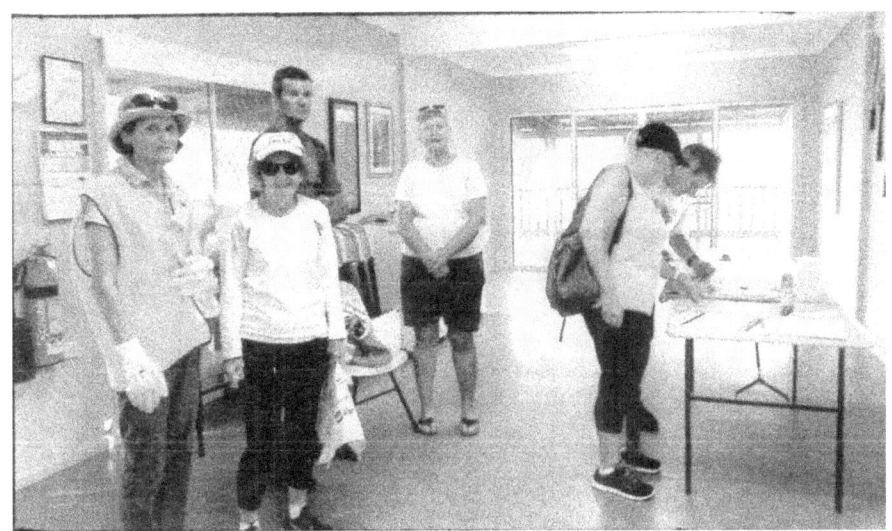

Ready to Go!

Rubbish Collections

Bushfire Alert

With every spell of very hot dry weather comes the threat of bush fires and accidents CAN happen!

.... Smouldering Peat

Around 1993-1994, when local lads had a cubbyhouse –complete with furnishings – in the area of Booti Booti National Park, 200 metres or so into the bushland on the northern side of Green Point Drive, and not far from the entrance to the village, an accidental flame ignited a small fire. Authorities did their best to put out the fire in the large area of peat bog nearby but the fire continued to burn underground. Phil McAsey, from our Green Point Rural Fire Brigade, used his knapsack equipment to check on the smouldering peat for the next week until it was finally extinguished.

.... Hot Embers

During the mid 1990's, there was a large bush fire on Wallis Island. The strong northwesterly blew up and hot embers were showered far and wide – even landing at Green Point and parts of Forster.

The 1997 Bushfire ......*Sparks Fly*

On 23/1/1997, some young people were riding their trail bikes out from the sewerage works near Janies Corner, at the northern end of Seven Mile Beach, when a spark ignited bushland. Their efforts to put out the fire were unsuccessful and the fire quickly got out of control.

Soon our local Fire Brigade volunteers were called in and crews came from Tuncurry and Pacific Palms Brigades to assist against the advancing fire. (Green Point's old Bedford fire truck often broke down and at the time was in the Council workshop being repaired). As a safety precaution for firefighters and the public alike, The Lakes Way was closed and the electricity supply was switched off.

Before too long the fire had jumped The Lakes Way and sped across the wetlands towards Green Point. The thick dark smoke billowed high into the air as the flames took hold of the Paperbark trees. Hot embers were borne on the strong northeasterly, landing on local properties and residents quickly strove to put them out. There were two high points in the fire – one going towards Pipers Bay and the other going south from Green Point Drive towards Camp Elim. Containment lines were cleared north of Camp Elim and three helicopters were brought in. The helicopter pilots were wonderful – flying from 10am until 9pm. When it was dark they flew with the aid of search lights, dipping down into the shallow water of Pipers Bay and out from Smokehouse Beach in Wallis Lake. In Pipers Bay, the helicopters did circular runs every three minutes – working in rotation – with one collecting its load of water as the other came in to follow. Sometimes there was one on each side of Pipers Bay, such was the urgency of the situation. Sometimes their landing gear had to go down below the water level in order to collect the water in their canvas buckets. When loaded, they sped off with their precious cargo to douse the numerous spot fires. By 9pm the nearby flames had been extinguished and the relieved residents of Green Point were able to relax once more. It wasn't until a week later that the 'rain' came and put out the smouldering remains of the fire.

Later, it was found that the fire had jumped Green Point Drive between The Lakes Way and the village entrance, damaging many electricity poles which later had to be replaced.

.... From Janies Corner

.... Towards Green Point

Roads

Early Times

Around 1962, when the Green Point subdivision was constructed the roads were very narrow and basic – just a thin layer of bitumen over road base. By 1973 most roads were eroded, especially Lucas Avenue, and high grass, Lantana and Blackberry grew by roadsides. On 24/4/1973 the Progress Association complained to Great Lakes Shire Council about the rapidly deteriorating condition of the un-made road, from The Lakes Way to Green Point village. In March 1974, an Association request was made that this length of road be tar sealed. Road work commenced when Council funds became available – with the work being done in sections. Road maintenance continued to be needed, until the work was completed around 1976. A letter dated 6/3/1979 from the Association to Council stated that no maintenance had been done on Green Point roads for the last 7 years. In October 1982, a petition containing 76 signatures was sent by the residents of the village to Council, requesting immediate attention to the dangerous state of the roads in Green Point. The Cape Hawke Advocate Newspaper was also notified.

The action of extra incoming traffic, with holiday makers towing their fishing boats and builders driving delivery trucks, resulted in the fragile roads being broken up and many potholes were formed. Green Point Drive and Seabreeze Parade, being the main roads through the village, had bitumen surfaces, but they also experienced heavy wear and tear from the traffic. The lesser secondary roads were also in need of repair. The strips of bitumen down the centre of Lucas Avenue, Campbell Avenue, Emerald Place and Frazer Avenue, were narrower still. On 2/10/1986, the Association wrote to Council saying that Wharf Road was in a deplorable state. Potholes, up to 100mm in depth after rain and the loose surface on the hilly section, made problems for traffic trying to negotiate the road.

At that time, Great Lakes Shire Council covered a huge area, with a relatively low population of ratepayers and the small village of Green Point was not a priority. Nevertheless, it didn't stop the Association from complaining about the state of the roads in the hope that 'eventually' something would be done. In June 1990 a petition containing 121 signatures was presented to Council protesting the lack of attention to Frazer Avenue, which had had virtually no maintenance work since the estate developer originally sealed the road. As a result Camellia Place, Waratah Close and Bottlebrush Close, which all had gravel surfaces, were bitumen sealed in the early 1990's and in 1991 Council reconstructed Frazer Avenue.

A solitary plug of bitumen seal amid bare gravel, on the badly worn Frazer Avenue at Green Point.

(Photo from Advocate Newspaper 6/6/90)

Traffic Problems

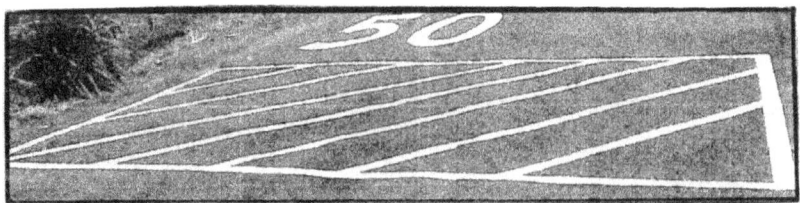

Early residents were concerned about the affect of speeding vehicles in the village, especially along Green Point Drive. On 10/3/1976, the Progress Association requested the Traffic Authority of NSW to reduce the speed limit to 60 kms per hour, but their request was denied. A sign was then erected near the Fire Hall to remind motorists to 'slow down and watch out for children'.

Over the years suggestions were made to make the narrow roads more traffic friendly. In 1981, the idea of one-way traffic around the circuit roads was put forward again. This time a resident survey was done and as a result it was deemed that it was better to leave the situation as it was – the roads could be widened and the speed limit reduced instead. In later years more surveys were done with the same results.

Speed Limits Reduced

A Public Meeting was held on 20/8/1994 to discuss traffic calming to slow traffic down in Green Point. By February 1996, the population of Green Point had grown considerably and the danger of speeding vehicles in the area had become ever more apparent. After proposing alternative speed reduction methods the Association surveyed residents again. It was concluded that speed humps would not be introduced and instead, recommended that a traffic calming device be constructed at the entrance to the village. In April 1997 after consultation and approved by the RTA and Council, work began on a chicane – to be situated 50 metres outside the entrance to the village. The road construction and garden beds were completed in June and the signage erected by August. In December, Northpower installed a street light on a nearby electricity pole.

Since 1987, numerous requests were made by the Association to reduce the speed limit on the road between the junction of The Lakes Way and the entrance to the village. This narrow stretch of hilly road became much safer in 1997 when the speed limit was reduced from 100 kms to 80 kms per hour. At the Public Meeting arranged by Council on 4/4/2001 which was attended by the Mayor, three other councillors and about thirty residents, the feeling was very strong and the vote was unanimous for the introduction of a 50 kms per hour speed limit in the village. By mid June 2002 the long awaited 50 kms/hr signs were installed. (P.A. records)

Tidy Towns Awards

The entries are made up of community groups which participate in the improvement and maintenance of their community on a voluntary basis. The entry to the Tidy Towns Competition is an accumulation of works throughout the year.

The First Tidy Towns Entry

Green Point first entered the Tidy Towns Competition in 1982.

The Great Lakes Shire Council helped out by having the roadsides mown and residents were involved in beautifying the tiny village. At the time, their 'new' adventure playground equipment, situated at the reserve next to the Fire Hall, was their pride and joy. This photograph from the Great Lakes Advocate, dated 4/11/1982, shows Mrs. Marie Maunder, the Keep Australia Beautiful Council judge with local residents Alan Robinson and Laurie and Margaret Kilham and family. The residents explained the community's plans for the future of Green Point and Mrs. Maunder, was very impressed with their efforts and admired their vision, encouraging them in their future endeavours.

Mrs Marie Maunder, Keep Australia Beautiful Council judge, inspects the Green Point adventure playground with local residents Alan Robinson, Laurie and Margaret Kilham and family.

Later, the Keep Australia Beautiful Council (NSW) advised that Green Point was unfortunately not successful at that time, but hoped that they would try again at a later date.

Tidy Towns Competition Winners

In 1997, Great Lakes Council fielded 15 entrants from its area to compete in the NSW Tidy Towns Competition. This area had the largest representation within in the state.

Encouraged by the earlier results of the 'Adopt a Road Scheme' the Progress Assoc. entered the Tidy Towns Competition for a population category of 351-1200.

Later, Green Point was judged as winner of the 'Roadside Litter Reduction' section – for the 'Green Point Roadside Litter Program'. This covered the length of Green Point Drive from The Lakes Way to the entrance of the village. Residents received the award on behalf of the community at Forster RSL Club on Australia Day 28/1/1998.

......In 1998, Green Point entered the Tidy Towns Competition again. Working bees were organized – the park mowing team did their bit, litter was collected from roadsides and reserves, posts repainted, signs cleaned and overhanging branches trimmed. A new public 'be-tidy bin' was installed near the shop and residential properties were mown and spruced up.

After judging, it was found that Green Point had won another Tidy Towns Award, this time for the 'Roadside Litter Reduction' in the 'Adopt a Village Project' section.

New Playground Equipment

The Community Survey done on the 8/4/1990, showed that a children's playground was needed. By 1993, the number of children in the area had grown to 135 children under 15 years and 95 between 5-15 years.

An inspection by Great Lakes Council on 25/2/1993 revealed that the old playground equipment, stored near the Fire Hall, did not comply with current standards and as a result it was removed. Council advised that a similar double swing and free standing slide would cost $3,500 plus installation. Council was unable to assist with funding at that time so it suggested applying for a grant. On 30/4/1993 the Progress Association applied for a $3,600 grant from the Hunter Area Assistance Scheme but unfortunately, they too, did not have funds available at that time.

The aim of the Progress Association for 1994 was to seek funding for the provision of playground equipment of an acceptable standard of safety and to ask Council about funding requirements. Accordingly Council was again approached in April 1995. In April 1996, Gayle Redman, on behalf of the Grubs Playgroup, enquired about the proposed playground equipment and asked Council again for assistance. Council advised in September 1996 that no funds were available in the current budget and nothing could be done until the 1997/1998 budget. The Playgroup then organized a petition to the Mayor, with the support of the Association.

In February 1997, Council had set aside $6,000 towards the proposed 'full sized' BMX track. As the track was to be reduced in size, Council was able to redirect these funds to the new playground equipment, which was estimated to cost around $10,000. The long awaited playground equipment was delivered to the site in July and after installation in August 1997, Council supplied the koppers logs and fill, with anything leftover to be returned. Later, the Association was able to donate $1340 from funds with the balance to be made up, in kind, with volunteer labour.

Volunteers, John Cavanagh and Rick Haffner built the log surrounds and spread the area with soft bark fill. For the children's safety the sections of koppers logs used in the equipment had to be sealed. Gayle Redman and Leslie O'Connor volunteered to paint the wooden structures with outdoor clear sealing paint supplied by Council. Other volunteers helped with the 2nd coat, having to apply the paint and allow it to dry before the eager school children arrived. Judging by the number of happy users the play equipment proved to be the most successful project that the Association had, up to that date, achieved.

BMX Track

On the 14/5/1995, at a public meeting, most residents present were in favour of a BMX cycle track to be constructed on the Green Point Park reserve. A committee was formed to acquire information from Council regarding setting up the track. By 7/8/1995 plans were drawn up for approval. Council agreed to look at the $6,000 cost for the work in the 1996 budget as funds were not available as at 25/10/1995. The committee arranged to meet with Kerrie Simmons (Council Parks Officer) on 7/2/1996.

It was originally proposed that a 'full sized' track be constructed, but the plans showed that the track would take up nearly all of the park area and cater only for dedicated riders.

Following an on-site inspection on 23/2/1997, by Council's Works and Services Committee, the decision was taken to reduce the size of the proposed BMX track to a 'recreational' track. The track would be located along the back fence, with an offer to relocate the 'professional' sized track to the North Tuncurry sporting field area. The proposal for the large BMX track was not supported by Council so the $6,000 set aside for the earth work mounds, was redirected, in April 1997, and supplemented to spend $10,000 on the playground equipment instead. The funding to start work on the smaller track was available on 1/7/1997 and by 29/8/1997 Council had constructed five mounds from road base coated with a thin outer layer of sandy soil, which allowed the grass to grow and hold the mounds together. The mounds were up to one metre high – suitable for young bike riders. The BMX track was ready for use on 21/1/1998.

Multi-Purpose Concrete Court

.... Plans made

The younger children living in the village had been catered for with their playground equipment and the modified BMX track. Now it was time to acknowledge the needs of the older children.

With this in mind the Progress Association considered previous community surveys and decided to work towards constructing a multi-purpose concrete court in the park area. It would be available for every activity from handball, hopscotch and skipping to rollerblading, riding bikes, scooters and skateboards. When completed the concrete court would measure 30.5mx15.25m. Future plans, as recent surveys reflected their popularity, involved basketball and netball facilities.

.... Funding arranged

In December 1997, the Association submitted a grant application to the Dept. of Sport & Recreation for funding. Great Lakes Council fully supported the project and on 17/4/1998 a cheque was gratefully received in the amount of $3,000. Being dollar for dollar funding, the Association pledged $3,000 plus extensive volunteer labour towards the cost.

Fundraising came in the form of a 'Monster Guessing Competition', with nineteen prizes totalling over $1,000 in value. Competition raffle tickets were organized in July and from August onwards they were made available for sale outside shops in Forster. Workers in both Tuncurry and Forster industrial areas were canvassed and generously donated to the cause. Thanks to the many sponsors of this fundraiser the raffle was a great success. Mayor John Chadban drew out the winning tickets at Council during the Oyster Festival weekend. Proceeds from the Competition, together with income from numerous Lamington Drives, amounted to $2,200 and Association funds supplied the balance needed for the $3,000 grant.

John Cavanagh, resident of Green Point, with Mayor, John Chadban as he draws the winning raffle ticket in the Monster Guessing Competition.

.... Construction

By 29/1/1998 Council appointed surveyors had pegged out the site, the area was levelled and a tree removed. Readi-Mix Concrete offered the concrete at $133/cu metre (the same rate as for the tennis courts) and the formwork for the concrete slab was donated.

On the 5th and 6th of December 1998 about 25 local dads turned up at the site. Organized by John Cavanagh they had volunteered to help with the installation of the reinforcing steel and the concrete pour. Starting at the western end of the court, they worked together under the supervision of local experienced volunteer concreters. The project was a community effort with many people being involved and the end result proved well worthwhile.

To ensure that the concrete was 'secure' for the future hard-wearing traffic the court had to be hosed down each day for a week. By then the excited local children were well and truly ready with their bikes and skateboards to advance onto the court and enjoy the facility – at last they had a safe place to ride away from the dangers of our busy roadways and just in time for school holidays. (P.A. records)

.... The Concrete Pour Begins

.... The Work Continues

.... "We're Off to the Park!"

In the 1990's 'the park' was just a grassed area – top dressed and mown. Local children would go there after school and on the weekends to play football with their mates. At one stage practice goal posts were erected but later had to be taken down due to Council regulations. When the wind was right children flew their kites and small toy aeroplanes on the oval. Unfortunately, the area was not quite large enough for a standard sized soccer field, so the local children had to travel to Forster for their home ground. However, for a short time, local sporting groups used the area for training purposes.

As anticipated, things really changed when the new park facilities were built. The playground equipment was a great success with the local school children. Mums brought their small children to enjoy the park – including some from Forster and others from the Tuncurry Mothers Club who included the Green Point park in their group outings.

BMX bikes were the 'in thing' at the time the track was constructed and proved very popular with the young boys who liked to modify the track to their own liking. When the mounds became too dangerous their deep trenches had to be filled in.

The multi –purpose court was very popular indeed, especially as it had been completed in time for the Christmas school holidays. After Christmas Day new remote controlled toys, scooters and fancy new bikes (complete with streamers and training wheels) zoomed around the slab whilst proud parents took photos of their children's progress. Young boys practiced their moves on their brightly coloured designer skateboards – showing off with click-clacks and 360's. Older children rode their bikes around whilst little girls played skipping and hopscotch or hand ball.

The tennis courts were also in use over the holidays as families and friends enjoyed a social game of tennis. The success of the facility continues to bring enjoyment to many people and was well worth all the dedicated hard work of the local volunteers.

Enjoying Activities

Green Point Park Sporting Complex

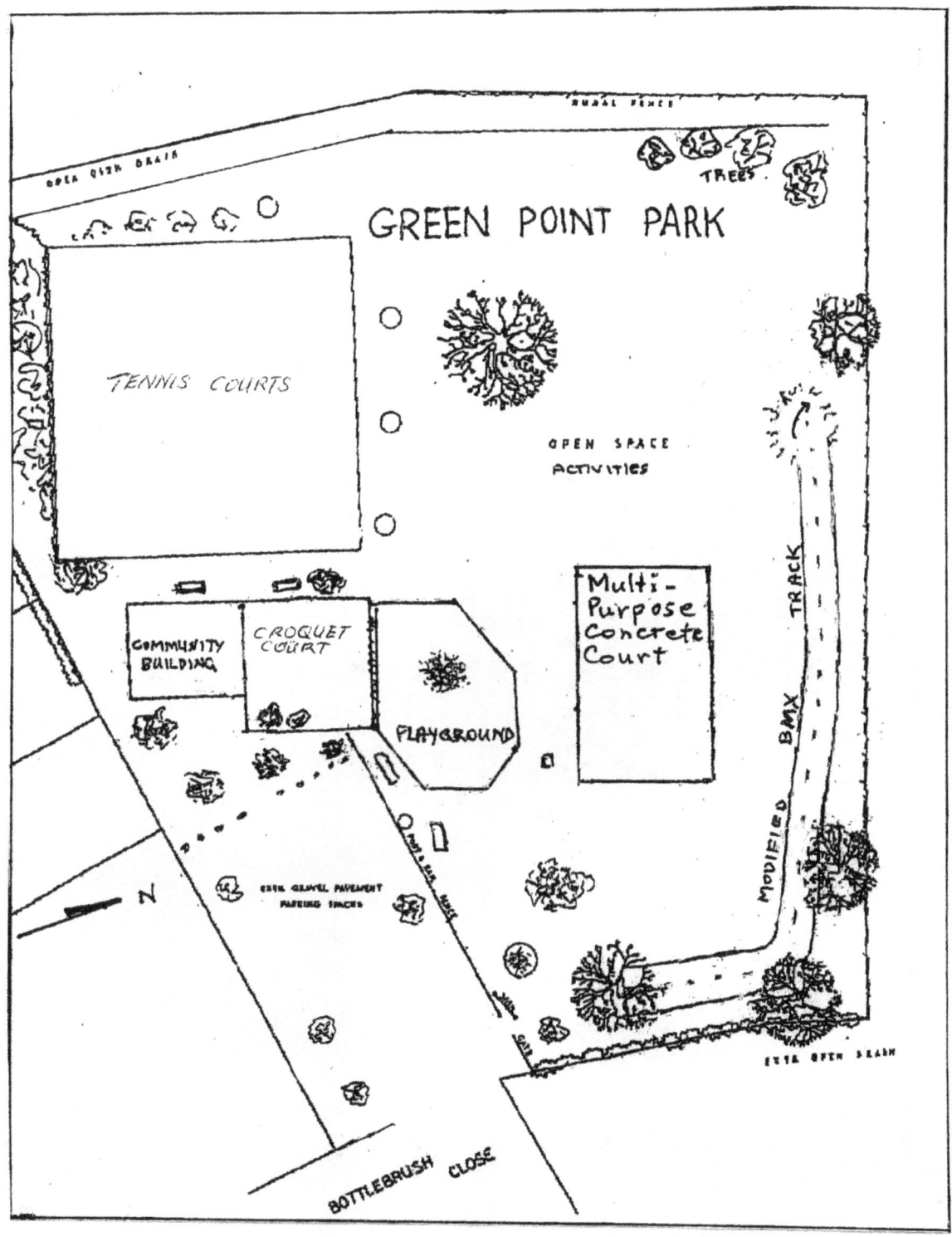

Tidy Towns Entry

In mid-1998 Green Point submitted a 'second entry' in the Tidy Towns Competition. This time it was in the 'Government Authority Section' which covered the Development of the Green Point Community Reserve. The tennis courts, playground equipment, children's BMX cycle track and multi-purpose concrete court were all situated in a pleasant and picturesque setting maintained by volunteers.

The judges were again very impressed by the overall community effort and as a result Green Point was successful, for the second time, in the 1998 Tidy Towns Competition. A 'Welcome to Green Point Proud to be a Tidy Town' sign was erected by Council at the entrance to Green Point.

Preparations for the Fete

As Association funds were needed to fulfill funding grant requirements a 'giant family fete' was planned for Saturday 20/11/1999.

The fete aimed to be a fun experience for all the families in the community so many activities were suggested for the children. BMX and skateboard demonstrations were arranged. Children's competitive games, cake cooking and colouring-in contests were planned with prizes of confectionery for the winners. 'Darts for Cash' would be for the older participants.

The following sponsors agreed to contribute to the prize list: Waynes World, Brian's Bedding, John Amato, Country Palings Petals & Pots, Greg Golby, X-sight, Kneebones, Retrovision, Enhanced Pine, The Trading Post, King Roster, Amaroo and Forster Village Shops - prizes not used were to be auctioned.

Invitations were sent out to local market stall holders to participate in return for a small fee. Jack and Lisa Hall, as members of the Lions Club, were able to arrange for the use of their club's Chocolate Wheel and for the participation of the Lions 'Charity Princess'. Association volunteers were organized to man the many stalls, judge the children's competitions and run the raffles. Play Group mothers offered to do a cake stall and the Rural Fire Brigade volunteered to run the BBQ and cold drinks stand. Extensive media advertising and letter drops were done.

As the 'big day' drew near every effort was made to spruce up the village for the visiting public. Grassed roadsides areas and around the Community Hall and park were mown. The hall building was cleaned 'inside and out' and the tennis courts were made ready for 'free' tennis.

The Big Day Arrives

As seen in the photos it was a lovely sunny day for the event. Market stall holders arrived early to set up and secondhand articles were delivered ready to be displayed for the Trash and Treasure tables. Dozens of Green Point lamingtons were packed ready for sale and the Lucky Door prize set up at the entrance to the hall. Inside, the Association ladies dressed the tables with bright tablecloths and small vases of flowers, whilst others worked in the little kitchen area preparing plates of scones, jam and cream for morning teas.

An original artwork, donated by local artist Ron Davis, was displayed as a raffle prize. Donations of food goods, wine and gift vouchers from local businesses were arranged on the Tombola stand. Young mothers from the Playgroup set up their cake display ready for sale, ticket sellers prepared for their guessing competition and the Rural Fire Brigade volunteers stocked up their supply of sausages, bread and cold drinks for the BBQ food stall. A steady stream of residents brought along more potted plants for the garden stall, whilst the Lions Club Chocolate Wheel was made ready for business. It wasn't long before a crowd of visitors started arriving and the various activities of the fete were happily in progress. With the appearance of the Charity Princess the scene was complete.

Official Opening of the Park

With the completion of the children's park facilities in the late 1998, the Progress Association suggested to Great Lakes Council that now would be an appropriate time to officially name the park area. Names put forward were Green Point Park, Green Point Reserve and Green Point Parkland. 'Green Point Park' was chosen and subsequent arrangements made with the Geographic Names Board.

For the occasion Council had a newly designed 'Green Point Park' sign erected at the entrance to the carpark. A draw-curtain was hung across the front of the sign in readiness for the Official Opening. As the crowd was dispersed throughout the park area it was necessary for a microphone and P.A. system to be set up. Being a joint project between Great Lakes Council and Green Point Progress Association it was appropriate that the Mayor, Cr. John Chadban, officially name the park. In his opening address the Mayor praised the efforts of all the volunteers and recognized the 'community spirit' involved in the park project. He also wished residents ongoing success with any improvements to the area and said that wherever possible Council would support communities willing to work hard towards achieving their goals.

Around 400 people enjoyed the family day – a pleasing number considering the small population of the village at that time. The net proceeds from this event was $1572.00 some of which would be put towards the proposed basketball court. (P.A. records)

A History of Green Point
.... Community Fundraising

.... Stalls Galore

Foreshore Clean Up

Since early times of the Green Point subdivision professional fishermen, locals and tourists alike used the lake foreshore as a dumping ground. No thought was given to the accumulation of rubbish in and around the lake foreshore. Over the previous 30 years the foreshore had been polluted with old damaged boats, rusty broken crab pots and anchors, old car tyres, rolls of wire, piles of old fishing nets and broken bottles. This all added up to making it dangerous for users of the area. As far back as 1979, the Progress Association was concerned about the problem and a suggestion was made at the time that boat moorings 'only' be allocated to Pipers Bay.

In July 1990 representatives of the Association made a polite verbal request to the local professional fishermen to tidy up the rubbish on the foreshore, but this request went unheeded. The Association then sent letters to the Fisheries Inspector, Maritime Services Board and Great Lakes Shire Council requesting their help to clean up the area. Again in 1994 Association letters were sent to the Waterways Authority and the Fishermen's Co-op.

'Clean Up Australia Day' in the early stages concentrated on the reduction of roadside litter, but as the untidy state of the lake foreshore became more of an issue, around 1997, a special mammoth effort was planned by resident volunteers to clean up this area. The professional fishermen agreed to help and designated which of their old crab pots and equipment could be removed. Two car trailers and the back of a truck were used by volunteers to collect the huge amount of rubbish and deposit it at the Council's pick-up area at The Point.

The combined efforts of those concerned achieved a remarkable result, which led the community to next consider the problem of the overgrown vegetation in the nearby area.

In 1982, when the Tidy Towns judges inspected Green Point they suggested that the lakeside walk was an untapped resource which could be improved to enhance the village. On 9/9/1997, the Tidy Towns Assessment Report suggested that when the Foreshore Clean Up Programme had progressed further, Green Point should consider entering it as a 'special project' in the future.

Following this report a motion was made at an Association meeting by Lesley Archer (a Green Point resident), that perhaps the community, with the help of the Landcare Organization, could clear the weeds from the area beside the foreshore. An application for $5,000 funding was submitted and approved, but due to insufficient labour support from residents, the grant funding had to be returned and the project set aside for the time being.

Noxious Weed Problem

Whilst Lach Fraser's dairy farm was in operation the cattle kept the vegetation under control, but when left unchecked the Lantana and Blackberries took hold. These bushes grew in many areas throughout the subdivision but as householders cleared their blocks most plants were removed. The main areas still affected by these weeds were either side of the rough track running by the lake from the bottom of Wharf Road to the northern end of Green Point Drive.

Ipomoea (Morning Glory) was unfortunately introduced into the foreshore reserve areas when the sewerage pipes were laid around 1993/94. Soil was imported to bed the 'mains' pipes after excavation in rocky areas and to cover the pipes where necessary.

A New Approach - Plans Made

Following consultation by the Tidy Towns group, Wallis Lake Estuary Management Committee and the Great Lakes Council, the Progress Association was approached to participate in the improvement of the previously 'run down' and degraded area of lakeside foreshore. As a result, a community survey was arranged for 24/3/1998 in which residents indicated their preferences for suggested improvements. The response from the 80 out of 210 residents who received the surveys formed the basis for the planned Foreshore Development Programme. The foreshore area was surveyed by Council on 18/10/998.

Being a community beside Wallis Lake, it was of great significance that we care for the estuarine foreshore. On 5/3/1999, an Association meeting was held regarding the proposed Foreshore Plan of Management.

Issues discussed included:

- Boat moorings, launching and unloading facilities and canoe storage racks.
- Channel location and sea grass protection.
- Land access for vehicles and boat trailer parking.
- Location of swimming and picnic areas.
- Funding sources for a toilet block.
- Landcare group for weed removal
- Planting of native indigenous plants.

On 14/3/1999 Ron Davis (a Green Point resident) accepted nomination as Landcare Co-ordinator to recruit assistance from local residents and Association members, to provide the manpower to implement the required environmental plans for a Landcare grant.

The acquisition of funding was considered more favourable by the State/Commonwealth Coastcare Assessment Panel, if well planned, and fitted in with existing local or regional coastal management areas. After consultation with Janne Yardy, Council's Manager of Parks and Recreation, Ron Davis was able to draw up a plan for the foreshore area, which was accepted by members of the Association on 11/4/1999.

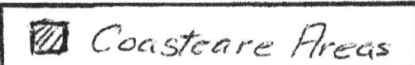
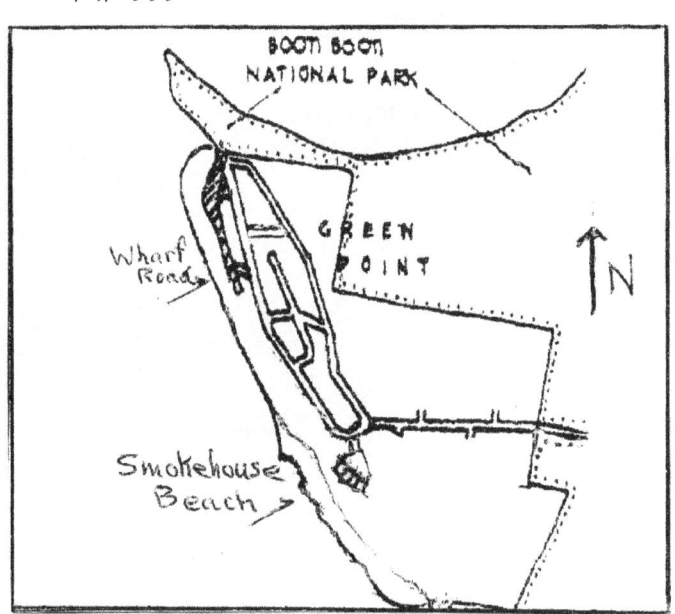

Foreshore Plan of Management

On 27/4/1999, a community workshop was held at the Council Chambers with consultation between the Association and Council representatives, David Turner of NPWS., Brett Ryan of Waterways and Keith Lynch of the Fishermen's Co-op.

The AIMS discussed were to provide a long term plan that would guide future development of the foreshore (Lot318) and nearby public reserve (Lot317) at Green Point.

The Objectives

- To best meet the requirements and aspirations of the local community, relevant State and Local Government authorities and professional fishermen.

- To improve the recreational and visual amenity of the area in a manner consistent with good environmental practices.

- To identify and harness funding sources and resources available for development and maintenance of the area.

- To determine the most appropriate location and design of facilities and to promote development which would provide long term sustainable benefits, while improving the natural environmental character and values of the area.

Files and studies were reviewed and after discussion concept plans and costings for a 'draft' plan outline was prepared.
- Wal Attard of Re-Flora Australia was commissioned to head up a work plan for a Landcare/Coastcare group.
- Maintenance would involve Council and NPWS, Waterways and the Fishermen's Co-op.
- Volunteers would be needed for regeneration of vegetation and mowing grassed areas.
- Council's Janne Yardy submitted an application for government funding through the Financial Assistance Grants to Small Villages and on 30/4/1999 was allocated $6,000 available for use by Council in the 1998/1999 financial budget for the Foreshore Improvements. (P.A. records.)

Coastcare - Work Commenced

As the new Coastcare Co-ordinator, Ron Davis, assisted by Wal Attard (Bush Regenerator), completed the necessary forms on 13/6/1999 and then applied for a Landcare grant. In the August 1999 issue of the Green Pointer newsletter, Ron called for volunteers to join in the Coastcare activities, working along the foreshore area for 3-4 hours per week.

By October, a dozen enthusiastic residents turned up on site ready with gardening cutters and sturdy gloves to start work clearing the overgrown vegetation. Council arranged for qualified plant advisors Wal Attard and Steve King to be on hand to instruct the group as to the best way to work on the problem. Plant identification was an important issue, as all native plants had to be retained.

The group was encouraged to collect leaves from plants in the area and bring them back to the experts for identification and be filed for later reference. They were taught which plants were weeds and had to be removed, and which plants were to be retained: e.g. the Lantana bushes were to be cut up and left to form mulch on the ground and then the base of the trunk poisoned. The Ipomoea vine was to be pulled down from the tree tops then rolled up into balls and placed in the fork of a tree to die. If left on the ground the vine would take root again. Any Ipomoea roots unable to be dug out were to be poisoned. Months of hard work clearing the area of noxious weeds made a dramatic difference and the Coastcare workers looked forward to the time that they could start the planting of the area with native plants.

The Challenge Ahead...... *Ipomoea*

.... and never-ending LANTANA !

.... LANTANA – ready to be mulched!

.... Clearing out the WEEEEEDS!!

Tidy Towns Winner

As a Foreshore Plan of Management had been developed and residents had proved their sincerity by their involvement with the Landcare/Coastcare project, the Development Programme for the Foreshore was entered in the next Keep Australia Beautiful Council (NSW) Tidy Towns Competition.

As a result, Green Point won yet another Tidy Towns Award! This time in the "Waterways/Foreshore Protection" for our region within New South Wales - population Category 351-1,2000. (P.A. records)

The 1999 Tidy Towns Award Certificate is proudly displayed along with other previous awards in the Community Hall.

Skateboarding at the Park

The local children continued to enjoy playing on the 'Multi-purpose Concrete Court', BUT as 'skateboarding' became more popular, the youth in the area wanted additional facilities. Many young people and their parents attended the Progress Association AGM held on 7/2/1999 to voice their concerns and discuss the construction of skateboard ramps on the concrete slab. The Association agreed to look into the necessary requirements and costs involved.

At the following meeting held on 11/4/1999, the children were encouraged to submit their designs complete with measurements to Ron Davis, who agreed to draw up rough plans. Although the Association was sympathetic to the ideas suggested, some designs proved to be over ambitious. On 10/10/1999 a 'U' shaped half-pipe was declined as similar skateboard facilities were available at Tuncurry for the older boys.

Many regional skateboard parks were looked at and eventually a pre-cast design was selected. As the skateboard facilities were to be allocated to the western end of the concrete court, the slab had to be extended towards the eastern end to allow for the proposed basket ball half-court. The area was pegged out on 18/2/2000 and working bees arranged.

As the prospect of having skateboard ramps built at the park seemed a direct possibility, some over enthusiastic young people embarked on making their own skateboard ramps and jumps, which they erected on the concrete slab. The wooden and metal equipment, although safe when first brought to the area, proved unable to withstand exposure to the elements and deteriorated rapidly.

On 12/5/2000 Janne Yardy, Council's Manager of Parks and Recreation, inspected the makeshift skateboard equipment and deemed it to be unsafe and could present a hazard to the children using the area. It was understood that removal of the equipment would deprive the young people of recreational outlets and as a result Ms.Yardy asked the Association to consider the possibility of working with Council to design and install more robust and safe equipment – either light removable structures bolted to the slab, or concrete elements outside the slab. Later, the homemade structures were removed by Council.

... Unfortunately, the ramps were deemed unsafe.

Skate Park Facility Planned

Following a Public Meeting held on 2/9/2000 a Progress Association 'skate park subcommittee' was formed on 10/9/2000 to work for the establishment of a skate park facility at Green Point. Members included Don Craig (President), Colleen Reardon (Secretary), Wally Paszyn (Treasurer), John Cavanagh (Liaison with Council), Bob Currans (Member of the Progress Association) and Tom Wren, Luke Paszyn, Jed Redman and Lyle Reardon who represented the youth of the area.

Many issues were considered in the design of the proposed facility. They comprised of age groups and type of skating preferred, the site which had to be safe and secure and close to assistance, toilets and available drinking water. Also, the design had to be within budget and involve users together with a professional skater and a Council engineer. On 18/9/2000 a submission was sent to Council for endorsement regarding a grant application to the Association for the project.

Eventually an agreed design was chosen which included delivery and installation of two ¼ pipe BCP Pre-cast Modular skateboard ramps, one transition wedge, a large block and rail, and extensions needed to the existing concrete slab – with an estimated cost of $14,000. Council agreed to supply the earth banks required at the side and rear walls of the platforms for the modular ramps.

Fundraising

The subcommittee worked hard and arranged many community fundraising activities. Local service organizations also made significant donations towards the project. Together, with Association funds, the amount of $3,000 was designated towards the new facility. On 30/10/2000 a DA was submitted to Council and on 3/11/2000 Council donated $4,000 towards the project.

An Application for Assistance from the NSW Sport & Recreation Capital Assistance Programme 2000/2001, was then lodged by Council seeking matching funds of $7,000 for the Green Point project – on the basis of the volunteer labour, Association funds and in-kind assistance from Council. The members of the subcommittee were delighted when soon afterwards the Government Grant was approved paving the way for the much anticipated 'skate park'.

Members of the Progress Association subcommittee

Concrete Court Extension

In order to have a safe area between the skateboard riders and other court users, it was necessary to extend the length of the existing multi-purpose concrete court. As with the earlier park project many local residents were again involved, donating their time and expertise.

The first working bee was held on 17th and 18th March 2001 when they dug out and formed up to specifications the area for the proposed half basketball court and also for the bases to support the two quarter-pipe pre-cast heavy skateboard ramps. The concrete pour was done on 24/3/2001 and allowed time to cure.

.... Dads Involved Again

Making Ready the Foundations for the Ramps

Skate Park

Despite the extremely wet weather, a bogged semi-trailer and a delayed crane, the concrete skateboard ramps, transition wedge and other equipment were delivered on the 22/5/2001. The crane driver expertly manoeuvred the structures into position on the western end of the multi-purpose concrete court. Council supplied the earth banks required at the sides and back walls of the ramp platforms. The excited local children of all ages were keen to ride the skateboard ramps as soon as possible, to practice and perfect their moves. On 9/9/2001 the large block and rail were installed by volunteers.

.... Early Movers

Skate Park Section Completed

Later, the older more advanced skateboard riders moved on to use the larger skate park at Tuncurry leaving Green Point Park safe for the junior riders. When small scooters and bikes became more popular, many young people began to use the ramps for their trick stunt manoeuvres . On 16/9/2013, at the request of the Association, Council extended the concrete landing pads on top of the earth mounds to make the areas safer for the riders.

To enhance the area, surface drainage was corrected and open space ruts filled with top dressing and volunteers planted forty-five native flowering shrubs around the perimeter of the park.

Basketball Half Court

On 13/8/2000, after considering many types of basketball hoops, a Truline (Australia) heavy duty basketball facility was chosen.

The unexpected $1,500 cost of the extension to the concrete slab left a shortfall in allowable funds. This meant that the completion of the basketball court had to be delayed.

On 10/10/2001, Council was approached to consider funding or providing help with the outstanding commitments to complete the basketball court and park area. In return, the Association would provide $500 towards funding the outstanding items. As the remaining balance in the skate park account was $666.70 it was decided to donate the full amount to Council towards the basketball stand and then close the account.

On 14/7/2002, John Cavanagh installed the basketball goal post, hoop and backboard on behalf of Council and the Association. For the convenience of users, Council supplied two park bench seats at the side of the concrete slab. Later, on 9/1/2003, Council contractors cleaned the cement with acid and when dry, painted the lines according to specifications, ready for use as a basketball half court.

The Skate Park subcommittee sincerely thanked all the local volunteers for their time and labour, Great Lakes Council for their financial help and advice, and John Cavanagh for his assistance as co-ordinator. They also thanked Grant Adams and John Monkley for their time, company equipment and expertise, Graham Barclay for the use of his truck and very patient driver who brought the prefabricated skate equipment safely up the highway and Twin Town Crane Service for the use of their crane and driver (both services at discounted rates). With their work completed the Green Point Skate Park subcommittee was dissolved on 10/2/2002. (P.A. records)

Both the skate park and basketball court facilities continue to be immensely popular with the local children, families who attend the park for picnics and to watch their children play and with visiting children's play groups.

Skate Park and Basketball Court

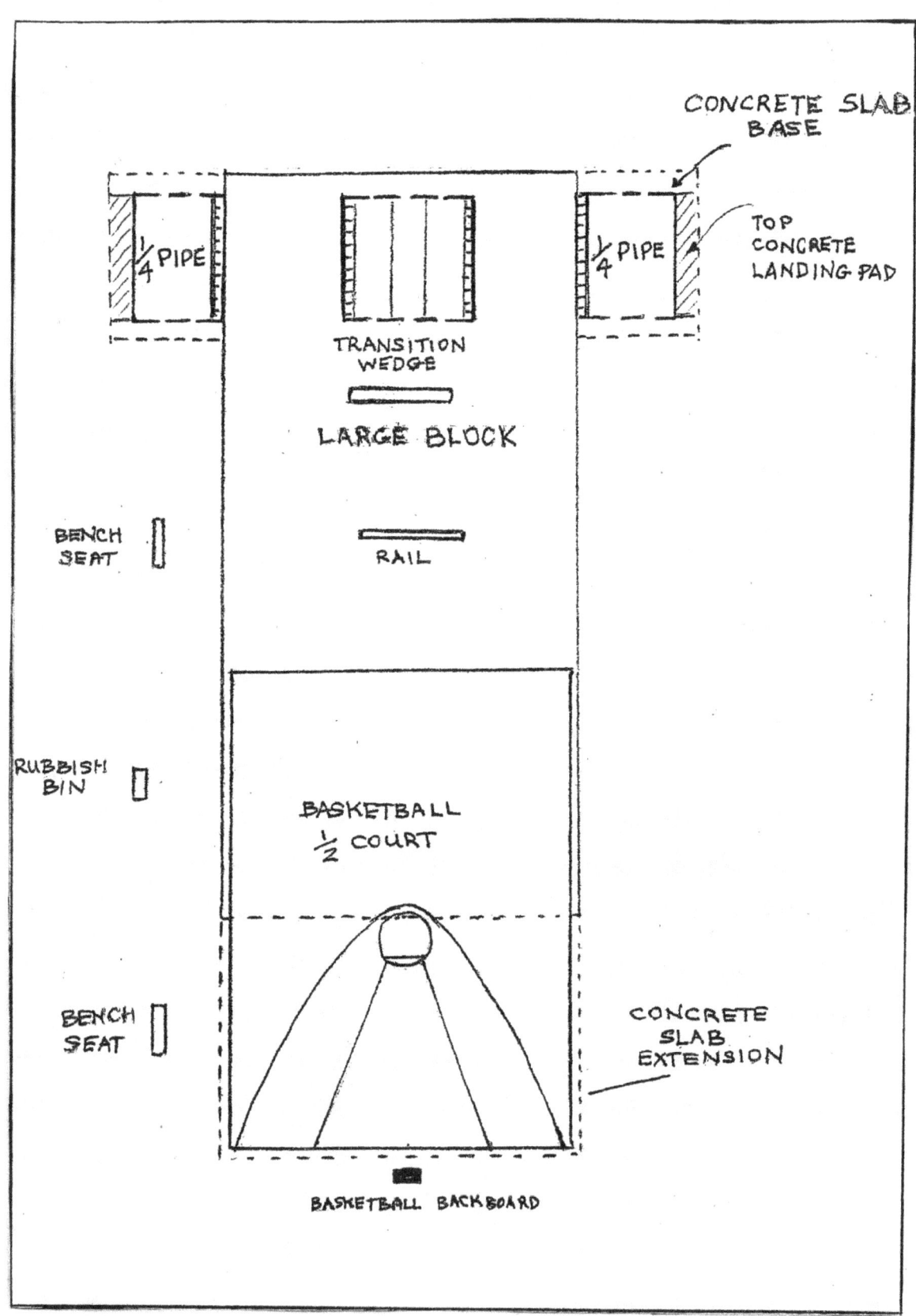

Village Mowing and Park Maintenance

Around 1980 Great Lakes Shire Council supplied a ride-on mower to the community to be used by volunteers to mow, where possible, the verges around the village and to maintain Jim Markey Park (adjacent to the Fire Brigade hall). At this time the ride-on mower was stored in the old Fire Brigade hall. During the early 1980's Council arranged the supply of maintenance parts at cost price to the Progress Association. This changed in 1987 when Council was then able to take on the responsibility of equipment maintenance.   (P. A. records)

In April 1991, Bob Currans and Bill Raward started hand mowing around the newly acquired Community Hall building and carpark just prior to the monthly Progress Association meetings. When the tennis courts were completed in mid 1993, Bob started hand mowing five cuts around the perimeter of the courts. Later, when the amenity block was built, the ride-on mower was transferred to the storage area adjacent to the Community Hall.

In order that the village children had a safe area to play, Bob started using the ride-on mower to cut the metre high grass on the reserve close to the carpark. In January 1994, the Sewerage Works Depot, which was positioned on the far side of the reserve was disbanded. As the majority of the worksite was located adjacent to the farm fence the area there was still covered in loose rocks. A working bee was organized in 1995 to remove the rubble and over the following six months Bob was able to slowly extend his mowing area to the whole of the reserve and up to and including around the Fire Brigade hall.

When the Croquet Court was constructed in 1995 Bill Raward took on the job of mowing the area before games days, until the Croquet Group closed down in November 2000.

In 1997 John Cavanagh used the Council back-hoe to top-dress the playing area. The sand was transported from the hillside of the southern access lane from The Lakes Way into Green Point Drive. On 22/2/1998 Council supplied a new ride-on mower. Bob continued to mow the park reserve and surrounding area until around 2002 when local residents Terry Rolfe and Ron Davis took over the work as part of the Community Mature Age Allowance Programme. They mowed the park, roadsides and beside drains, the access to Smokehouse beach and part of the foreshore area. In late 2003 Bob returned to continue mowing the park reserve and surrounding community areas.

Meanwhile, Great Lakes Council had set up a number of volunteer grass cutting groups in the Forster area. Acknowledging the efforts of Green Point residents, (Bob Currans, Bill Raward, Les Hardacre), Council positioned a large concrete equipment shed in the park reserve in February 2006. They also supplied an updated ride-on mower, three second hand motor mowers, a whipper-snipper and a set of free standing shelves to hold maintenance tools and equipment. Soon afterwards, volunteers concreted an apron at the entrance to the shed to enable easy access for the equipment

Over time, other community minded residents joined the 'Grass Cutting Group'. All volunteers were required to be inducted by Council and instructed on how to use the mowing equipment, safety measures and appropriate clothing to be worn. In 2008 Council supplied an extra motor mower and in November 2015 a 'new' ride-on mower. Fuel continues to be supplied by Council and equipment repairs done at the Council's workshop.

Over the years the number of volunteers has fluctuated according to their availability and health. The work continues with an average of 4-7 workers attending each mowing day. Overall, up to 2020 there have been a total of twenty-five volunteer workers who have helped maintain Green Point Park and adjacent community areas. (Bob Currans)

New Flagpole

In the mid 1990's, after the transportation of the tiny Community Hall to Green Point, the Progress Association erected a small wooden flagpole adjacent to where the children's play gym is situated today.

In February 2001 when the Association President, Malcolm Tompson, heard of a newer flag pole being available for community use, he suggested that the Association consider taking advantage of the offer. Bovis Lend Lease was redeveloping the site of the old CSR Pyrmont Sugar Refinery and no longer required the two flagpoles positioned at the entrance to the site. After consideration, the idea was welcomed and a DA was submitted to Council – which was subsequently approved on 12/8/2001. It was agreed that the Association was to pay for the trucking costs and for the supply of concrete to install the pole.

On 12/9/2001 a working bee was organized and the digging of a large hole, required prior to the concrete pour, was started. Unfortunately, problems occurred when the sandy soil kept falling in from the edges, and, as the water table was not far under the surface, water kept filling the hole! It quickly became apparent that sheets of corrugated iron were needed to jam against the sides of the excavation and a frantic effort ensued to pour the concrete into the rising water and complete the job. According to a template supplied, large bolts were secured into the concrete for the base plate, and then the concrete was allowed to cure. (Bob Currans)

Unfortunately, after the flagpole was erected, the pulley system was found to be faulty and a small equipment grant was arranged to cover the cost of the new necklace/halyard and keys. Council supplied koppers logs for the fence surrounding the flagpole which was then constructed by volunteers on 11/10/2001. As the existing State flag appeared small in proportion to the twelve-metre high flagpole, a larger Australian flag was obtained from Bob Baldwin MP, the then Federal Member for Patterson on 12/9/2004. (P.A. records).

As a matter of interest: The flagpoles are made of tempered aluminium and would have cost $2,700 when new. The second of the two flagpoles was erected on the Forster break wall for the Volunteer Coastal Patrol Base (Malcolm Tompson). Since May 2005 the base has been known as the Marine Rescue Co-ordination Centre (Wendy Borchers).

100 Years of ANZAC (1915-2015)

The commemoration of 100 years since the landing of the ANZAC forces at Gallipoli on 25/4/1915, was remembered in a quiet, dignified way at Green Point – by the raising of the Australian flag and then left at half mast until sunset. Normally, the protocol states that after the ANZAC Service, the flag must be fully raised. However, it was an appropriate and significant gesture from Green Point.

Bob Currans remembers his uncle, David Lutton Currans – a young shearer and sheep farmer from out west of Nyngan NSW. On 10/6/1915, he joined the army and served in the AIF 3rd Battalion during World War I. He was first sent to Turkey's Gallipoli Peninsular, then to Egypt and later to fight in the Battle of Pozieres, where he died on 17/8/1916. Another occasion to celebrate, was Australia Day 26/1/2016, when the flag flew proudly over Green Point Park.

A History of Green Point
.... *"We Will Remember Them"*

A History of Green Point

Foreshore Development

Great Lakes Council's AIM, for the foreshore at Green Point, was to address the major existing problems relating to the accessibility, appearance, safety and useability of the foreshore reserves beside the lake.

The area had to have access for recreation and provide access for fishing - for recreational and professional. The draft plan had allowed for the closure of the track north of Wharf Road, with the installation of a boom gate for access by essential services and Coastcare vehicles. This proposal was later found to be unpopular with residents and professional fishermen alike and as a result the track was left open for everyone to use and enjoy.

Another proposal in the draft plan was for canoe racks to be constructed beside the lake for the storage of locally owned canoes. This idea was discounted because of possible vandalism to privately owned property. Also, residents preferred the atmosphere created by having boats resting along the shoreline.

Funding through Coastcare for the Green Point Estuarine Regeneration Project, was arranged by Kerrie Simmons (GLC Parks Officer), Jane Whiteley (Coastcare Facilitator) and the Green Point Progress Association. The extra funds needed came from the Department of Land and Water Conservation and were paid in three stages as the work progressed.

The first priority for the development of the foreshore area was for the building of a public toilet block. With this in mind, Coastcare volunteers worked to clear the proposed building site of the existing dense vegetation. With the aid of 'STAGE 1' of the funding grant and the $10,000 allocated by Council on 12/2/2000, the much needed facility was completed by 30/8/2001. Mid-Coast Water was requested to wave the cost of the sewerage connection fee. In September 2001, to allow easy wheelchair access to the amenities block, a concrete path was laid and later turf was brought in to enhance the area.

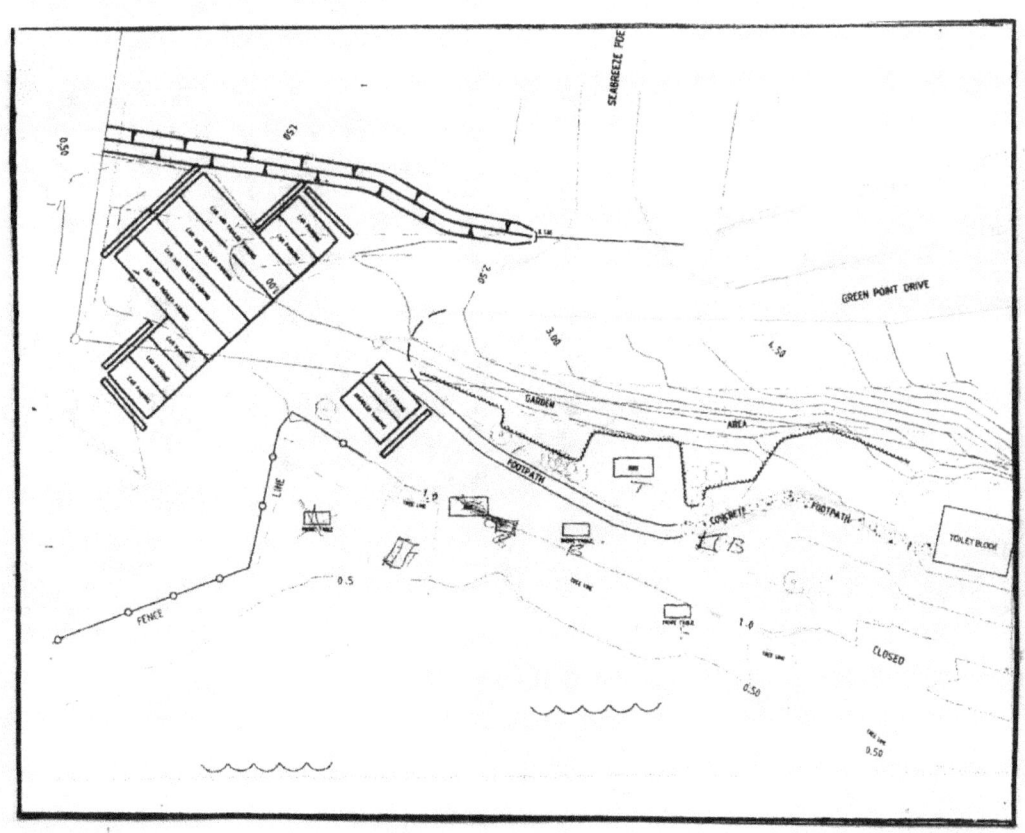

'Stage 1' ..... Toilet Block Built

'Stage 2'.....Landscaping Commenced

'**STAGE 2**' of the funding grant allowed for landscaping of the nearby area. As the extensive weed infestation on the hillside, adjacent to Green Point Drive had been removed by Coastcare workers, Council was able to arrange for Wal Attard and his 'Work for the Dole' team to prepare the garden area of the park reserve (Lot 317). Once this job was completed the Coastcare group went to work to plant out the area. The selected numbers and types of plants required by Council were sourced from Tarara Nursery by Re-flora Australia.

.... *Edging and Bago Fencing*

In April 2002, Council landscapers constructed treated pine slab borders around the planted area, as well as a log retaining wall below the bank at the rear of the toilet block. Later, Wal Attard and his team returned to erect Bago fencing along Green Point Drive and beside the foreshore track to enclose the bushland regeneration area.

'Stage 3' .....Smokehouse Beach

By December 2002, after STAGE 3 of the funding grant was made available, Council constructed a set of single rail wooden steps for access to Smokehouse Beach. Signage was erected at the pedestrian access in May 2003 and for traffic safety 'No Parking' signs were erected opposite on the dangerous bend on Green Point Drive.

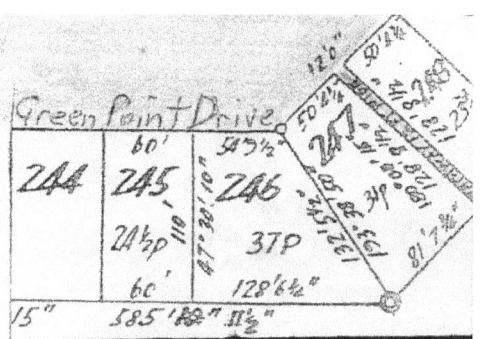

.... Boat Moorings

Allowing for land access to Booti Booti National Park, and for the possibility of high water levels, Council then constructed car parking and boat launching areas. NSW Waterways made new boat moorings available (for a fee) to residents and professional fishermen. The mooring posts were positioned away from the tiny beach area to allow space for swimming and recreation. (P.A. records)

Coastcare Funding Grants

These grants enabled Council to:

- Supply Coastcare volunteers with garden tools, gloves, shirts and hats and the required First Aid Kit.
- Cover the cost of trucking large amounts of cut green waste to the tip and for the delivery of wood chip mulch for around the plants.
- Employ Wal Attard to poison-spray large areas for weed eradication along the foreshore between Wharf Road and Smokehouse beach.
- Remove dead and dangerous trees.
- Fill potholes and grade the surface of the foreshore track when required.

On 12/8/2001 Ron Davis, due to ill health, resigned as Coastcare co-ordinator and Les Hardacre took up the challenge. The foreshore area along the lakeside was by no means completely cleared of Lantana and other unwanted vegetation and, by then, the number of Coastcare workers had reduced to an average of around seven volunteers per working day. A daunting task still lay ahead with such a long length of foreshore to be undertaken by so few.

The weeds needed to be removed periodically and previously weeded areas had to be weeded again and again. By working their way along the side of the track the group cleared designated areas ready for the planting of native plants indigenous to the area. It was hard work clambering up the steep hillside to remove weeds and escaped garden plants which had invaded the bushland and it was no wonder that volunteer numbers reduced to four by 2003.

Later, many native grasses were introduced along the edge of the foreshore. This was to help secure the bank and stop lakeside erosion - also, to filter the run off water from houses along Green Point Drive – before allowing the water to enter the lake. (Bob Currans).

... Working Along the Track

.... Spreading the Mulch

The Community Trailer

In order to transport Coastcare equipment down to the foreshore area, help out with the distribution of mulch and take green waste to the tip, it was necessary to have a trailer available. Les Hardacre, as co-ordinator, applied on behalf of Coastcare for a Commonwealth grant to buy a new 7'x4' galvanized box trailer. The grant application was successful and in May 2004 a trailer was purchased for $1,311.50. A donation of $250 from MidCoast Water was used to fit an extended tailgate for loading the ride-on mower.

The trailer was then handed over officially to Council who arranged for its registration, insurance, maintenance and repairs. Until further arrangements could be made, the trailer was stored on the premises of Ron Davis. In exchange for a small hiring fee ($10 a day or $5 day for current financial members of the Progress Association), the trailer was made available to residents of Green Point for delivery of their green waste to Tuncurry tip.

Over the years the trailer has proved to be a great asset to the community and hiring fees have added useable funds for the Association. (P.A. records)

In 2006 Council erected a lock-up enclosure to store the trailer close to the concrete maintenance shed at Green Point Park and to increase the haulage capacity the trailer sides were extended.

Coastcare

.... Plantings

In order to learn more about littoral rainforest plants, Les Hardacre and Bob Currans attended a number of Plant Identification Workshops organized by Council. As a consequence of working at Council's Plant Propergation Sessions at their Tuncurry nursery, they both started growing native plants from collected seed, and from cuttings, with Council supplying the potting mix and plant tubes for the work. Any plants not used in our Coastcare area were donated to Council for use on other Coastcare projects. When needed, members of our Coastcare group have joined other groups to help plant or weed their areas.

Originally, Council supplied woodchip mulch to be spread around the new plants. In more recent years similar mulch has been dumped by arborists at the nearby carpark. Local gardens as well as Coastcare plants have benefited from the 'mountains of mulch'. Likewise, when the sea grass was available after the clearing of the little beach area, it too was used as mulch.

Due to ill health, after fifteen years of working with Coastcare, Les Hardacre had to retire. During his time as the co-ordinator, Les kept records of the number of plants planted and the number of hours worked by the group on each working day. Bob Currans then acted as co-ordinator and it was estimated that by the end of 2019 the amount of native plants planted would be close to 24,500 and hours worked by volunteers would exceed 15,000 hours.

The following list indicates some of the numerous types of trees, shrubs and understorey plants which, over the years, have been planted in the Coastcare Regeneration Area.

Banksia	Lilly Pilly	Understorey plants -
Bird's	Melaleuca	Cordyline
Black	Native frangipani	Dianella
Bleeding heart	Native hibiscus	Dillwynia
Bottlebrush	Plum pine	Flannel flowers
Blueberry ash	Red cedar	Hardengbergia
Cabbage palm	Rosewood	Juncas
Cassine	Sandpaper fig & other figs	Lamandra
Cheese	Tuckeroo	Pigface
Corkwood	Wattle	Vines & creepers
Grevillea	Whalebone tree	Wesytringia
Golden penda		

.... Growing - on the Indigenous Plants

.... *Reserve Gardens Established*

.... Removing Ipomoea & Planting Natives

.... Some of the Coastcare Volunteers

.... *Never-ending Maintenance*

In 2017, (apart from replacement plantings), at least another 1,000 more new understorey plants needed to be planted. Ongoing maintenance from then on would be confined to weeding, pruning, mulching and selective weed spraying: as once the overhead canopy thickened and blocked out the sunlight, weeds should become less of a problem. However, climatic conditions changed and the lack of water, due to the drought, had detrimentally affected the Coastcare regeneration area. Bob Currans continued to propagate hundreds of native plants, which were then planted to replenish the landscape. By mid 2018, due to the very dry conditions, planting, deemed to be futile, was ceased.

On 20/12/2018, damaging high winds (over 120 kph - similar to a tornado) ripped through the MidNorth Coast and the Hunter Region. Being in the direct route of the storm, Green Point was extremely hard hit – resulting in huge damage caused by the strong winds and fallen trees. Beside the tree trunks blocking roads, electricity and phone wires lay broken and a danger to residents. It was days before services would be restored, due to the magnitude of the storm ravaged area. The roofs of two houses in Green Point Drive were damaged and emergency tarpaulins were used to cover the homes until repairs could be carried out.

A heartbreaking scene met the Coastcare workers when they went to survey the damage. The extremely high winds came directly across the lake and devastated the hillside. The recent dry time had left the trees vulnerable to damage and many had either broken branches or had toppled over with some falling across the lakeside track. The Council's contract arborists later cleared the way, making the road accessible and safe for residents. By the summer of 2019, the drought had tightened its grip and the region became severely affected by the up coming potentially extreme bush fire season!

Hope for better times ahead came in January 2020 with a number of light showers of rain –followed by downpours in early February. Within a short time signs of green appeared in the landscape and 'life' was restored to the dry scorched earth. New plantings could then resume to restore areas lost to the drought conditions.

Over the last twenty years the number of regular Coastcare volunteers has fluctuated, mainly due to ill health, lack of free time available, holidays away and leaving the area. As new residents become members, the group is able to retain a core of around six dedicated workers. Whilst Coastcare work continues, the foreshore bushland regeneration area will be maintained for the enjoyment of residents and tourists alike. Each year, our volunteers are invited to a 'Thank You Morning Tea' arranged by the Council in appreciation of the hard work done by 'all' the volunteers who give their time on behalf of their community and the environment. (Bob Currans)

.... *Heartbreaking High Wind Damage*

Development Of Foreshore Completed

Over the past twenty years the untidy, weed infested lakeside area, has been completely transformed into the pleasant surrounds we have today. Great Lakes Council, the Community Association, professional fishermen and residents have all worked together in order to produce this successful outcome of which we can all be proud of and enjoy.

In order to help keep the foreshore area clean and tidy Council garbage bins were made available in 1999 and to complete the reserve picnic area, Council, under pressure by the Association, constructed a covered picnic table and bench seats on 13/10/2013. Many residents and tourists have since visited the area to enjoy the picnic facilities, and in the evenings, when the sun goes down over the lake, magnificent sunsets prompt many to take photographs.

With all the planned facilities now in place, all that remained was to maintain the work already achieved. In the early days, Rod Bell, a keen fisherman of Green Point, initially used a hand-mower to maintain the reserve area. Nowadays, Council-inducted community volunteers are able to use the ride-on mower provided by Council. In 2019, Rod Bell was forced to retire from the mowing due to ill health. Fortunately, Richard Knights, another grass cutting volunteer agreed to take over Rod's wonderful contribution. The area beside the lake and south of Wharf Road, has been mown for many years by David Buchanan. Thanks to these volunteers the grassed areas beside the lake are kept regularly maintained.

The unique lake views and natural beauty of the area beside the lake's foreshore are no doubt appreciated by the many resident recreational walkers who over the years continue to tread a path around Green Point on their early morning rounds. Many resident dog owners use the route beside the lake to walk their dogs. In 2014, and for their convenience, plastic bag dispensers for dog droppings were positioned at the lakeside reserve and at the entrance to Smokehouse Beach on Green Point Drive. This was achieved, after much negotiation with Council, by Helen Tompson – a then member of the Association. As Helen has now moved away this continuing service is carried out by Gayle Redman.

As mentioned on Council's ordinance signs, erected in 2014, we can now see that the area previously referred to as 'The Point' has been officially named the "Green Point Foreshore Reserve". In July 2015, the Association, working with Council, was able to have a long awaited fish-cleaning table installed adjacent to the lake for use by the local fishermen. The 1999 Development Plan for the reserve proposed that fencing, to restrict car access into the picnic area, should be provided. This work was completed in late 2016 when Council replaced the existing large rocks around the perimeter of the grassed areas with new standard height wooden bollards, making it safer for vehicle parking and pedestrians. This brought the reserve in line with other areas under Council's jurisdiction. Due to the need for improvements to the nearby carpark, Council repaired and bitumen sealed the area on 31/10/2019, making it better for residents and tourists alike. (C.A. records)

Foreshore Reserve

.... Public Amenities

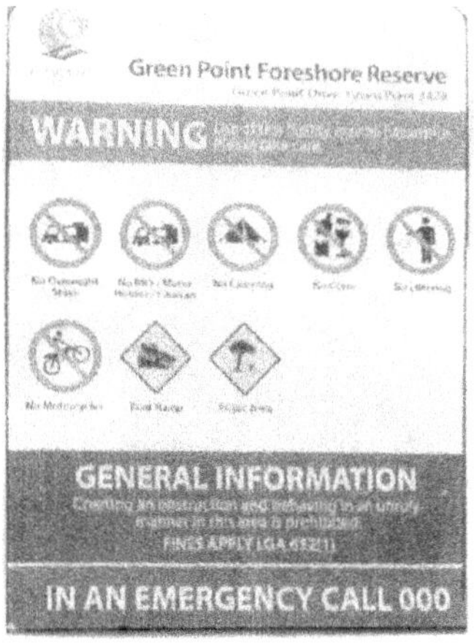

.... The Lakeside Walk

.... The Track in Bloom

Flora - Wildflower Display

When passing through the nearby Booti Booti National Park in springtime, large areas of wildflowers can be seen in bloom. Around August each year the many varieties of wattle put on a lovely show of golden yellow. By September numerous species of wildflowers start to bloom along both sides of Green Point Drive from the chicane to The Lakes Way. These include: Dillwynia, Eriostemon, Grevilleas, Native Cassia, Epacris, Hakea sericea, Baeckea, Crowea, Heath Banksia, Boronias, Bottlebrush (Callistemon), flowering Tea-Tree, broad-leaf Geebung, the Austral Grass Tree and small orchid type flowers like the Silky Purple Flag flower and many others.

The most impressive display however, is that of the white Flannel Flowers. In the springtime, following the March 1991 bush fire the Flannel Flowers smothered the hillsides in all directions – from a distance the hills appeared to be covered in snow! The Flannel Flowers (Actinotus helianthi) would have easily adapted to the open spaces with lightly filtered sunlight, poor sandy soils and perfect drainage. Summer bush fires, which devastated the landscape, seem to have rejuvenated the soil and remarkably, these delicate flowers, have returned each season for our enjoyment. Over the years the hilly heathland areas in Booti Booti National Park, either side of the Green Point access road, became well known for their wonderful Flannel Flowers and local 'Walking for Pleasure' groups included a visit to Green Point on their springtime calendar.

In the early 1990's, before the access to the track across the wetlands on the northern side of Green Point Drive was blocked by National Park authorities, we did a bush walk to explore the area. Whilst walking the track we were thrilled to find a solitary native Christmas Bell plant growing nearby. Christmas Bells (Blandfordia grandiflora) are perennial plants with crowded grass like leaves. They grow between 50-80 cms high with bunches of three to ten large waxy bell-like flowers which vary from yellow to orange or red with yellow tips – flowering, as their name suggests, around Christmas time. The swampy wetland area, with its sandy soil and full or partial sun, provided the perfect conditions for them in which to grow.

When I asked Owen Mathias if he remembered the wildflowers growing in our area, he recalled that in the 1930's, there were many outcrops of beautiful Christmas Bells growing in the bush on each side of The Lakes Way and also close to his home on the farm at Pipers Bay. As a young lad he would go out on his horse to gather a bunch of flowers for his mother. His horse 'Joker' would amble along slowly and stop when he found a cluster of the blooms so that Owen could lean down and pick the flowers.

In the 1950's, Anne Bramble remembered the flowers being called 'Moor Christmas Bells'. During the 1960's-1970's Charlie Bramble often travelled The Lakes Way to Green Point, and when asked about the wildflowers, he recalled that Christmas Bells grew en masse across the wetlands. He remembered "the moors being a blaze of red as he passed by – just like FIRE!" This was confirmed by Leanne and Bill Legge, who said that "the Christmas Bells were blood red as far as you could see on the left hand side of The Lakes Way going towards Forster". (In earlier days travellers had an uninterrupted view across the moors. In more recent times The Lakes Way has been upgraded and the roadside drain constructed which allowed the Paperbark trees to colonize and block out the view across the wetland area.)

By the mid 1970's-1980's, according to Olive Steel and Val McPherson, the Christmas Bells still grew in abundance. This photograph of Doris Perry, taken in 1987, shows the large expanse of Christmas Bells in bloom at that time.

As mentioned, just a few years later in the early 1990's, we were only able to find ONE solitary specimen. Later in 2002, Margaret Blackwood was able to find a few more plants growing on the southern side of Green Point Drive in Booti Booti National Park. Whatever the cause of the near extinction of these colourful wildflowers, it is hoped a remnant still remains hidden in the bushland for future propagation.

Fauna – A Walk on the Wild Side

Around 1960, when the dairy cattle no longer grazed our area, the vegetation in the subdivision was allowed to return to the wild. Tree seedlings grew taller and invasive weeds, like Lantana and Blackberry bushes, took over. By the mid 1970's animals from the surrounding bushland had ventured closer to the new resident's homes and gardens.

.... Lizards

Nowadays, little Jacky lizards, patterned garden skinks and Eastern Blue-tongued lizards are all welcome in our gardens, but not always so when it comes to the larger variety.

Chris Sutton, an early resident of Green Point Drive, recalled that with no fences to stop them large Monitor lizards easily accessed residential properties. Olive Steel, a nearby resident, related how a near two metre long goanna had strutted up to her house from the bush below and walked along the top of the back balcony railing – only to flop down on its belly beside her on the decking. "They were very scary", she said "and new residents were told that you do get used to them". Between 1992 and 1995 large goannas were sighted in bushland behind No. 129 Green Point Drive (Brian Gordon). In the late 1990's a resident who lived near the bushland end of Waratah Close, was surprised one day to turn around and find a near two metre long Monitor lizard walking along the top of the farm fence 'directly' behind him. In 2005, residents in Seabreeze Parade reported seeing two very large goannas behind their home in the swampy area of the wetlands which they fondly referred to as 'The Everglades'. (Noelene Turner). As late as 2016 a goanna was seen in bushland below No. 65 Green Point Drive (Jeanette Hardacre). Next door to Jeanette's, at No.67, an adventurous Monitor lizard wandered through the open front door and down the hall into Jan Akerman's lounge room. Jan immediately rang Susan Blackwood and her two teenage sons, Jacob and Callum, with cries for help. They quickly arrived with a large doona cover in hand. After quite a bit of coaxing they managed to get the fellow into the cover amidst loud yells and female screams as the lizard was much heavier than they expected and it certainly was not happy being contained. The intruder was eventually returned to its lakeside bush retreat. Undoubtedly there have been other sightings of these large reptiles in bushland surrounding the village. Cooking smells from barbeques held at the Sailing Club grounds, (south of Green Point), often entice them out of the nearby bushland to scavenge for meat scraps.

Another lizard is the Land Mullet. This species is one of 82 threatened animals in the Great Lakes Region. (Great Lakes Council). Around the mid 2000's, this black lizard, about the size of a Blue-tongue, was sighted by Margaret Gibbons behind her property at No.105 Green Point Drive and also by Bill Raward behind his property at No. 77 Green Point Drive.

In 2019 residents reported hearing the "clauk, clauk, clauk" sound, close to their properties, announcing the arrival of the little gecko.

A Land Mullet - a significant species found within the Great Lakes.

A History of Green Point
.... Noisy, Friendly or Fierce

.... *Wriggly Tales*

Over the years village residents also became accustomed to seeing snakes around the area. These tales are but a few of their encounters. Chris Sutton reported that around 1975 he remembered seeing a five metre long python which hibernated each winter in his neighbour's shed at No. 7 Green Point Drive. This black and dirty grey coloured snake could often be seen stretched from one side of the road to the other, warming itself in the sun. Later on, when up the ladder cleaning the guttering on his two-storey house, he had to keep very calm when he met this long snake 'face to face'.

In the mid 1980's a large Diamond python used to curl itself around a roof beam in the Green Point Gallery Restaurant keeping warm for the winter. At the time patrons didn't seem to mind it being in the rafters above their heads. In the 1990's, Carpet snakes often turned up unexpectedly on properties around the area. Having the backdoor to the decking blocked by a two and half metre long Carpet snake, Olive Steel at No. 15 Green Point Drive, had to request the assistance of a neighbour who removed the persistent reptile with a broom. A visiting python captured a wayward guinea pig from our neighbour's yard and years later, when gardening, I was surprised to find a similar snake curled up under foliage in a garden bed. In 2005, residents Noelene and Lou Turner at No. 52 Seabreeze Parade, referred to their visiting python as 'Sammy the Snake' and said that they actually missed him when he left their backyard after three months. Residents Philippa Jones and John Hughes at No. 4 Frazer Avenue enjoyed having their visiting three metre long Diamond python which often resided in their backyard tree and was last sighted in October 2007.

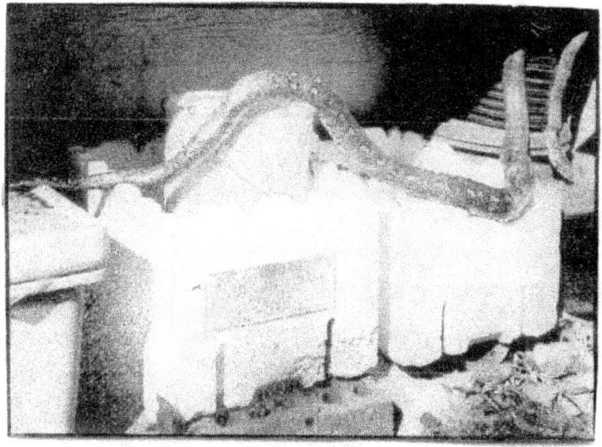

.... *Snakes Alive – Don't Panic*

Years ago the mantra was "the only good snake is a dead snake!" These days, with education, more people realize that if we leave snakes alone they will leave us alone. Snakes generally are timid and usually will only attack if provoked. In April 1997 a two metre long Red-bellied Black snake was killed at the lakeside picnic area, the reason being that residents feared the local children and dogs would be a risk. In fact these snakes are an asset and worth protecting as they have been known to eat the deadly Eastern Brown snake. Both these species occasionally leave the surrounding bushland and venture into local gardens in search of food and water, before moving on.

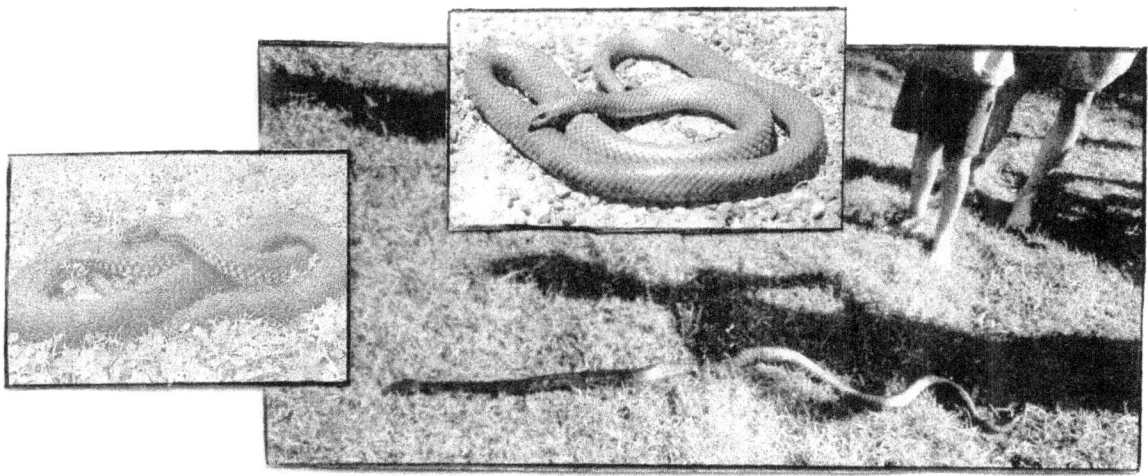

Less of a worry is the long, slender Tree Snake. They have tiny heads, with bulbous eyes, are quite slow moving and are generally regarded as not harmful to humans. Their colouring varies from black to pale grey-green with a yellow green or blue underside thus blending into garden foliage where they feed on small prey. Recently, I was fascinated to watch the way in which a Tree snake climbed slowly up our house brickwork and up to the guttering then onto the roof.

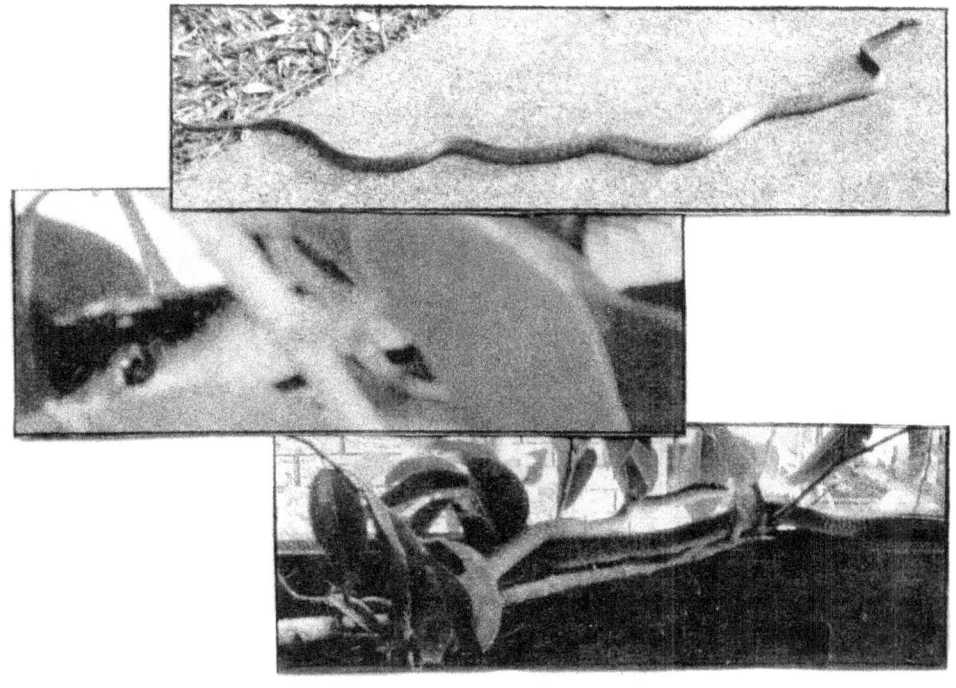

.... Foxes

These animals were introduced into Australia for recreational hunting in the 1850's and since then have spread across southern Australia and have become a serious threat to domestic livestock and wildlife. (NPWS)

In the early 1920's to 1930's there were large numbers of foxes living in the sand dunes near Seven Mile beach and shooters from Forster used to join with local working farmers to eradicate the pests. In 1928 foxes roamed around the dairy farm and Lachlan Fraser had to protect his large chicken run with high paling fences. (Owen Mathias). By 1979, early residents Lowell Reardon and Renata Schmakeit, also had to protect their ducks and chickens from the foxes. Around that time many foxes were seen, in the evenings, crossing The Lakes Way. (Charlie Bramble) Ross Kneebone reported that a number of small wallabies had been killed by foxes on his farm property in 2007 and 2008.

To control foxes and protect native wildlife short sessions of 1080 baiting is carefully planned and controlled by the NPWS. The meat based baits are buried 10cms under a mound of sand (termed bait stations). Signs are displayed on National Park boards showing the dates on which the baiting is to be carried out. There were fox baiting sessions from 17/4/2008 to 25/4/2008 and on 15/7/2009. On 20/2/2013 and 17/6/2013 foxes were sighted in good condition on The Lakes Way 300 metres north of the Green Point turn off. Later, Council arranged for a fox's den in bushland beside the lake and below Green Point Drive, to be exterminated.

.... Dingoes

Over many years dingoes have roamed our area and south towards Pacific Palms. In the early 1990's a dingo was sighted on Seven Mile beach, foraging through a fisherman's bag for food. In June 1996, dingoes were seen circling around picnicers having a barbeque at Santa Barbara – obviously looking for handouts. In the late 1990's Ted Hook's Kelpie-cross, named 'Slug', had wandered into bushland near the 'Turtle Crossing' property. Loud yelping and cries of pain brought the owner running, just in time to save the much loved pet from being mauled to death by a starving dingo.

One evening in mid 2006, Paul Murrell sighted a wallaby bounding across Green Point Drive near to the chicane, closely followed by a dingo. In February 2008, an extremely thin mother dingo was seen standing in the carpark at the corner of Green Point Drive and The Lakes Way and later, Charlie Bramble mentioned that a nursing mother dingo had been removed by the National Park Ranger, as it was looking very poorly. In April 2009, Peter Welton, whilst walking his dogs early in the morning, reported seeing dingoes in the same vicinity.

These animals are actually dingo crossbreeds, and as such, are referred to as wild dogs by the National Parks Wildlife Service. When needed, the NPWS steps in to protect native animals from wild dogs and foxes, by arranging for the Local Land Services, in co-operation with Council, to attend to the situation. (NPWS. Booti Booti National Park).

.... Predators

.... Wildlife Crossing

When on my walks along Green Point Drive from the chicane to the corner of The Lakes Way and back, I have observed that not all 'wildlife crossings' have been successful! Over the years it has been disheartening to see a number of deceased animals by the roadside.

In the late 1990's I saw a dead wombat on The Lakes Way near the corner of Green Point Drive. (A resident in Seabreeze Parade reported evidence of a wombat hole and wombat droppings on his property in the 1980's). The 'Kangaroo' road sign, erected on Green Point Drive in the early 1990's, warns motorists of the danger of kangaroos crossing. Unfortunately two animals were killed by vehicles either side of the nearby hill on Green Point Drive. Smaller wallabies have been killed on the same road closer to the chicane. (Grey swamp wallabies have been observed in the early morning and at dusk grazing on property at the end of Camellia Place, feeding in paddocks adjacent to Waratah Close, in the bushland behind homes in Seabreeze Parade and in Booti Booti National Park.

In 1997, a large echidna visited a resident's garden at No.15 Green Point Drive. In order to show the neighbours the animal was put into a large cardboard box. We rushed over to see the echidna only to find that it had pushed the box over and was escaping – burrowing into the nearest garden bed! It was amazing to watch as the echidna rotated and disappeared from view before our very eyes. In the mid 2000's 'Spikey the Echidna' was often seen crossing Green Point Drive in the vicinity to the village entrance. Residents were deeply saddened when Spikey was killed by passing traffic.

Little Long-necked tortoises need to cross Green Point Drive access road, in order to travel between the large swamp areas either side of the roadway. Although residents, over the years, have rescued many little tortoises from the perils of busy traffic, there have still been a number of fatalities. These little creatures wander around looking for food and water and in February 2013, after a huge storm, one turned up in our backyard. (Freshwater reptiles that have clawed, webbed feet instead of flippers, are called freshwater tortoises) The local NPWS confirmed that our tortoises are the long-necked variety as they can turn their heads from side to side.

In the wild, tortoises and echidnas usually live for many years. Recent sightings of both of these animals in gardens around the village will, hopefully, ensure the future survival of their species in Green Point.

A History of Green Point

.... Road Casualties

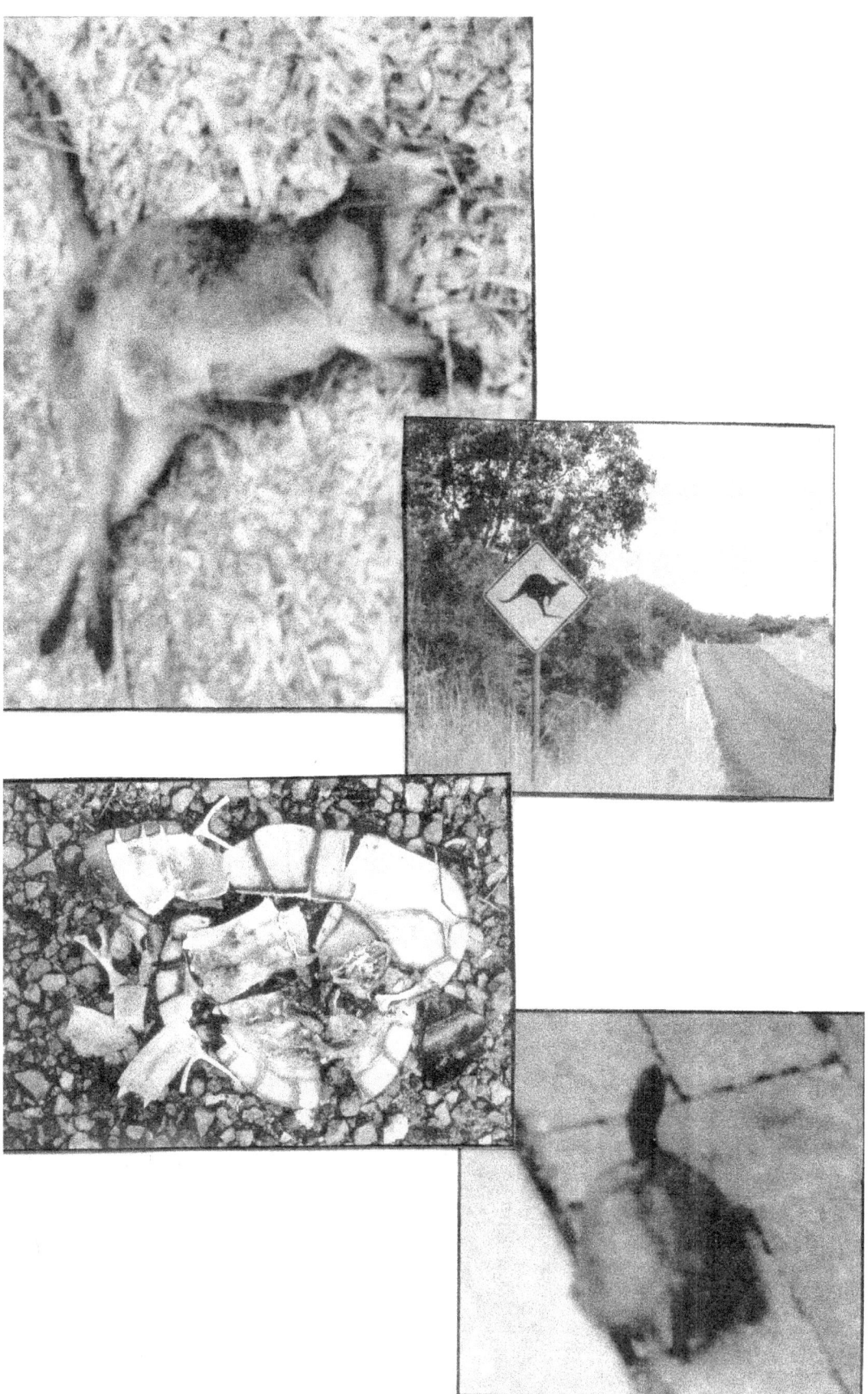

.... Lake Swimmers

Around 1978, when many animals were washed away with the flood debris and into Wallis Lake, a large goanna was sighted swimming from Little Snake Island to Green Point. Ernie and Olive Steel noticed a baby wallaby struggling in the channel and took their row boat out to save the scared little animal – later to set it free in the bushland.

Between 1999-2002, a small number of deer were sighted swimming from Big Snake Island to Green Point. They came ashore below No.65 Green Point Drive and walked along the lakeside path (Jeanette Hardacre). Many years later, on 7/2/2013 Jim Klyne was very surprised to see a deer grazing in his back garden, at No.19 Seabreeze Parade. Due to the shortage of food after the December 2012 bush fire at Coomba Park the animal may have swam over to Green Point looking for greener pastures. In August 2014 and October 2015, deer were sighted by John and Ann Van Dyck near Big Snake Island and swimming across the lake towards the village. Upon investigation it was found that these Rusa deer had been seen at Shallow Bay, then Coomba Park and on to Flat Island, (off Wallis Island). During 2016, families of deer were observed by many residents, roaming around the village in the evening and visiting gardens for fresh pickings – an action which set the many local dogs barking as they sensed the presence of the grazing animals nearby.

As the deer numbers have grown over the years they have become more of a problem than first anticipated. Whilst driving along The Lakes Way around 8.30pm in mid 2018, I narrowly missed a large female deer, as it ran across the road in front of my vehicle. Later the same year, Carmel Pike, a local resident, reported a similar experience which happened around 9.30pm on The Lakes Way near Sweet Pea Road. Carmel drove straight into a mature deer as it raced across the road in front of her. The impact severely damaged the front of her car but as she was alone and nervous about stopping, she slowly drove home with steam streaming from the radiator. She made it home safely but her car was deemed to be a 'right off' and had to be replaced and also, within the village, fighting stags badly damaged two parked vehicles in Frazer Avenue.

At times, the deer can be observed close to residential properties and a discarded antler from a young deer was also found in the vicinity of Green Point. As a 'warning' to motorists entering our area, a deer image sign was erected in 2019 beside Green Point Drive on a hill top on the way into the village. Later, just prior to Christmas, and - in true Aussie tradition and humour – the deer pictured on the road sign received a red nose.

By 2020 the feral deer had colonized areas of Coomba Park and Wallis, Regatta, Big, Yahoo and Snake Islands, also Green Point and South Forster. The NSW NPWS and MidCoast Council are aware of the problem and its impact on the local areas.

The Hunter Local Land Services prepared the Hunter Regional Pest Animal Management Plan 2018-2023, which stated "the focus of management of Rusa deer is to reduce impacts on public safety and limit further spread, until improved control methods are available." Although a programme was mapped out no funding had yet been secured to deliver these actions.

A History of Green Point
.... Feral Deer, Visit Homes

.... Night Visitors

The last koala was sighted at Green Point in 1979, however, there are still other furred animals in our area. Over the years, bandicoots and native swamp rats, have been invading gardens at night, digging for food. Another night feeder is the brushtail possum which can often be heard bounding across rooftops and running along tops of fences. Some concerned residents have built nesting boxes in trees and enjoy observing these mischievous nocturnal animals. However, friendships can wane when the cheeky possums raid their prized crop of near-ripened pawpaws and mangoes – just prior to picking! A sugar glider was sighted in December 2007 by Ross Kneebone on his farm and tiny squirrel gliders have been seen feeding at night on tree blossoms in many areas around the village.

Fruit bats/greyheaded flying foxes have been heard feeding on seasonal fruit from the large Port Jackson fig at No. 105 Green Point Drive - (Dr. Margaret Gibbons) - also, a fruit bat colony camps at Smiths Lake. They feed on nectar, pollen and fruit of eucalypts, paperbarks and banksias. (In and About Pacific Palms by Anne and George McKay). On occasions this large group of bats has visited Green Point on their way over to protected bushland areas in Forster. In March 2010, some residents in Seabreeze Parade were alerted in the evening by the high pitched squeals of the bats and took their torches outside to observe these little furred creatures feeding on the blossoms of the nearby paperbark trees. In early June 2016 this dead fruit bat (pictured) was found in Green Point Park – apparently a victim of the recent violent storm. Both the larger fruit eating flying fox and the smaller insect eating bat have the potential to transmit the deadly bat Lyssaviris, so handling of these animals must be avoided as scratches and bites can result in being infected (Hunter New England Health).

.... Frogs

In the early farming days from 1928-1960, the reedy swamp area south of the Green Point Drive access road, was the perfect environment for frogs. The area then was referred to as the 'Big Boggy Swamp', as cows would venture in too far and become bogged. (Owen Mathias) Closer to home frogs often inhabit water tanks, down pipes and cisterns – especially the big green tree frog. Whilst ever we continue to hear their repeated 'crawk' call and hear the chorus of the dwarf green tree frog and other small brown frogs, and observe them in our gardens, we can be assured that the ecology of our area is healthy – regardless of modern day development.

.... *Fruit Foragers*

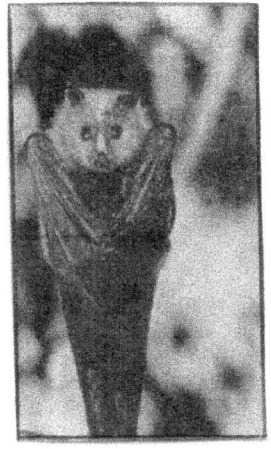
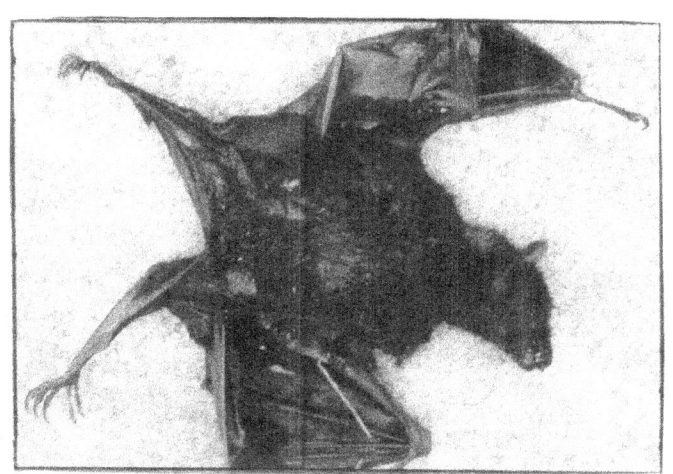

Birds

We are privileged in Green Point to have a large population of birds visit the area. Whenever you stop, look and listen in our village you are bound to encounter one bird or another. Birds entertain us with their unusual antics and melodic calls and, in doing so enrich our lives with their presence. Some residents encourage these colourful creatures by growing flowering native plants, others put out bird seed, bread and honey, or hand feed small portions of meat. Most will supply a bird bath with clean water ready for hot dry days.

However, the emergence of a Brush-turkey population in Green Point has become an annoyance to many residents as the birds continue to destroy garden beds whilst looking for food and spread mulch in all directions. Since 2018, the male bird has made a number of nest mounds in the bushland beside the lake and many little offspring have been produced.

.... *Birds In Action*

Residents at 19 Seabreeze Parade were intrigued by the antics of a male Satin Bower bird as he systematically went through their peg bag throwing out all the pegs. Only the blue ones were selected for his bower situated in the back garden.

When the Little Wattle birds built a nest close to our house, it became a learning tool for our grandchildren to see the eggs in the nest and later the baby chicks as they developed.

Watching the majestic White-bellied Sea-eagle flying back home with a large fish clutched tightly in its talons, was a memorable experience. Also, gazing at the many Pelicans spiraling ever upwards on the thermals over Pipers Bay - one can only wonder how much they actually enjoyed the ride and the expansive view way down below.

In the late summer of 2016 residents overlooking Big Snake Island were enthralled by the actions of the Pelican colony at the northern end of the island. The population had grown due to the hatching of the new chicks and it was now time for them to be taught to fly. Groups of six baby birds were chosen for instruction and there was to be no wandering off as any wayward chicks were quickly brought into line by the older birds. Firstly, they learnt to swim in the shallows, then, two weeks later they were taught to fly just above the water level. Next came the big test; they had to learn to land! It was quite funny to watch their attempts and consequent belly plops – until, in the end, they learnt to take off and land gracefully.

Whilst walking beside the lake I was thrilled to see a family of Tawny Frogmouths, perched together on a She-oak branch and so couldn't resist taking a photo. Nearby I was able to capture a pelican with its recent catch still in its beak.

Since moving to the village around 1991, avid bird watchers Philippa Jones and John Hughes, could often be seen walking along the roadsides, and near the lake, constantly listening and watching out for our local birdlife. In her regular informative articles 'Birds of Green Point', Philippa encouraged and educated interested residents about our local birdlife, by including detailed description, habitat and migration habits (if any) of our local birds at that time. In 2015, after Philippa and John passed away, the families, as a mark of respect, had a memorial bench placed at the Foreshore Reserve for visitors and residents to sit and enjoy the picturesque view of the lake.

.... *Birds in Action*

.... *Pelican Rescue*

Betty Simpson joined the NSW Animal Welfare League in 1976. For seven years she worked hard as the honorary secretary of the Forster/Tuncurry branch of the League. When she resigned her position, The Advocate newspaper reported that "Mrs. Simpson was the 'backbone' of the local branch for many years and her untiring efforts resulted in many animal's lives

being saved, as well as providing help to many people with pet problems." In 1984, when Betty moved to Green Point, she became the Duty Officer for the League, answering phone enquiries and giving wildlife help advice, reporting incidents and arranging call outs.

One such incident was in the mid 1990's, when she noticed an injured pelican, just off shore in Wallis Lake, near what is known as the Foreshore Reserve. The pelican appeared to have a broken wing which probably would have made it aggressive if approached by one person and very hard to handle. It was time to bring in the troops, as the large bird needed to be corralled, then caught before it could be helped. Betty was able to rally 'her kids' as she called them – the young members of The NSW Animal Welfare League. Lance Ferris from Ballina Seabird Rescue also attended and between them the pelican was captured and taken away for treatment and rehabilitation.

This photograph shows Lance Ferris with the pelican and Betty Simpson (on the right) with 'her kids' close by.

.... Bird Safety

In April 2015, Green Point residents were excited to watch a pair of Ospreys start building a nest on top of poles near the electricity substation on The Lakes Way, north of the corner to Green Point Drive. Passing tourists were also interested in its progress. When Tony Wren, a local resident and retired electricity linesman recognized the dangerous position of the nest within the 'high' voltage area, and that the birds could have caused the electricity to arc, he alerted Essential Energy. Marguerite and David Lamb also contacted the energy provider regarding the danger to the birds. The electricity was cut off and over the next six hours the linesmen carefully moved the large nest to a platform constructed on a new pole nearby. Thankfully the birds accepted the change and carried on as usual.

Enthusiastic bird watcher and keen photographer, Marguerite Lamb, took a special interest in the Osprey family and kept the Green Point community informed with regular documented articles and photographs, printed in the Green Pointer. The dedicated parent birds produced a baby chick in August which by 14/10/15 was practicing liftoff. By the end of October the little bird was able to fly short distances and on 10/11/15 was observed arriving back at the nest with its own fish catch. As time went by, the young bird left the nest to start a new life on its own. Around the same time the following year the parent birds produced another chick. Sadly, on 19/10/16, this inexperienced juvenile Osprey had flown into the windscreen of a moving vehicle and had died as a result. After a time of mourning the parents were sighted collecting sticks, breaking them, and rearranging them in the nest. The Ospreys returned to the nest in March/April 2017 and two chicks were produced in August. The fledglings usually leave the nest in November to fly further afield, then to return a year later to the area where they were hatched. In early 2019, the electricity substation was removed along with the disused electricity pole and wires – leaving the remaining supporting pole and Osprey nest intact. The birds continue to frequent the nest and in early 2020 a young Osprey was sighted by David Lamb eating fish at the nest with the parent bird watching nearby.

.... Bird Watching

Visiting bird watchers can often be found by the Foreshore Reserve listening for bird calls and watching for the many species of birds – sometimes capturing them with photographs. Local NPWS Ranger, Brett Cann, advised that over the last eight years he had arranged for contractors to remove weeds from the Booti Booti area, north of the Foreshore Reserve. The last group to do so, in 2016, was from 'TIDE' (Taree Indigenous Development and Employment). It is hoped that as the native plant understorey becomes established, more birds will be enticed to the area – making it even more attractive for birdwatchers.

Our Resident Osprey Family

: Photographs by Marguerite Lamb

..... Birds of Green Point Area

This is not a definitive list, but consists of birds that have been observed clearly enough to identify. Some of these are resident, some migratory, and others have been seen only once. Certain species have disappeared since more of the area has been cleared and habitats reduced.

Australian Brush-turkey
Brown Quail
Black Swan
Australian Wood Duck
Pacific Black Duck
White–headed Pigeon
Spotted Dove
Brown Cuckoo-dove
Crested Pigeon
Peaceful Dove
Topknot Pigeon
Tawny Frogmouth
White-throated Needletail
Fork-tailed Swift
Pheasant Coucal
Eastern Koel
Channel-billed Cuckoo
Shining Bronze-cuckoo
Dusky Moorhen
Eurasian Coot
Royal Spoonbill
Australian White Ibis
White-faced Heron
Australian Pelican
Little Pied Cormorant
Australian Oystercatcher
Sooty Oystercatcher
Pied Stilt
Pacific Golden Plover
Masked Lapwing
Bar-tailed Godwit
Silver Gull
Little Tern
Caspian Tern
Common Tern
Greater Crested Tern
Barking Owl

Black-shouldered Kite
Little Eagle
White-bellied Sea-eagle
Galah Little Wattlebird
Red Wattlebird
Yellow-faced Honeyeater
Noisy Miner
Spotted Pardalote
Striated Pardalote
White-browed Scrubwren
Striated Thornbill
Whistling Kite
Brahminy Kite
Rainbow Bee-eater
Oriental Dollarbird
Sacred Kingfisher
Laughing Kookaburra
Yellow-tailed
Black-cockatoo
Brown Thornbill
Australasian Figbird
Olive-backed Oriole
Eastern Shrike-tit
Rufous Whistler
Golden Whistler
Grey Shrike-thrush
Eastern Whipbird
Black-faced
Cuckoo-shrike
Pied Currawong
Australian Magpie
Pied Butcherbird
White-breasted
Woodswallow
Willie Wagtail
Little Corella
Sulphur-crested Cockatoo

Eastern Rosella
Musk Lorikeet
Rainbow Lorikeet
Scaly-breasted Lorikeet
Australian King-Parrot
Green Catbird
Regent Bowerbird
Satin Bowerbird
Brown Treecreeper
Variegated Fairy-wren
Superb Fairy-wren
White-cheeked
Lewin's Honeyeater
Southern Boobook Owl
Honeyeater
New Holland Honeyeater
Brown Honeyeater
Blue-faced Honeyeater
Little Friarbird
Noisy Friarbird
Eastern Spinebill
Osprey
Rufous Fantail
Spangled Drongo
Leaden Flycatcher
Magpie Lark
Black-faced Monarch
Torresian Crow
Australian Raven
Eastern Yellow Robin
Rufous Songlark
Welcome Swallow
Silvereye
Myna

The above list was compiled by Marguerite and David Lamb

A History of Green Point

Association Becomes Incorporated

In 1973, Green Point residents banded together to form a Progress Association in the hope of becoming more successful when negotiating with Council and other Government Authorities. At that time, the main concerns of residents were the lack of electricity, telephone services, proper mail deliveries, a school bus service and household garbage collection. Another long term problem was that of addressing the terrible condition of the roads in the area, and the lack of street lights and traffic signs. When the original brick Fire Hall was built by resident volunteers, it became the venue for Bush Fire Brigade and Progress Association meetings. Fundraising activities were held for more firefighting equipment and for future community projects. In late 1983, meetings were held with Council to discuss the possibility of a future tennis court, playing field and Community Hall.

On 6/9/1990, the Association received their Certificate of Incorporation and became known as Green Point Progress Association Inc. This better enabled insurance coverage and negotiations with Council for future development. Past fundraising efforts covered the cost of transporting the old tennis club shed from Tuncurry to Green Point and volunteer work improved the building, ready for use by December 1990. Over many years the Association members worked tirelessly in the planning, fundraising and execution of the proposed community sporting projects. All challenges were met head-on, with determination and vigour by the dedicated volunteers – everyone working together to achieve the best outcome for the community.

The Association is made up of a President, Vice-President, Secretary, Treasurer, Publicity Officer, Public Officer and around ten committee members who are elected to assist the executive. Over the years, from 1973 until 2005, there were over sixty separate office bearers who have given their time and energy to work for the Progress Association. During those 32 years the following members were President of the Association: Perce Adams, Roy Harden, Albert Goodworth, Steve Seadon, Dianne Markey, Alan Robinson, Ellis Moregan, Roy Staddon, Allan Steed, Ron Mitchell, Tim Robinson, Rick Haffner, Lana Raward, Malcolm Tompson, Jack Hall and Trevor Cooper.

Changes to Letterheads

As the Association evolved over the years so too did the illustrations on the letterhead and on the 'Green Pointer' newsletter. Being an historical landmark and remnant of the original dairy farm, the Port Jackson fig tree, near No. 105 Green Point Drive, was depicted on the early letterhead and the newsletter from 1981.

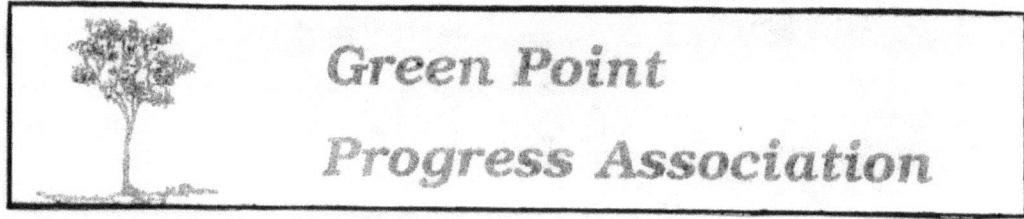

Association Change of Name

The introduction of a new Civil Liabilities Act around February 2004, resulted in the constitution of the Association needing to be changed. From July to November 2004, at the suggestion of Malcolm Tompson, a review of the Association's constitution was made and amendments to the document completed. The alterations were to simplify and make clear the workings of the Association. The President at that time (Trevor Cooper) noted that the amendments also allowed for a 'change of name' which was agreed upon and would better represent the 'spirit of our village'. Accordingly, in February 2005, the Association became known as Green Point Community Association Incorporated.

In June 2005, the Treasurer (Paul Murrell) reported that the change of name was unable to be registered as there was another Association in NSW with the same name and that he had to contact the Dept. of Fair Trading for further information.

The name was offered, a vote taken, and the motion carried. On 21/7/2005 a 'Certificate of Incorporation of Change of Name' was issued. Green Point on Wallis Lake Community Association Inc. was formalized when the new rules were tabled on 14/8/2005 and lodged and accepted on 16/10/2005.

Trevor Cooper continued to serve as President until the end of 2006 when he was succeeded by Margaret Blackwood from 2007 until the end of 2013. Gaye Tindall followed in 2014, and remained as President at the time of writing this record.

To formalize the new stationery and newsletter it was requested of the then resident artist, Ron Davis, to illustrate lakeside scenes more relevant to Green Point. (C.A. records).

Bush Fire Brigade

.... Amalgamation

After years of dedicated service, Fire Brigade Captain George Schoonhoven retired due to burn injuries sustained during the 1991 Green Point bush fire. John Amato, who had been a member of the brigade since 1982, served as Senior Deputy Captain, then became Captain for around three months in 1991, before having to resign due to pressing business commitments. Don Craig followed on as the next Brigade Captain but was also only able to serve for around three months,

Without a full compliment of trained members the brigade couldn't operate to full capacity. In view of the decreasing area allocated to Tuncurry Headquarters Branch and lack of new members, Great Lakes Council's Works and Services committee arranged for Green Point Bush Fire Brigade to help by amalgamating the two brigades in 1991. In order for Green Point Brigade to remain operational it was necessary to abide by Council's decision.

.... Independence

The number of Green Point Brigade members had been steadily increasing since 1993 and over that time the brigade had sought to become independent and autonomous.

Due to building discontent over operational problems between Council's Fire Officer and Tuncurry Headquarters Branch, a 'crisis meeting' of the Green Point Brigade was held on 26/6/1996. Under the leadership of Captain Geoff Hargraves a decision was made by the brigade members to break away from the Tuncurry Headquarters Branch of the Fire Brigade

In July, Tuncurry Headquarters Brigade Captain Bob Berriman, reported that he had no objections to the separation, as the amalgamation of the brigades had never been totally successful. Council's General Manager, John Fitzpatrick, advised that all ties had been broken and by August 1996 Great Lakes Council agreed to re-establish Green Point Bush Fire Brigade as an independent brigade. However, this position was to be reviewed at the end of the 1996-7 'bush fire danger period' when such factors as the crew availability and turn out times would be assessed.

.... Changes of Name

In 1997, due to changes in the law, the Green Point Fire Brigade Constitution was again up-dated. Following this in October 1998, the brigade was given the opportunity for a change of name. In the early years, the group was known as the Green Point Volunteer Bush Fire Brigade. Later, it changed to become the Green Point Bush Fire Brigade and in 1994 it became known as the Dept. of Bush Fire Services. Ultimately, in 1999, the brigade chose to come under the umbrella of the NSW Rural Fire Service and finally came under the Act on 1/7/2001.

A History of Green Point

.... *A Boost to Morale*

Phil McAsey joined the Green Point Bush Fire Brigade in 1993 and later became Captain in 1998. He encouraged Open Days, recruitment for membership and extensive firefighting training. The arrival of a new Cat 7 twin cab tanker truck in 2001 was a great boost to the morale of the brigade.

The previous vehicle, an old Bedford Tanker, was petrol fuelled and dangerous to operate in a large fire. The extreme heat would evaporate the petrol in the motor and as a result the truck would stop and could trap the firefighters. Thankfully, the new Cat 7 twin cab tanker truck was a low combustion diesel and less likely to blow up in a fire.

A History of Green Point

.... A Helping Hand

It was thought to be an advantage for efficiency and safety to have more members with a Heavy Vehicle Licence to drive the new tanker truck when needed.

At the suggestion of Max Burroughs, member of the Green Point RFS and member of the Country Labour Wallamba Branch, Phil McAsey (Brigade Captain) personally approached the above branch of the Labour Party meeting on behalf of members of the Green Point Brigade. He requested their help as a branch initiative to negotiate with Government Authorities, for concessions regarding the then unfair costs of around $100 incurred by brigade members wishing to upgrade to a higher class truck driving licence.

Although at the time the actual driving test was free of charge to RFS members, the associated costs still needed to be paid. They included the cost of the new photo licence of $17, the RTA driving knowledge text book $50 and the driving knowledge test $30. Of course certain criteria would have to be reached by members to enable these costs to be covered. To save on Driving School costs and time off work, with possible loss of wages, it was also suggested that experienced brigade higher class drivers could tutor the lower rated drivers, using the brigade tanker truck. Also, that group knowledge testing and group driver testing could be arranged.

Correspondence was sent to the Minister of Emergency Services, Bob Debus, Minister of Insurance, Carl Scully, Minister of Local Government, Hon. Tony Kelly and Premier, Bob Carr, regarding the problem. The ensuing response was 100% co-operation and as a result these training procedures and cost savings were applied to those with the correct documentation, not only RFS members but also to the SES and VRA groups. (Max Burroughs)

.... Threatened Closure of Bush Fire Brigade

By late 2004, the Brigade membership had declined. Captain Phil McAsey explained to the Community Association meeting held on 14/11/2004 that this was due to volunteers retiring or moving away. Also, that due to Government spending cuts the rationalization of smaller Bush Fire Brigades within the NSW Rural Fire Service, had threatened the closure of the Green Point Brigade.

As predicted by Commissioner Koperberg of the Head Office of the Rural Fire Service in 1996, the resulting decisions regarding smaller Fire Brigades, were based on such things as crew availability and call out times.

On 19/11/2005, the community was alerted via the Association's newsletter, about the proposed Fire Brigade Closure and residents were invited to discuss the matter at the next Community Association meeting to be held on 11/12/2005. At the meeting, Trevor Cooper (President), reported that the Rural Fire Authority had decided to dissolve and disband the Green Point Volunteer Brigade at the end of the coming fire season. The Authority had decided that the fire truck and facilities were underused and that Green Point could be covered by Tuncurry or Pacific Palms Brigades.

The reasons given for the proposed closure were that there were:
1. Only twelve active members, with an additional seven new members lined up.

2. Too little activity.

3. High cost asset

4. Fire brigade members could join the Pacific Palms brigade.

5. Members must be workcover trained in each necessary activity. e.g. chain saw certification.

Fight to *Save* Our Brigade

At the meeting residents were alarmed and outraged at the news of the proposed closure. Afterwards, some residents wrote letters of objection and put forward their arguments against the proposal. A well supported Community Association petition, to halt the closure of the brigade, was sent to Authorities but the response was disappointing. Through the combined and concerted efforts of the Green Point Fire Brigade and the Association, pressure was bought to bear on Government Authorities to reassess the proposed closure.

On 24/11/2005, after consultation with the Green Point Fire Brigade, our local MP at the time, John Turner, wrote a letter to the Hon. A.B. Kelly MLC on their behalf, putting a lengthy detailed argument for the brigade to remain open. On 9/12/2005, Max Burroughs (a member of the Green Point Brigade) also wrote to the Hon. A.B. Kelly MLC, explaining his views about the unrealistic demands put on the small brigade, which would require three, to possibly four crews to be on call 24 hours/365 days a year. He enclosed an aerial photo showing the Green Point area and the access road, Green Point Drive. His greatest fear was the fact that the village was a fire trap and he felt that economic rationalization should not take precedence in this case.

After the Community Assoc. meeting on 11/12/2005, Trevor Cooper wrote on behalf of the Association to the Hon. Tony Kelly MLC, Minister of Emergency Services and Alan Gillespie of the Regional Fire Service, Lower Hunter Zone NSW RFS. Among other factors, he explained our unique position geographically, being surrounded on three sides by National Park bushland with a high fuel load, also the fact that we had had three large bush fires in the past with only one access road in and out of the village. The community of 260 households needed a quick response to spot fires and ongoing protection. Copy letters were sent to John Turner MP and Bob Baldwin MP.

In his reply to the Association on 26/1/2006, John Turner enclosed a copy of his correspondence to the Hon. A. B. Kelly MLC and the resulting reply. Mr. Kelly had been advised of the proposal to amalgamate with Pacific Palms Brigade and was of the view that it must be considered that this plan would guarantee fire cover around the clock and provide a response time of less than 30 minutes (C.A. records) Taking into consideration the other arguments he put forward and those of Superintendent Alan Gillespie of the Lower Hunter Zone NSW RFS on 31/1/2006 it appeared that there would be a hard fought fight ahead to save the Green Point Fire Brigade from closure.

For village fire protection the Green Point Brigade remained opened until the end of the fire season. Meanwhile, nothing could be achieved until after Parliament resumed in February 2006 when negotiations could continue.

.... *Reinstatement* of Brigade

In order to deal with the problems concerning the proposed closure of the Fire Brigade, the effect on the Brigade members and the community, Commissioner Phil Kopenberg established specific procedures and an interim management committee which included volunteer representatives to review all the matters of concern.

As suggested by Commissioner Koperberg, at a meeting at Bulahdelah on 7/5/2006, the Green Point Rural Fire Service Brigade members wrote collectively to Superintendent Mark Lewis at Tuncurry Rural Fire Control, requesting that the Brigade be allowed to continue to function. Copy letters were sent to Commissioner Koperberg, T.Brown Representative Brigade Management Group and the Green Point Community Association. Following a meeting held at Bulahdelah Brigade, the Green Point RFS Brigade was reinstated on 11/6/2006 – back as it had been six months earlier.

... *New Members and Training*

On 14/10/2006 an 'Open Day' and strong recruitment drive was held which resulted in renewed community interest. By early 2007 nine new members had joined the brigade bringing the total to twenty-two.

Training was held every second Saturday for the crew and new members undertook twenty hours of training over three consecutive days in April with more to follow. RFS Brigades offered training, ranging from basic firefighting, village firefighting, first aid to breathing apparatus operation and rural fire. On 26th and 27th May, twelve members from Green Point Brigade joined other firefighters in the Community Hall for an extensive eighteen hour training course on RFS First Aid. All the members passed with flying colours. On 15/9/2007 another 'Open Day' and barbecue was held at the Green Point Brigade building with information distributed on preparing for the next bush fire season and fire safety.

.... *The Inaugural Fire House Challenge*

On 29/9/2007 local area RFS Brigade members met beside the lake at Pacific Palms to compete in this friendly competition. Due to major fires in the area at the time, only four brigades participated. Each with a crew of four firefighters, Pacific Palms, Coomba, Bungwahl and Green Point went head to head, testing their skills. To win an event crews had to demonstrate their knowledge, speed and ability to enact fireground procedures accurately, using the safest response to the simulated emergency. (Pacific Palms photograph – Advocate 7/11/2007)

All their hard work and training was rewarded when Green Point's Brigade team of Christine Reardon, Alan Bawden, Captain Phil McAsey and Deputy Captain Simon Murrell won the overall point score. The trophy was accepted by Captain Phil McAsey from Senior Group Captain Stuart Gentle on behalf of the Brigade. (C.A. records)

'Congratulations' - Green Point RFS

A History of Green Point

Commercial Fishing From Green Point

Wallis Lake has always had an abundance of fish and as a resource, has supplied large quantities of food for early populations living around the lake. In the past, pioneer fishing families in Forster/Tuncurry worked together to form a highly successful fishing industry. Over time, more fishermen living around the lake became involved and the industry spread.

.... Professional Fishermen

Over the years the Bramble family has fished areas in Wallis Lake. In the early 1960's Rex Bramble fished the waters around Green Hill Point - as it was known at the time when Lachlan Fraser had his farm. As there were no outboard motors in those days, working boats could take up to two and half hours to motor back to Forster - especially when it was against the tide. In bad weather, Rex sheltered overnight in the cabin on board the fishing boat moored close to Shepherd Island. Other times he left his boat at the farm and drove his vehicle back to Forster. (Charlie Bramble) The Legge family also fished our area around the same time. Allen Legge and his sons Robert, Terry and Bill were based at Charlotte Bay. They fished our area during the winter months when the water was cooler, which helped preserve the fish. When necessary they stayed overnight in a tent just north of where the Foreshore Reserve is today. (Bill Legge) George Belton and Keith McBride also used to shelter from the strong prevailing winds when out fishing. They used to moor their boats whilst they camped overnight on Shepherd Island. (Chum Bramble)

.... Dead Fish on Shoreline

In early 1976, a large number of undersized dead fish were found scattered on the lake foreshore, at Smokehouse Beach and near Wharf Road. This fish kill prompted Steve Seadon (an early resident) to enquire about the situation and approach the Fisheries Board about reducing the number of commercial fishermen using the lake. (P.A. records).

On 5/4/1976, in answer to his enquiry, the NSW State Fisheries advised that restrictions were being imposed on the fishing gear and the length and mesh size of nets that licenced professional fishermen could use and that net sizes were carefully determined after scientific investigation. The escapement of a sufficient number of immature fish stocks, at a reasonable level, was a prime factor in this regard. Regrettably, some immature fish were killed in netting operations, but these numbers were insignificant when the enormity of the stocks was considered.

Government Gazette notices were attached to the reply letter setting out the fishing restrictions on the lake – certain areas in Wallis Lake were closed to net fishing on weekends and for other specific periods during the year. The entrance waters were closed to net fishing as a conservation measure and to allow fish freedom of movement to ocean waters. Some other areas inside the estuary were also closed to net fishing and other restrictions protected the tidal waters of the oyster farms. (NSW State Fisheries).

Local professional fisherman, Greg Golby, explained the situation. Originally the fishing nets had small mesh and were up to 1,000 metres in length. When the fish were funnelled into the cod bag at the end of the net, some types of fish panicked and jumped out. This meant that the dead fish could be seen on the shoreline. The Dept. of Fisheries later changed the regulation size of the nets to overcome the problem. After further discussion with local fishermen, it was decided to increase the size of the mesh and reduce the length of the nets to 500 metres, which has since been proven satisfactory.

.... *Fishermen Numbers Fluctuate*

Charlie Bramble commenced fishing professionally from Green Point in 1972. Not long afterwards he decided to settle there to live. Greg Golby used to fish from Tuncurry but, in 1984 he also decided it would be better to live and work in Green Point. In 1992 Bill Legge moved to Green Point where he began fishing professionally with his brothers Robert, Colin and Terry who travelled to Green Point to fish with him.

By the mid-to-late 1990's, there were more professional fishermen working from Green Point. Some resided here and others travelled from Charlotte Bay, Smiths Lake and Tuncurry. These included Paul Stevens, Shane Geale, Malcolm and Dallas Trotter, Warren McWilliams, Tony Monin and Vaughan Barnsley. Others like Greg Bowland lived in Green Point and worked the ocean from Tuncurry. By the late 1990's there were 5-6 hauling crews working the lake from Green Point. They covered areas of Pipers Bay, Smokehouse Beach and as far south as Tiona. One hauling crew was the Chapman brothers, Bert and Percy, who had a boat which, because of its shape, was referred to as the 'African Queen' by other local fishermen. As with other industries, the number of professional fishermen working from Green Point fluctuated from time to time. Some retired and other moved to different areas to work and by 2005 there were only around five commercial fishermen working locally. (Greg Golby)

One of the main factors influencing the reduction of numbers within our 'Great Lakes Region 4' in more recent years, were the three NSW Government Buy Out Schemes:

- The first, known as the **Recreational Buy Out** occurred in 2002, when Bill Legge and his brothers Robert, Colin and Terry all retired from commercial fishing from Green Point.

- The second or **Marine Park Buy Out** occurred around 2007 and was designed to replenish fish stocks. The buy out mainly affected the ocean fishermen from Smiths Lake down to Myall Lake, including an area around Seal Rocks. Also, when parts of the Manning River were closed to prawning and fishermen could no longer fish their designated areas, they were allocated specific parts of Wallis Lake and its estuaries.

- The third commercial fishermen's buy out was referred to as the **Reform Buy Out.** The NSW Government reforms, made by the Minister of Primary Industries, were designed to build a strong foundation for long-term viability and sustainability of the fishing industry.

Through the NSW Primary Industries Commercial Fishers Business Adjustment Program, commercial fishermen were given the opportunity to bid in a blind auction. After the third round was held, the Government was able to ascertain the buy and sell price that the fishermen expected and then give them the choice to sell their business if they wanted to get out, sell part of the business – say if they didn't want to prawn for example – or buy up other fishermen's shares to increase the size of their fishing areas. (Greg Golby)

Although the buyout scheme made problems for many commercial fishermen, the process however, did enable those who persevered and wanted to retire from commercial fishing, to do so satisfactorily. In July 2017, locally based fishermen Vaughan Barnsley and Warren

McWilliams chose to use the benefits of this Buy Out Scheme to retire from commercial fishing. On average between 2014-2017 there were seven commercial fishermen based at Green Point.

In 2016, there were thirty-eight 'active' fishers within the Wallis Lake Fishermen's Co-op (Great Lakes Advocate) - around twenty-five being lake and estuary fishermen and others being ocean fishermen. In addition to their fishing endorsement, most commercial fishermen have endorsements to go prawning and crabbing, as these supplement their seasonal fish catch (Vaughan Barnsley)

.... Prawning

Commercial fishermen, wishing to go channel prawning, attend a draw held at the park near the NSW Fisheries Dept. at Tuncurry. It is held every full moon, with the prawns running five days later, for twelve to fourteen days. Fishermen are allotted a peg number which determines when and where they can fish each night.

For many years, the Legge brothers used to net for prawns in the weed beds of Pipers Bay. To attract the prawns, bright lights were attached to their boats and ends of the nets. Around 2001-2002 changes were made to the Seine prawn nets. Measures were taken to increase the size of the mesh, from 28mm to 32mm. This was done so that the small prawns could get away, to be allowed to later grow in size.

.... Crabbing

In the past, the old wire covered square-cage type traps were used, but in 2010 new circular style traps were marketed and became quite popular with fishermen and effective catch wise. In 2016, to encourage the resource, modifications were made to the crab trap design. Newly fitted 50mm mesh with rectangular escape holes allowed smaller crabs to crawl out the back of the trap, to later reproduce. In 2016, around 60% of Blue Swimmer crabs caught in NSW, were supplied by the commercial fishermen of Wallis Lake and its four rivers. The NSW Fisheries Dept. and the commercial fishermen work together for the betterment of the industry and the environment. (Vaughan Barnsley)

Turtle Tales

Many commercial fishermen come in contact with sea turtles whilst out on Wallis Lake and are extremely concerned about the safety of these majestic sea creatures. Some time ago, when out on the lake, Vaughan Barnsley noticed some bubbles rising to the surface. After circling in closer, he saw the head of a brown backed sea turtle coming up for air. It was obvious to him that the very large creature was in danger of drowning as one of its flippers had been caught in the rope of a crab pot, which was attached to an anchored buoy. The more the turtle circled to get free, the more it became entangled and the rope cut further into its flesh. Quickly, Vaughan cut the rope, which enabled the turtle to swim safely away. He felt that "it was only that the turtle was very large and strong that it was able to swim away – a younger, smaller turtle may not have survived." (Over time algae builds up on the backs of green sea turtles which gives the impression of being brown-backed. – NSW Dept of Fisheries.)

Unfortunately not all sea turtles escape the effects of 'man's interference.' So concerned was Les Cheers, (a commercial fisherman from Smiths Lake for over forty years) when he came across a dead sea turtle that he took it down to Sydney's Taronga Park Zoo to have an autopsy performed on the creature – the sad result was that its stomach was found to be full of plastic bags!

Late one afternoon, long-term local fisherman Ted Hooke, was returning home from fishing on the lake when suddenly his boat collided with a large brown sea turtle. There was a tremendous bang at the bow of the boat. On impact, the craft reared up into the air, throwing Ted and all his fishing gear overboard. He found himself floundering in the middle of the lake, with no help in sight, and wondering what to do next. Luckily for him the boat didn't take off for the nearest shoreline as expected, but proceeded to propel itself in a circular motion. After assessing the situation, he swam the three metres needed to approach the boat and was able to grasp a trailing rope and use it to climb on board – relieved to be able to return home safely and hoping that the old turtle survived and would live for many more years to come.

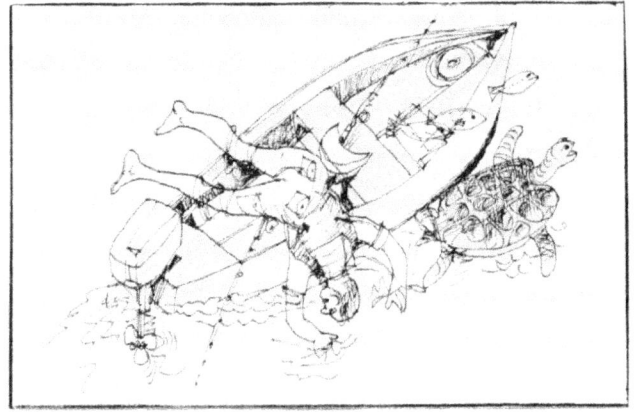

Whilst checking on the recovery of the environment on Little Snake Island, resident Dr. John Van Dyck and his 9-year-old grandson, came across a large intact turtle shell. Judging by its size it could have been very old and may have gone there to die.

Formation Of a Fishing Club

As the population of Green Point increased it followed that there would be a large number of keen recreational anglers fishing the nearby lake and ocean. In early 2007, Michael Van Bilsen, approached the local recreational fishermen with an idea of forming a community based 'Fishing Club' – one which would include the young people in its activities. As a result, an 'inaugural' meeting was held at the Community Hall. A large number of local fishermen attended and voted to accept the proposal. In April, the Green Point Fishing Club was formed, with Jeff Christensen as President. Regular meetings were to be held at the lakeside reserve (weather permitting) with the AGM to be held in July each year. A Fishing Club notice board on Green Point Drive displayed the upcoming events and information was also available at the General Store and reported in the Green Pointer newsletter. Annual membership fees were set at $25 (family), $10 (adult) and $5 (junior).

Fishing Competitions -

The first competition of the newly formed club was held on ANZAC Day, with some 27 club members taking part. After four more competitions the membership had grown to 58 – with 42 adults and 16 juniors. Competitions were held on the first full weekend of each month, for members and guests - entry fee $2 for members and $5 for visitors. The competitions started at 6am on Saturday morning and ended with the weigh in at 1pm on Sunday. Participants could choose from lake, ocean, beach or breakwater fishing and were allowed to weigh in their best five fish of any species. Originally, there were senior and junior categories, but later a 'ladies only' category was introduced.

To keep the competition interesting, winners for the different categories were determined by a series of 'random weight' draws; where the winner was the person in each category whose fish weight was the closest to the 'mystery weight' drawn. There was also a 'Clubman of the Year Award' and the senior and junior members 'Annual Fishing Award' Each Sunday at 12 noon, before the competition weigh in, members enjoyed a friendly sausage sizzle lunch Later, the winning prizes were awarded for both adult and junior category entrants, and the meat raffle and competition entrance prize tickets were drawn.

Man Overboard –

There was always a laugh to be had when the club members got together beside the lake – but on one occasion at the reserve, it was NO LAUGHING MATTER! Ignoring his wife Robin's advice to first sit down in their boat before attempting to board, husband Harry Jones - DID IT HIS WAY! When putting his leg over the side to climb into their tinny, he unfortunately got his leg caught in a rope – and over he went, head first into the shallow water. Despite witnessing their floundering mate, who may have been drowning, the other club members couldn't stop laughing! (Robin Jones)

Celebrations by the Lake - Many residents would remember the Fishing Club Christmas parties, New Year's Eve Celebrations and Australia Day festivities held at the reserve by the lake. All events were made more enjoyable and memorable because of the music played by the locally grown 'Smokehouse Band' whose members comprised of Phil and Karen Bousfield, Peter Welton, Bill Legge, Troy Dooley, Chris Long and Tom Searle. The first Christmas Party was held on 2/12/2007, with sixty family tickets being sold at $25 per family. Seafood, barbecue meals and soft drinks were provided. Also, a Christmas raffle was drawn. A year after the club was incorporated as an Association, the number of members had increased to 73, with 20% of the members being juniors under eighteen years. In mid 2008, with the help of generous sponsors, the club was able to supply polo shirts complete with club logo, which were sold to members as a fund raiser.

The 2008 Australia Day celebrations, organized by Bill Legge, involved a barbeque lunch and a fun re-enactment of the landing of Captain Arthur Phillip in Australia – which included sundry unsavoury convicts performed by local residents in period costume. The band played sea shanties and everyone joined in the singing. Three local residents, after receiving their Australian Citizenship Certificates, were then able to join in the celebrations as true 'Aussies'! At the second annual Christmas party, held on 6/12/2008 at the reserve. Members were able to partake of a sumptuous meal of prawns, crabs and roast meats free of charge. The lady members supplied garden and fruit salads and the local Smokehouse Band provided the entertainment. Pirate Pete and his assistant attended to the needs of the younger members using magic bubbles and Santa also made an appearance. The Club went from strength to strength, to become the largest of its type on the Mid North Coast, with some one hundred and twenty members, of which approximately one third were juniors.

'Australia Day' Fun

'Australia Day' Fun

Leadership Changes -

Jeff Christensen had been President for many years until ill health became an issue for him and he passed the leadership to Rod Bell. Rod proved a good captain and it was only during the final two years of activity that he found it necessary to hand the baton to Mel Waters. Still wanting to be involved Rod Bell supplied the fish and manned the barbeque. Whilst the club's primary aim was a social one, it actively supported the Community Association in a number of its enterprises. Through its affiliation with the Association, the Fishing Club – being a member of the NSW Amateur Fishing Association, was able to assist with their corporation insurance cover at community fundraisers.

Fishing Club Closure -

As time went by enthusiasm waned (mostly due to travel and ill health) and the club was left with a dozen or so members and no longer seemed viable. In mid 2014 a decision was made to disband the club and by the 10th August, Mel Waters and the treasurer, Linda Dooley had completed the arduous and complicated job of winding up the club's financial and legal affairs. In early 2015, the Community Association was fortunate to be the beneficiary of the club's ssets – monetary and cooking equipment.

Fish-cleaning Table -

Since 2011 the Fishing Club had repeatedly requested for Council to supply a fish-cleaning table by the lake. It seemed that lack of funding was a reason that Council could not comply with their request. In 2015, Rod Bell asked Margaret Blackwood, the then President of the Association, if she could help. With the Fishing Club's generous gift in mind and extra grant money available Margaret approached Steve Howard, the parks supervisor with Council and with whom the Association had a good working relationship, to see if a table was at last possible. With the cost of the table and labour agreed, work was commenced and by July 2015 a stainless steel table, complete with shute, hose and connected water was finally installed. The Coastcare team, led by Bob Currans, completed the job by 'landscaping' the surrounds with mulch and native plants. (C.A. records)

A History of Green Point

Roads – The Lakes Way Intersection

As far back as 1978, Green Point residents had voiced their concern about the lack of visability to the south, at the corner of Green Point Drive and The Lakes Way. The intersection was considered very dangerous, as the roadside sand dune obscured vision of the oncoming northbound traffic and accidents had occurred. A letter from the Progress Association to Great Lakes Shire Council was sent on 24/8/1978 requesting that the sand dune be removed. On 13/12/1978 Council investigated and arranged for routine maintenance to carry out benching on the sand dune at the southern approach to the intersection and to install a street light.

At an Association meeting held 25/9/1986, a safety turning lane was proposed. As a result, a letter was sent to Council requesting a widening of the intersection at the junction of Green Point Drive and The Lakes Way, with a turning lane towards Forster and a passing lane for south bound traffic. Correspondence also went out to The Hon. Bruce Cowan MP member for Lyne, regarding the situation. At the time, Council lacked the funds needed and on 9/10/1986 requested the Dept. of Main Roads for the improvements to be done under the Main and Trunk Roads Construction Programme – Priority No. 3. By October 1992, when the intersection had become a Priority No. 2 'Black Spot', Council submitted a request of $140,000 from the RTA. to complete the project. (The Advocate Newspaper 14/10/1992)

.... *Residents Protest*

In February 1994, to draw attention to this long standing problem, Association correspondence was sent to the Dept. of Transport Minister, Bruce Baird, with copies to Great Lakes Council, The Hon. John Turner MP and the Advocate Newspaper. Council in reply advised that 'Black Spot' funding was no longer available and funding from the RTA Regional Roads grants was being used to improve sections of The Lakes Way and no further funding could be expected for the next two to three years.

In desperation, on 3/8/1994, an organized group of Green Point residents assembled at the intersection - plackards in hands - to protest against the lack of action taken by authorities to remedy the longstanding dangerous intersection. A local newspaper and the Prime Television crew were present for media coverage.

.... *New Access Lanes*

In early April 1995, Council accepted a Daracon Civil Engineering quote of $179,210 for the design and construction of two sections of The Lakes Way at Green Point Drive – the intersection and pavement rehabilitation in a southerly direction for 750 metres. (Advocate Newspaper 19/4/1995) Council advised that the work on the intersection would be done during their 1995/6 works programme. The Northern lane turning out of Green Point Drive was constructed first and the road widened, to allow passing traffic to the south. The Southern lane, coming into Green Point Drive and the rehabilitation of the sand hill beside the road was done later. At the completion of the project two orange overhead safety street lights were installed.

.... Coach Stops

In April 1995, the Association wrote to Council and the RTA requesting allowances for bus stops either side of the intersection. (In the past coaches to and from Newcastle and Sydney had refused to take on or set down passengers at the intersection and would not consider a scheduled stop until the roadway was widened to allow the buses to pull in safely.) Following the widening and upgrading of the road in March 1996, The Lakes Way/Green Point Drive intersection was designated as a rural coach stop and a bus shelter was later constructed on the eastern side of the main road.

.... Unsafe Turning Lane

Since the earlier improvements carried out on the above intersection in 1996, concern had been vented as to the safety of vehicles waiting to turn into Green Point from the north. In October 2001 the Association wrote to Mike Keegan, Manager, Transport Assets at Great Lakes Council regarding the traffic problem. It was felt that with through traffic moving at up to 100 kmph, the cars waiting to turn right were in danger of being struck from behind. A separate right hand turning lane was requested, to allow through traffic to proceed safely. The submission was later referred to Council's consultant.

Since 1994 the number of households in Green Point had increased by around 100 to 260, and with the additional population road use had increased. In February 2006, further Association correspondence went to Council and they replied that the length of pavement would have to be widened to meet the necessary design guidelines with an estimated cost of $30,000. Council continued to monitor traffic volumes and agreed that when traffic increased to a level requiring an upgrade of the intersection, further consideration would be given. In the meantime, Council continued to push for additional road funding for work on The Lakes Way.

In January 2007, the then President of the Community Association Trevor Cooper, informed Council of a serious accident at the intersection, involving a truck and three cars. The stationary car waiting to turn into Green Point Drive was hit from behind, catapulting it into oncoming cars and sending the truck into the bush on the other side of the road. Following this event a Community Petition with 280 signatures was lodged with The Hon. John Turner, Minister of Local Government, which was then presented to the Minister for Roads and Traffic requesting him to intervene. Unfortunately, as there had not been any fatalities reported, the intersection could not come under the RTA 'Black Spot' funding programme. During 2007 discussions were held between Council's Director of Engineering, The Hon. John Turner MP, and the RTA, but no resolution was reached mainly due to the costs involved.

In May 2007, the new President of the Association, Margaret Blackwood, wrote a letter to Ron Hartley (Director of Engineering) suggesting an alternative solution. She wrote, that on a recent visit to Coomba Park, she noticed double headed arrows on the road at the right hand turn into Coomba Road and a passing lane on the left to allow following cars to proceed without having to stop. On the 30th July 2007 the Association received a reply from the Manager of Design & Investigation, Kumar Kuruppu, saying that at a recent meeting of Council's Traffic Advisory Committee, the Committee had 1: no objections to this proposal and the recommendation was adopted and 2: that linemarking should comply with Figure 4.8.24 of RTA Design Guide.

The Association continued to keep up the pressure on Council and the work on this dangerous corner was finally completed by Christmas 2007 and has proven a very safe outcome.

Two more orange coloured safety lights were installed which added to the safety of motorists, especially in times of heavy fog at night, but, regardless of the newly improved roadwork, care still had to be exercised by drivers when turning into Green Pont Drive from the north, mainly due to low visibility of oncoming vehicles approaching from the south, at up to 100 kmph.

Roads – Kerb & Guttering & Drainage

As far back as July 1992, the Progress Association had discussed resident's concern regarding the flooding of their properties after heavy rain. After further complaints in 1997, it was again brought to the attention of Council. In June 1998 the Great Lakes Council developed a Community Survey, which was posted out to all residents within the Council area. After the results were collected, the most pressing projects were considered in the current budget and for the 1999-2000 financial year.

The main concerns affecting Green Point residents appeared to be the lack of road maintenance, the need for kerb and guttering and proper drainage for the overflow of storm waters. The Association continued to address Council about these matters, but the response was always - 'lack of sufficient funds'! At that time the Council area was comparatively large compared to the small population of ratepayers, and over the years, the Council had not been able to arrange the rate increases needed and many programmes had to be axed to make up the shortfall.

Trevor Cooper, during his time as President of the Association (2004-2006), and with the assistance of Malcolm Tompson, proposed a number of major drainage works for Green Point. Through the Association, Trevor made it his objective to push for these road works to be completed, but due to budgetary restraints, these projects were often delayed. The Association continued with its presentations to Council, including meetings with individual Councillors and on 28/9/2004, the Association submitted detailed information on the number of drainage problems within the community.

Eventually their perseverance paid off and Council committed $55,000 to the Green Point programme but it was conditional to the funds becoming available. To keep up the momentum, a deputation of twelve Green Point residents addressed the Council on 26/8/2005 to again argue that the $55,000 that was earmarked for essential drainage in Green Point should be found in 'that' financial year. On 3/9/2005 Mike Keegan (Manager Transport Assets at Great Lakes Council) advised, that due to financial constraints, Council was unable to fund any drainage work at Green Point in the current financial year, but that he would re-submit the item for Council's consideration in the 2006-2007 budget process.

Following on from Trevor Cooper, Margaret Blackwood became the next Association President - the office which she held from 2007-2013. Margaret took up Trevor's cause and continued to fight for improved roads and drainage for the community. By 14/10/2007, the funding for the long awaited drainage work had been granted – the Council survey work was completed and plans were to be finalized for the work to commence in early 2008.

In the years that followed a number of road works and major drainage programmes for Green Point were undertaken by Council -

- Kerb and guttering, drainage and road resealing of a section of Green Point Drive.

- The laying of large stormwater pipes through easements and the necessary construction of water- flow controlling boxes.

- The clearing, grading, concreting (where necessary), of open roadside drains.

- Ongoing maintenance.

.... Kerb and Guttering – Northern Side

Road work commenced in March 2008 and as properties on the lower side of Green Point Drive had been inundated with excessive runoff water during times of heavy rain, the kerb and guttering and drainage work was initially constructed on the northern side of the road. The work started from the chicane at the entrance of the village and continued as far as Bottlebrush Close, but due to a shortfall of Council funds, the project was left incomplete. In 2009 the road work continued in front of the next four homes and up to the RFS building site.

On 26/9/13 work resumed on the northern side of Green Point Drive. To overcome further drainage problems the width of the road was extended to form a gutter on the inside of the bend at the top of the hill to divert overflow stormwater down the hill, (via a bitumen riser constructed near the eastern corner of Seabreeze Parade) into the new guttering in front of the RFS site.

Kerb and Guttering – Southern Side

In 2011, kerb and guttering and drainage work commenced on the southern side of Green Point Drive – working from the chicane and up as far as the bus stop. In 2012, when more funding became available, the work continued to proceed up the hill as far as the Green Point Gallery. (In late 2012, private contractors (at the owner's request) completed kerb and guttering in front of his property adjacent to the Green Point Gallery)

Major Stormwater Drainage

From 1928 until 1960 Green Hill farm, having no permanent creek or waterway, was reliant upon heavy downpours of rain for survival – the much needed rainwater fed the underground springs and small catchment dams in the lowlands of the property.

However, by the time the Green Point residential subdivision was formed geographical changes had taken place. Road excavation and construction had cut into the side of the high ridge, disrupting the natural watercourses and as a result, the roads running down the hillsides and along the lowland flats, often became affected by excess water erosion. In the past, basic under road piping had been constructed where necessary, but in times of heavy rain, excess stormwater continued to gush down hillsides, beside properties, and across roadways. Easements became cascading waterfalls and at times the deep open gutters couldn't cope. The barely basic roads of minimal width were continually being damaged by stormwater runoff and natural seepage water from springs – which resulted in potholes and eroded edges. As the population of the village increased and the majority of the prime blocks were built upon, it became apparent that there was an urgent need for improved drainage in areas affected by excess stormwater.

In June 2012, Council commenced Stage 1 of its planned major stormwater drainage construction work – laying large pipes from Emerald Place through to Seabreeze Parade. The pipes conveyed the stormwater efficiently down the steep hillside, and to slow the flow, the water passed through three large drainage pits. The pipes ran down the easement to the northern side of No.49 Seabreeze Parade. The water then flowed down the gutter drain to under road piping, where it continued through drainage pipes in the easement area between No.50 and No.52 Seabreeze Parade – ultimately flowing into the wetland area behind the properties.

During times of torrential rain, the easement between the properties at No.15 and No.17 Green Point Drive had been awash with water, collected from the nearby road drain. The water flowed down the steep hillside towards the lake, gouging its way into the landscape between the properties and cutting across the lakeside track below. To remedy this problem, in March 2014 Council commenced Stage 2 of their planned major drainage work.

Large water pipes were laid, running down the hillside in conjunction with 5 large drainage pits to slow the flow of the water. In addition to this effort, and to protect the fragile environment, deposits of large stones were placed further down the hillside to allay the flow of water and capture any silt and debris. To protect the lakeside track from extra erosion, a concrete dish drain was constructed to allow the remnant stormwater, after being filtered through the native plantings, to safely enter the lake. With Stage 1 and 2 of the drainage work finished, garden restoration of the properties concerned took place complete with new top soil and overlay of turf.

.... Open Roadside Drains

Apart from the extensive major drainage projects Council systematically attended to other problem areas within Green Point. In times of heavy rain excess stormwater built up at the chicane and spread out across Green Point Drive. This overflow of water on the roadway made driving conditions difficult and dangerous. In September 2014, Council attended to the situation by clearing and grading the gutter to allow the water to access the gutter drain.

Another open drain which needed attention, at that time, was situated beside the carpark adjacent to the Foreshore Reserve. Council workers dug out and graded the dish drain and (for safety) a number of white reflector posts were erected nearby. The drain area was seeded with grass and by October 2014 the waterway was completed and ready to filter the stormwater, before seeping into the wetland area.

In Green Point Drive, where an open gutter drain was situated below a rocky hillside and natural water flow was difficult to drain away, it was deemed necessary to construct a small concrete dish drain. In March/April 2017 Council excavated and concreted the length of roadside gutter drain below properties at No. 60 and 62 Green Point Drive.

.... Ongoing Maintenance

In November 2014, roadside gutter drains were cleared of long grass and where necessary, large stones were deposited in many of the deep drains to stem the rapid flow of stormwater running down the hillsides. Also, in 2014, Council filled potholes and graded the road surface along the lakeside track. Another form of ongoing roadside maintenance is the clearing of any overgrown vegetation which obstructs vision of the road for road users. In 2016 Council severely cutback the encroaching trees and shrubs on the southern side of the access road from the The Lakes Way to the chicane. For road 'safety', the high grass beside the roadside and either side of the corner intersection with The Lakes Way is routinely slashed and the roadside reflector guide posts installed in 2013, are promptly - after being reported by the Association - replaced after being damaged.

By the late 1998, Green Point Drive from The Lakes Way intersection to the village, Lucas and Campbell Avenues and Emerald Place were all bitumen resealed. Since then, road maintenance has been mainly limited to patching potholes and roadside edges. As the maintenance resealing of road surfaces was usually recommended after 7-10 years (Ron Hartley –Director of Engineering Services, Great Lakes Council), Green Point roads were well overdue. On 15th October 2019 and for the next 5 days, as part of Council's ongoing Asset Maintenance Programme to keep street surfaces in reasonable condition, Council arranged for contractors to spray the road surface of most of the streets in Green Point with bitumen, which was then covered with aggregate. In addition, Green Point Lane, which was previously a gravel road was graded and bitumen sealed. Also, the carpark adjacent to the Foreshore Reserve was repaired and bitumen sealed (C.A. records)

It is to be appreciated that all the major drainage and road maintenance work within Green Point could not have been carried out without Council's funds being made available, and also, that it is through the hard work and diligence of members of the Association and their negotiations over many years with Council, that these projects have become a reality.

A History of Green Point

Art In the Park

In 2008, after receiving approval from Great Lakes Council, Ron Davis (a local Green Point artist) organized an Art Project for Green Point Park. The aim of the community project was to engage the youth of the village in a constructive activity during the July and September school holidays. Under his direction and with the assistance of Gayle and Howard Redman, Susan Blackwood and Brian Gordon the children were encouraged to participate in painting the children's playground equipment and surrounding car park bollards and rails.

Before the proposed bright colours could be painted all the woodwork in the play area, plus the four park picnic tables and ten bench seats, had to be sanded down and undercoated. When this work was completed the older youth and assistant volunteers painted the play equipment with brightly coloured stripes, whilst the younger children worked together painting the bollards and rails around the carpark. After preparing stencils of drawings of local wildlife, the older youth joined Ron and Susan in painting the animals and birds on the coloured posts. To be in keeping with the theme, Ron revamped the little 'cubby' house storage building by painting the outside with colourful murals to delight the children.

After the park tables and benches were painted in attractive colours, and as points of interest, Ron then painted the tops of the four picnic tables with colourful murals, depicting activities and scenes around our area. One table top mural, close to the tennis courts, was designed with tennis racquets and international flags and another nearby showed many types of fish and a fisherman. For visitors using the park there were two table top murals, one showing our native animals and birds with the wetlands in the background and another nearby, of the lakeside view from the picnic area. The vibrant colours made Green Point Park unique and transformed the area into a visually happy environment for local and visiting children. Our young people involved at the time can be very proud of their achievements which were sincerely appreciated by the community.

.... *A Visit by the Graffiti Buster*

Towards the end of the work, an invitation was extended to Ted Bickford, well known volunteer 'Graffiti Buster; who then made himself available to speak to the young people present about the work he did and the importance of not defacing public and private property. Ted's philosophy about graffiti removal has been to minimize the exposure by removing the graffiti within twenty four hours so that the perpetrators don't get any recognition for the vandalism. With co-operation from Council, who supply his especially detailed Graffiti Buster vehicle and biodegradable cleaning products to safely and effectively remove graffiti, Ted has worked tirelessly for the Great Lakes area since 1995.

Being convinced that the lesson of vandalism needed to be taught from a young age, he developed a school programme which he administers on request. Councillor Leigh Vaughan was on hand to witness Ted's teaching skills, whilst he showed a variety of pictures to the gathered group on his laptop computer. Afterwards he opened the canopy of his truck to reveal all of his chemicals and equipment for cleaning, plus the matching paints for completing the restoration work. The young boys were especially interested in going over the vehicle checking out the contents and its colourful exterior artwork.

Recognizing that Ted was not a figure of authority, the children responded to him and his message to protect and value the property in the future. Since then, our 'special' park has continued to be free of graffiti and a joy for local and visiting children and their parents.

A History of Green Point

Proposed New Subdivision

As part of the NSW State Government Strategic Planning, Mid North Coast Regional Councils were obliged to survey their areas for vacant land which could, in the future, be rezoned for residential housing. The rural property at the end of Bottlebrush Close, owned by Ross Kneebone, came under this category. In answer to an enquiry by the President of the Association, Trevor Cooper, on 19/1/2007, regarding a proposed subdivision for Green Point, Great Lakes Council's Mayor, John Chadban, replied that he understood the Association's concern as he had viewed a large development company's website showing plans for a subdivision for Green Point. He pointed out that Council's Development and Conservation Strategy had identified land at Green Point capable of being 'investigated' for future residential development; but nothing had been approved and, if it were to consider such an application, the community would be consulted and their views sought.

Notification - At the Community Association's Annual General Meeting held on 11/2/2007, Trevor Cooper resigned his position after three years as President and Margaret Blackwood was elected to replace him. During the General Meeting members were alerted to the proposed new development. Malcolm Tompson, gave an overview and tabled a layout of the proposed Hardie Holdings Pty. Ltd. Development, together with a copy of NSW Government Dept. of Planning "Draft Mid North Coast Regional Strategy 2006-31". This strategy was designed to guide sustainable development of the Mid North Coast Region over the next 25 years, catering for a housing demand for up to 58,400 new dwellings by 2031, to accommodate the forecast population increase to 91,000.

It encouraged new housing developments with a shift to smaller households for an ageing population, so that 60% of new housing would be in greenfield locations and 40% in existing urban areas. Government regulations would ensure conservation of the natural environment, Aboriginal heritage values and visual character of rural coastal towns and villages.

On 15/4/2007 an Association subcommittee was formed with Malcolm Tompson (Convener) Margaret Blackwood, Trevor Cooper, Jan Armstrong, Michelle Latimer, Paul Murrell and Ken Oldfield. It was agreed that the Association send letters to State and Federal politicians, outlining concerns regarding the proposed development and asking for their advice. Local residents were advised of the situation with a report in the 'Green Pointer' newsletter and an article written for inclusion in The Advocate. On 17/6/2007, Councillor John Stephens agreed to address the Assoc. meeting regarding the proposed subdivision. The July/August edition of the 'Green Pointer' reported that Council's Release Area Manager, Roger Busby, had advised, on 12/8/2007 that no specific plans or residential development would occur until rezoning was decided upon and when that happened Green Point residents would be advised and invited to comment. On 9/12/2007, The Catchment Management Authority lodged an objection to the Government Dept. of Planning, as ground/stormwater levels were in question.

Amended Plan - Originally, the proposed development site was planned for 85 homesites, but later planning reduced the size of the area so that only 78 blocks could be allotted. The Advocate reported on 12/12/2007 that a development of around 70 homesites was a step closer to reality after Great Lakes Council voted to publicly display a Local Environmental Plan that gave the project the 'green light'. Council now needed the all clear

A History of Green Point

from the State Government to show the plan to the public. The Local Environmental Plan (LEP) detailed the predicted impact of the planned development and addressed environmental sustainability, strategic benefits and social impacts.

Proposed Development Plan

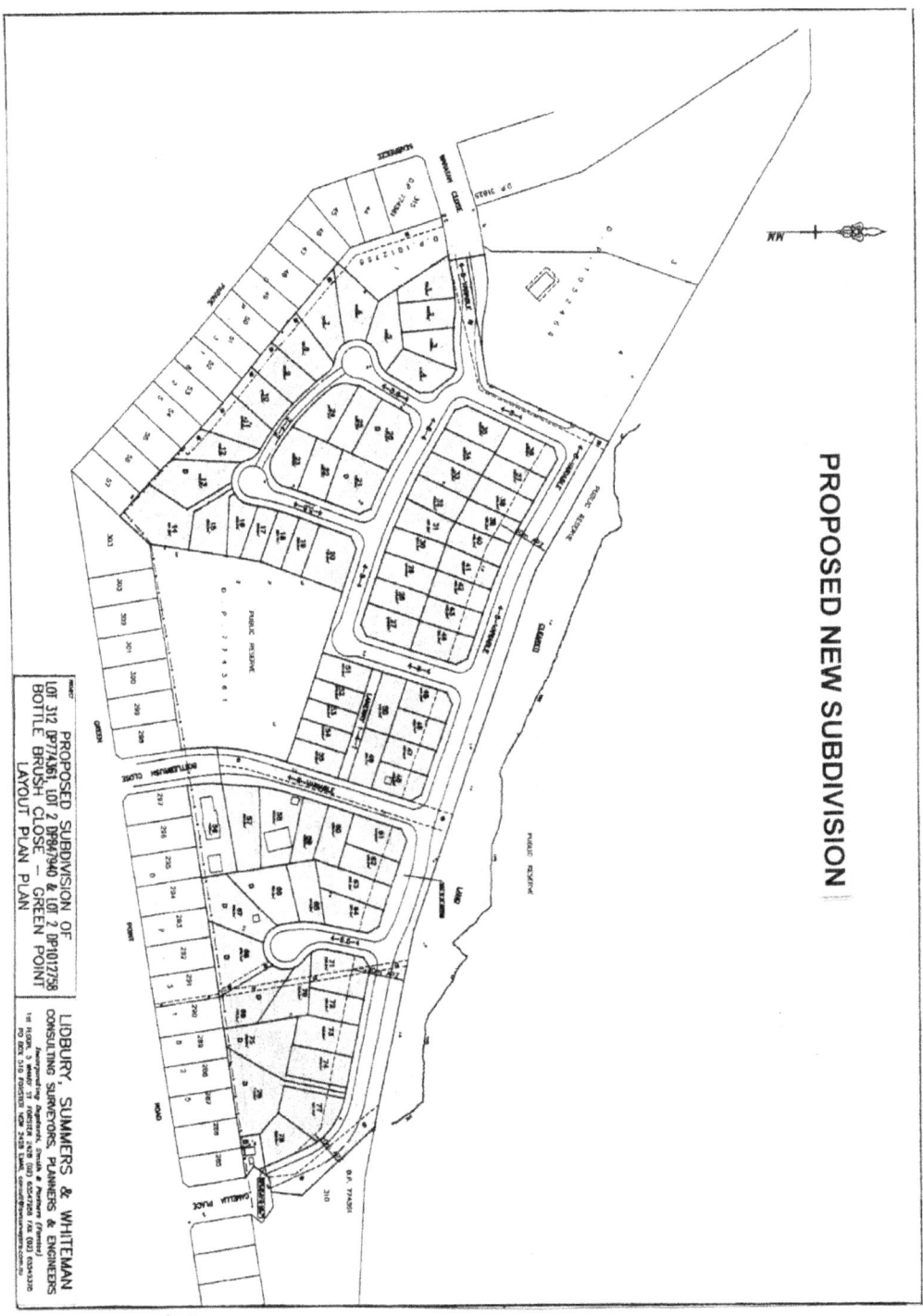

Draft Plan Exhibited for Rezoning

Great Lakes Council advised, on 18/1/2008, that a Draft Great Lakes Local Environmental Plan ((Amended No.58) – Rezoning of land at Green Point, would be on exhibition for the public from 23/1/2008 to the 7/3/2008. A Rezoning Justification Report would also be available for viewing at Council and on the website.

On 4/2/2008, the Association advised all residents that Council was proposing to rezone land at Green Point from RU2 (Rural Landscape) to Residential Development and that they were invited to a Public Meeting at the Community Hall early evening of 13/2/2008. Roger Busby, Manager Strategic Planning at Great Lakes Council, was to address the meeting and answer any questions about the proposal. It was made clear that this meeting was about the 'rezoning' only and that there would be a 'separate' exhibition and opportunity to hear concerns about the proposed subdivision and development after the Development Application was lodged.

The Public Meeting was well attended with around 50-60 residents present. Mr. Busby explained that Council had looked at a study eighteen months ago, regarding the lack of housing around Forster/Tuncurry and that as this parcel of land was the last available in Green Point, it had to be considered for development in addressing the shortage of affordable housing locations.

Under The Local Government Regulation Act 1993, housing blocks were allowed to be much smaller than the usual 600 square metre average block size existing in Green Point.

Objections

On 18/2/2008 a notification letter regarding objections to the development was circulated to all residents to help them construct their submission to Council. By 27/2/2008 521 petitioners signed a Community Petition calling for Council to safeguard the village against 'over development' and by 7/3/2008 160 residents had lodged their objections – reported to be the largest amount ever received by Great Lakes Council.

On 4/3/2008 the Association's formal objection to the proposed rezoning at Green Point was sent to the General Manager in response to Council's Rezoning Justification Report for LEP Plan 1996 Amendment 58. This objection set out the major reasons why the planned subdivision should NOT go ahead. Concerns included – further damage to fragile roads due to extra traffic - noise and disturbance to residents - road safety threatened – acid sulphate soil identified and affect on the adjacent wetland area – flooding due to the 1 in 100 year flood level and high water table in the area – reduced bush fire protection zone and increased danger to residents in times of bush fire and the fact of only one access road in and out of the village.

In an article in The Advocate dated 5/3/2008, Association member Malcolm Tompson pointed out that most of the controversy stemmed from the recommendation that Council rezone Mr. Kneebone's land with the view of installing affordable housing. The smallest new lots proposed were 345 sq. metres, whilst the smallest currently were 600 sq. metres which would have a huge impact on the character of the village and the population would increase by at least 35%.

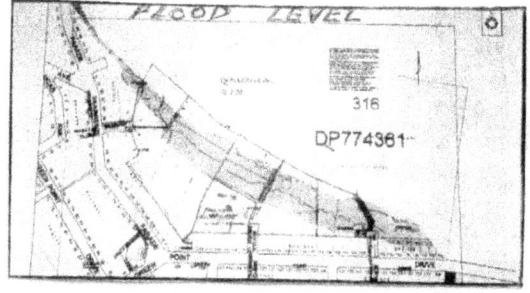

Above: Wetlands only 10 metres from proposed development.

Residents Make a Stand!

As a result of Association correspondence with Council and other Government representatives, Council decided to set aside time at the Strategic Committee Meeting to be held on 8/4/2008 to hear oral presentations from people who had made submissions on the draft rezoning plan and added, that further consideration would be given at the Council meeting to be held on 27/5/2008. Within days a 'Stop Press' flyer was delivered by the Association to all residents, advising them of the meeting to be held on 8/4/2008 at Council Chambers between 10.30am and 11.45am. All residents were encouraged to attend where possible and those who wished to voice their concerns at Council were invited to attend the next Association meeting so that issues could be co-ordinated without duplication. At the meeting on 8/4/2008, Margaret Blackwood (President) presented the Association's 'objections' in detail, followed by Jenny Maher, who reported on the mosquito problem in Green Point - Jenny amazed Councillors by producing a cup full of dead mosquitoes she had collected that morning, from their mosquito attracting machine. Paul Murrell spoke on Stormwater Strategy and Trevor Cooper on Acid Sulphate Soils.

On the morning of the next Council meeting on 27/5/2008 and despite the heavy rain blasting the pavement outside, dozens of Green Point protesters huddled at the entrance of the Council Chambers, holding hundreds of green balloons, which were to signify the number of submissions and signatories to the petition opposing the housing development. Close to 100 residents attended the meeting and eight Association members were due to present their case. Unfortunately, time was taken up by lengthy arguments put forward by Council representatives in support of the development and the Government's need for more low cost housing for the ever increasing population. Because of this, Ken Oldfield was left with very little time to present his Power Point address. His main concern was the feared impact on the adjacent wetland environment. Trevor Cooper also spoke, but due to the limited time remaining, his address was cut short. Jamie Boswell, Project Manager representing Hardie Holdings, addressed the meeting saying "the Community has their opinion and we'll always try to take that on board." Council explained to the packed gallery, dotted with 'Save Green Point' T-shirts, that ultimately the NSW Dept. of Planning would have the final say.

Media Attention

The Manning-Great Lakes 'Focus' Magazine published a sympathetic article written by Peter Lyne. It featured a coloured aerial photograph (taken by Craig Mason of East Coast Photography) of Green Point and surrounds - showing the small village and its close proximity to the wetlands flowing into Pipers Bay and citing the concerns of the Community's residents.

To follow on from the Council meeting, and to draw attention to the proposed subdivision, a series of articles, interviews and letters from residents, were published in The Advocate. On 25/6/2008, a full page advertisement presented a beautiful coloured photograph (taken by Paul Murrell of Green Point) of the wetland area only metres from the proposed development. The associated article put forth arguments as to why the residents were so opposed to the subdivision. .

Fundraising

To raise funds to help cover the cost of stationery expenses etc., sealed contribution containers were displayed at the General Store and the Coffee Shop.

The Association continued to involve the media with exposure in The Advocate and on Prime Television. Despite the Association being able to negotiate with The Advocate for a FULL PAGE advertisement for the cost of an HALF PAGE ($750), it was apparent that more funds would be needed to support the campaign. Accordingly, the Association established a 'Fighting Fund', and so a fundraising picnic day was organized for Sunday 24th August commencing at 11 am. The activities, to be held at the Community Hall and in the adjoining park area, were designed for all residents and children to enjoy.

The residents of Green Point literally 'flew into action'. The Fishing Club provided and cooked the sausage sizzle and made soft drinks available. Derrick and Dorothy Burns organized and garnered the prizes from generous firms in Forster for the very successful raffle. Lisa Seadon-Hall did a superb job selling the raffle tickets. 'Smokehouse' (our resident music group) admirably entertained the crowd. Glynn Blackwood and Alan Maher planned and ran the much enjoyed children's races. James, from the General Store, generously contributed lollies to add to Glynn's supply of chocolates for the prizes. Gayle Redman and her daughters delighted the young ones with their 'face painting' designs. Trash and Treasure, contributed by residents of the village, proved a great success with Elke Davis and Helen Simons tirelessly manning the tables. Helen Tompson 'guarded' the cake and jams stall all generously supplied by 'the cake makers of Green Point', whilst Jo and Bob Currans ensured everyone went home with a new plant for their garden. Lana Raward and her team of helpers kept the pikelets, scones, and tea and coffee rolling in the hall kitchen. Everyone agreed that the 'Fun Dog Show', run by Denise and Rob Dunsterville, was a crowd winner. Ron Davis generously donated one of his paintings for auction which was later 'knocked down' for a healthy price to an appreciative resident. Thanks to the generosity of the people who attended and contributed to the event, the day proved to be a huge success resulting in $3,200 being raised for the 'Green Point Fighting Fund'.

The Fight Goes On

During the following months the Association invited a number of Great Lakes Councillors to attend their meetings and give their informative advice regarding the proposed development. Dr. John Kaye MLA had addressed the rezoning subcommittee and portrayed a State Government perspective of land developments and various approaches at State level. On 7/9/2008, thirty residents joined with Association members to have their questions answered by Councillors Linda Gill and Leigh Vaughan. By 12/10/2008 the Association had formed a Community Reference Group as part of an advisory committee to review a revised Development Application from Hardie Holdings. The re-negotiated plan had then to be re-submitted to a council meeting before Council could submit it to the State Government for the rezoning approval. In the meantime the Association continued lobbying at Council, State and Federal levels as well as seeking professional environmental advice.

On 23/11/2008 Ken Oldfield invited Professor Bruce Thom, Emeritus Professor, University of Sydney and Member of the Wentworth Group of Concerned Scientists, to visit Green Point and make comments on the proposed rezoning and its impact on the local environment. He was able to give assurance that by adopting the 'precautionary principle', the developer had to prove to Council that this proposal did NOT impact or damage the environment.

On 9/12/2008, Council advised the Association that there would be no rezoning of the proposed development site until Hardie Holdings presented a Water Management Plan that satisfied the Council's requirements for clear flow into the adjacent Environmental Protection Zone and wetlands. Headed by Margaret Blackwood as President, the members of the Association had worked diligently with Council to ensure the best outcome for, not only the residents who would have been most impacted by the development, but also for the

A History of Green Point

future of all residents and the delicate environment in which we had chosen to live. At the Association's AGM on 8/2/2009 Margaret was able to announce the pleasing outcome that Hardie Holdings Pty. Ltd. had withdrawn their Development Application. (C.A. records)

Children's Road Safety

In the early days, Green Point was virtually a small fishing village with holiday makers and fishing enthusiasts coming out to enjoy the area. Roads were rough and it wasn't until 22/7/1974 that work commenced on the access road to the village and a STOP sign erected at The Lakes Way intersection. Council bitumen sealed the road in sections as funds became available. In October 1986, unregistered motor bikes and unlicenced drivers became a problem.

By 20/5/1987, 80 kmph speed reduction signs were installed at the approach to the village but local children who played in the street were still very much at risk. On 10/1/1990, Ron Leonard, an owner of property in Seabreeze Parade wrote to the Progress Association regarding his concerns. He had observed the large increase in the number of young children either living or holidaying at Green Point, and the increased amount of traffic and tourists, and at times the speed with which they travelled. Another worry was that many residents parked their cars half on the grass and half on the road which made it difficult for drivers to see young children who were riding their bikes or walking along the road. Ron felt strongly about the matter and as he 'didn't want to wait for an accident to happen' he offered to pay for a professionally printed sign to be made and displayed in the village. The large colourful sign welcomed visitors to Green Point and requested drivers to be on the lookout for children. It was installed on the electricity pole outside the Bush Fire Brigade hall on 5/3/1990.

Holiday times were the most dangerous for pedestrians. Due to the lack of footpaths residents were often forced to walk on the narrow roadways, sometimes with a cliff on one side and a steep drop on the other, On 20/6/1994, Council installed two pedestrian warning signs in strategic positions beside roadways. (P.A. records)

On 10/5/2009, there was a fatal accident at the entrance to the village. It involved a young twelve year old local lad, riding a small trail bike and who at the time, was not wearing a protective helmet. The community was deeply affected, and in response, the Association placed a commemorative plaque on a bench seat adjacent to the skate park.

This tragic accident brought to the community's attention the fact that many young people were not wearing their helmets when using skateboards and riding bikes on the roads and in the playground area. With this in mind Margaret Blackwood, the President of the Association contacted the Youth Liaison Officer at the Taree Police Station requesting an officer come and talk to the young people and explain the various aspects of personal safety both on the roads and in the skate park area. Twenty two young people and eight adults were present at the Community Hall on Wednesday 22nd July (during the school holidays) to hear Constable Barry's advice and join in with the discussions. A thank-you letter was sent by the Association.

As a result of the accident the bush and grassed area around the entrance to the village was cleared to allow for better vision. Also, in September 2009, a NSW RTA and Council initiative issued SLOW DOWN IN MY STREET stickers for residents to attach to their red lidded garbage bins as a reminder to motorists to slow down and drive to the legal limit.

With children's behaviour being unpredictable on the roads and drivers continuing to ignore speed limits, Council, in November 2014, took the opportunity to replace the damaged 'Welcome to Green Point - Proud to be a Tidy Town' sign, with a bold new reflective sign, requesting drivers to 'Drive Safely – Kids About' (C.A. records)

Slow Down in Our Street

Green Point Rural Fire Service – Local Fire Danger

In 2002, the property known as 'Turtle Crossing' (161 Green Point Drive) was cleared and piles of branches were accumulated ready for burning off. When the weather conditions appeared favourable the dry branches were set alight. All was well until a sudden strong southerly wind came up and sent burning embers into the adjacent bushland. The fire quickly took hold and burnt along the southern side of Green Point Drive – possibly being contained by the large swamp area to the south. The local Brigade attended the scene and with a 'watch and act' procedure, allowed the fire to continue burning as far as the corner at The Lakes Way where it burnt itself out. Over past years this bushland area south of the access road has grown back to become a bush fire prone area again.

The Brigade is always on call and when needed helps with local fires. At times it can be quite busy - e.g., in one month during the end of 2007, the Brigade attended fires at Minimbar, Tuncurry Tip and the Seven Mile Beach Development.

New RFS Building Needed

The Brigade Cat 7 Tanker truck could barely squeeze into the small Fire Hall and for RFS meetings to proceed the truck had to be driven outside!

By August 2007, the team numbered twenty-four members of whom ten were active firefighters and the others being support members. Due to the lack of available space at the Fire Hall, a training First Aid instruction course needed to be held in the Community Hall. The old substandard Fire Hall building had an outside toilet and no change rooms for members. The lack of a storage area for firefighting equipment and office space for logistical staff to set up operations only showed how drastically a new Brigade building was needed.

A vigorous campaign was then undertaken by the Brigade for a new building. Compared with the small volunteer built brick hall completed in 1982, the 'proposed' new large contract built metal building would house the fire truck, provide a large meeting room, office space, kitchen, change rooms and toilet facilities.

Local RFS members were thrilled when, in November 2007, their application for the project was approved – awaiting funding! The Development Application went to Council in early 2008 and proposed a 12x12 metre, metal cladded Colorbond building, including a six metre single truck bay, training area and amenities. Funding was to come from a combination of funds from Great Lakes Council, Sydney Rural Fire Services, State Government contributions and community household insurance levies.

Captain Phil McAsey continued to maintain the service and train his team in readiness for any bush fire alert. In 2009 an Education Day was held at the Brigade Hall for local residents to come along and learn how to protect their properties.

Demolition of Old Building –

Work commenced on the demolition of the old Fire Hall on 10/8/2009. The roof was removed first, then an excavator was brought in to knock down the brickwork. It was sad to see the old bricks tumble down but it was necessary for future needs. A selection of three different coloured bricks were salvaged for posterity by Margaret Blackwood, (Association President at the time) who then arranged for the workers at the Tuncurry Men's Shed to encase them in a wooden frame – as a reminder of the outstanding efforts of local volunteers, who years ago, built the original building. In preparation for the demolition of the building the tanker truck and all paper records, had to be stored in the home of Fire Captain, Phil McAsey.

New Building Construction

After the site was prepared the reinforcing steel was laid and the concrete floor poured. Soon after the steel framework took shape, it was followed by the green metal cladding. The large roller-door was fitted on 6/10/2009 and the internal work commenced on 9/10/2009.

The inside work took longer to complete as extra construction was needed to prepare for the proposed upper mezzanine level. Plumbing pipes were put into position for the kitchen, toilet areas and change rooms situated at the back of the building. On 28/4/2010 the water and sewerage pipes were installed followed by the installation of a water tank at the rear of the building. Generous community donations helped furnish the building with furniture, blinds, kitchen appliances and a barbecue etc. The Christmas raffle and other fundraising activities helped out with new equipment.

On 4/7/2010, excited Brigade members held their first official meeting in the new building and to commemorate the occasion, members, their family and friends, joined for a celebration barbeque afterwards.

On 14/10/2010 an Open Day was held at the new building giving an opportunity for local residents to share in the Brigade's proud achievements. Visitors were welcomed inside to see the new space available for operations and examine the firefighting equipment. A barbeque was held and visiting children enjoyed being able to sit up in the large fire truck.

Later, the 'Green Point Rural Fire Brigade – NSW Rural Fire Service….for our community' sign was displayed on the front of the building. Apart from fighting fires, the local RFS serves the community in many other ways. They assist Ambulance personnel where extra manpower is needed for patient transfers and members have been called upon to work with Fire Rescue teams, attend motor vehicle accidents and travel to natural disasters to help out after severe storms and floods. The Brigade, on an average, attends around two call outs per week throughout the year. The local Brigade continues to build its resources to ensure the safety of Green Point and surrounding communities.

A History of Green Point

Early Population Increase

In the mid 1970's the population of Green Point slowly increased as more early residents settled in the area and by 1991 the population had grown to 429. When town water and sewerage services were made available residential building developed dramatically. By 1996, the growing population had increased to 522.

During the years that followed regional tourism expanded and some tourists experienced the benefits of living in the Forster area and with many visitors becoming permanent residents, the population increased. Being ideally situated close to Forster and near the lake, beach and bushland, Green Point also grew in population. In 2008, there were around 280 dwellings built on the 312 blocks available in Green Point.

Since 1991, the tiny Green Point hall building had served the community well, but it was becoming increasingly evident that it was inadequate for the growing needs of the community. In 2009, headed by the current President, Margaret Blackwood, the Community Association, in consultation with residents, proposed plans for hall extensions to be built, to cater for the anticipated future population growth.

Extension To the Community Hall

.... Preparations and Planning

In the early 1990's it was a huge struggle for the community to raise the funds needed to transport the old tennis shed from Tuncurry and to complete the structure for use as a Community Hall. By 2009 an increased number of Government grants were being made available – the terms being that for every $1 raised in cash or kind, the Department concerned would match it 'dollar for dollar'. On 14/6/2009, encouraged by the favourable circumstances, the Association formed a working committee comprising of Paul Murrell, Ron Davis, Glynn Blackwood and led by Margaret Blackwood to put forward a proposal submitting builder's quotes, material costs and fundraising details.

On 8/11/2009 plans were made to extend the interior of the hall by three metres, add substantial veranda areas and modifications to the kitchen, and to present an application for a Government grant. The estimate for materials for the work was approximately $20,000. Curr253ent available funds amounted to $5,500, which included the balance of monies raised by by the community for the establishment of the 'fighting fund' – at the time of the proposed housing development on adjacent land. As the threat of the development had eased, it was proposed that, with the consent of Green Point residents, the Association apply the funds towards the project costs. With the current funds, plus an estimated 'work in kind' value of $15,000, the Association, on 11/7/2010 was able to apply for a grant of approximately $20,000 to meet a realistic project cost of $30-$40,000.

On 17/12/2010, the Association was informed by the Premier's Department that the application for the $20,000 had been granted. However, work could not be started until a contract was received. On 11/4/2011, detailed plans went to the Council and were said to be finalized by the end of the year.

Fundraising – Picnic/Fun Days

With the plans for the extension moving along and the Government grant to assist with bringing the project closer to reality, a subcommittee was again formed to organize fundraising events for extra financial eventualities. . After the success and community enjoyment of the 'fighting fund' fundraising day in August 2008, the format was set and two more days were organized for 28th March 2010 and 22nd May 2011. As before, and with the co-operation of the Green Point Fishing Club and the Community Association, the residents of the village gave generously of their time and effort to ensure that both days were a great success - enjoyable for all the families involved as well as the healthy amount of approx. $5,123 added to the hall extension funds.

.... A Call for Volunteers

Residents and Association members had readily supported the three previous fundraising events and now it was time to ask 'again' for their help. This time to receive the required amount of Government funding for the construction of the extension to the hall, the Association required the 'in kind' assistance of experienced volunteer tradesmen, general dogsbodies and a 'qualified tea lady'.

On 5/11/2011, a well attended volunteer labour group meeting was held and plans made for the initial construction work to commence in January 2012. Roger Haddon, who drew up the building extension plans, became the Project Manager and Geoff Tonge, the Building Supervisor. To allow access to the site area the existing wire fence and metal posts, used to contain the old croquet court, were removed in readiness for when the necessary safety fences could be erected around the building site.

On 24/1/2012, to the relief of the subcommittee members, the volunteer group arrived at the Community Hall to fulfill their promised commitment and to attend the Occupational Health and safety training session – which ran from 8.30am till 4pm with lunch provided.

On the day work commenced a further induction process was completed by Steve Howard from Council and on 30/1/2012 the volunteer workers received their Construction Induction 'White Card', issued by Work Cover NSW, which enabled them to work on site. Safety helmets and gloves were supplied. This was just the beginning of 1400 hours of tireless labour spent over the next three to four months in order to complete the planned extension to the hall building.

.... Construction Starts

Finally, our building supervisor, Geoff Tonge, did the honours by digging the first hole for the footings in readiness for the cement truck pour. When the call went out for 'wheelbarrows' to help distribute the wet cement, men with barrows appeared from all directions and everyone became involved making the concrete pads ready for the piers. Murphy's Law prevailed and it rained for the next two to three days – which was deemed to be a benefit in the long run. The attached photos show that the men, under the professional direction of Geoff Tonge, worked well together and in no time the framework was taking shape. The old roofing was removed and a new Colorbond roof and guttering was attached. Next came the new cladding, then the large heavy duty sliding doors were installed between the hall and veranda area. This made a great difference to the atmosphere within the extended hall and improved the outlook to the park and distant bushland. The new extended deck, flowing around the building, with covered awning above, made the building more useable and certainly more visually appealing. The existing concreted veranda floor on the western side of the building was covered with decking boards to meet up with the newly formed decking and balustrade. Wider wooden steps with hand rails were then attached.

.... Extension Takes Shape

.... Extension Takes Shape

.... *Window Changed & Decking Completed*

At the front entrance to the building, a generous landing was constructed and new wooden steps with railings added – all covered by a gabled awning. After the interior plaster work was completed both the inside and outside of the building was painted in soft 'paperbark' colours to blend in with the surrounding natural setting.

Note: As a point of interest the end wall of the hall, adjacent to the toilet block, is not lined with the new facia board but kept as an historical reminder of the original timber structure.

Whereas the extended hall was looking great, the kitchen area was still not upgraded and funds were running low. During an unexpected visit to the Community Hall by Stephen Bromhead MP, Member for Myall Lakes, he encouraged the Association to apply for another Community Grant. As a result of Margaret, again working closely with Council's Dianne Denton, a very welcome cheque for $5760 was received which meant that the old kitchen could be dismantled and modern units installed. Enough funds from the grant remained to acquire new blinds, tables and comfortable folding chairs. Later, using Association funds, a new security screen door and heavy-duty glass sliding door were installed in the entrance to replace the original timber door.

As a 'finishing touch' a new Green Point Community Hall sign was attached to the front wall of the building. This beautiful sign was designed and painted by Ron Davis, depicting a typical 'sunset' lake scene with moored fishing boats and two pelicans watching from the shoreline. Artwork also adorns the interior walls of the hall. One painting being 'Scenes from around Wallis Lake,' painted and donated by Brian Gordon, a resident artist of Green Point, and the other, 'After the Bush fire – Green Point' donated by Betty McKinnon, an artist from Forster. Both paintings relate to our area.

Enough thanks and praise cannot be said of Geoff Tongue (our tireless leader) and his team – Peter Wilkin, Tom Ryan, Paul Boda, Rod Bell, Paul Murrell, David Lamb, Glynn and Margaret Blackwood, Bob and Jo Currans (assistant painters) and lastly, Roger Hadden, for for his advice, patience and ongoing assistance when required. Everyone worked diligently at all times and enjoyed a wonderful camaraderie – especially at morning tea time when jokes and stories were exchanged – remember when Rod and Margaret fell off the scaffolding! etc.

As a new ruling for Disability Access Ramps was introduced on 1/5/2011, Geoff Tonge anticipated that, as a Council-owned public facility, the building would be required to have a ramp some time in the future. To keep up the momentum, and while he had the prmise of building assistance by David Lamb, he suggested that, once again, Margaret look into the cost of materials and an acceptable design for this additional project. A Development Application was submitted to the Council and with the assistance of Dianne Denton and Trevor Braybrook, a government funding grant of $5,500 was secured to cover the cost. Development approval was given and the construction work was quickly completed. Native plants were planted by Coastcare members to enhance the project. The completion of the extension, with the essential ramp proved undoubtedly a great success. "Built by the Community for the Community."

.... Building Completion – Open Day Celebrations

After three months of unceasing activity on the build, excitement was building as the new look Community Hall took shape.

The volunteer building team, lead by Geoff Tonge and managed by Margaret Blackwood, created a quality finish far beyond expectations. The Association was fortunate to gather such an experienced and qualified group of residents who offered their services and continued with the build until the job was done. Finally, after completion of the work, in May 2012, a working bee was arranged to tidy up the hall and surrounding area – all in readiness for the upcoming 'Open Day' celebrations.

The local residents were invited to view the finished work on Sunday 3rd of June. Due to the hard work of Helen Tompson, Marcia Byrne, Lana Raward, Bob and Jo Currans, Rod Bell and many more, a sausage/fish sizzle, followed by homemade cakes and slices, tea, coffee and soft drinks, was provided. Live music from the Smokehouse band added to the friendly atmosphere of the celebrations. The official opening took place at 3pm, with Glen Handford, General Manager of Great Lakes Council officiating. Also in attendance was Stephen Bromhead, State Member for Myall Lakes, who presented the Government grant cheque for $5,760, which went towards the cost of the refurbishment of the hall kitchen area.

It was later reported in the Great Lakes Advocate on 13/6/12 that the new building extensions were the result of a total of 1,500 hours of voluntary labour by the residents of Green Point.

With the extensions and refurbishment of the Community Hall complete, residents were encouraged to be active in the use of the facility.

(Photograph : Courtesy of Great Lakes Advocate)

.... Additional Improvements

In June 2013 Council provided and attached a glass fronted Notice Board to the front wall of the hall. In October, volunteer Peter Wilkin designed and built 3 moveable chair-bins to help with the storage of the new hall chairs. On 24/2/2014, Council's Andrew Braybrook was successful in acquiring a Community grant for $1,200 which covered the cost of new oven for the hall kitchen.

In April 2014, volunteers again worked on improvements outside the hall. Pavers topped the original exposed brick foundation walls and edge of the back garden bed. Areas were concreted to extend the front pathway and to enlarge the area at the entrance to the tennis courts. The existing breeze-way was freshened up with a coat of grey paint. During January/February 2015, Council workers concreted the disabled carpark space, painted the line markings, installed the two safety posts and the disabled parking sign. In April of the same year, Council concreted an approach to the carpark from Bottlebrush Close. In August 2018, the rotted electricity pole in the carpark was replaced by a taller, more permanent metal pole.

..... *Community Hall Status*

In 2014, Great Lakes Council reviewed all the public halls within the area with the intention of determining which halls were viable, with responsibility of management and maintenance and the financial recourse implications; and which halls were no longer viable, due to lack of use by the community or the need for costly building maintenance. From the Great Lakes Council Categories – Public Halls, Green Point Community Hall is classed as a Level 3 facility – Small Public Hall. After measuring the high ranking performance and use of the facility, Council agreed that the Community Association continue to arrange the hiring of the hall and management of the building, together with Council's ongoing support towards yearly maintenance costs. The hall continues to be a popular venue and is hired out regularly – with funds received going to necessary acquisitions and improvements such as office equipment and to maintain the sporting facilities for the betterment of the Green Point community.

..... *Changes to Amenities Block*

In 2015, Council's agenda was to assess all public toilets in the shire and to amend the buildings, where needed, so as to comply with specifications. A new 'disabled toilet' was required and, rather them demolishing the existing amenities block, it was decided to undertake modifications instead. It was established that the existing toilet block would be extended outwards by one metre to allow for the previous ladies toilet to become the new public unisex disabled toilet. The renovations included cement rendering the existing red brick walls and painting them to compliment the Community Hall colour scheme. The walls of the toilets were lined with smart white tiles and new utilities tastefully appointed. (C.A. records)

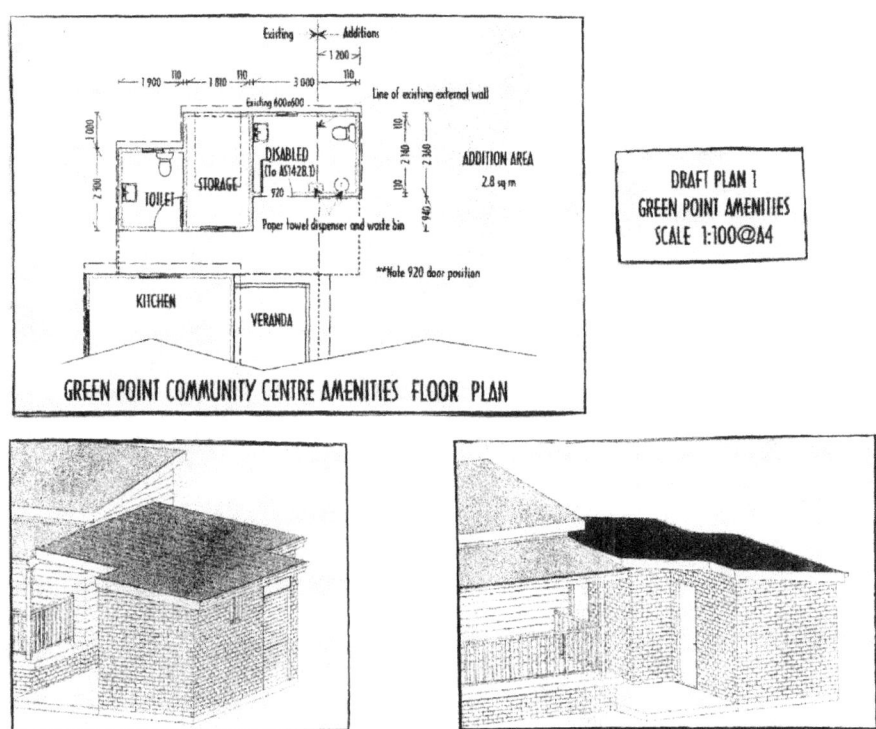

Green Point Rural Fire Service – The 2013 Bushfire

After a period of very hot and dry weather conditions, and with a high fuel load on the ground in areas around Green Point there was always the potential that a major bush fire would become a reality. On 4/1/2013, a fire, which Police suspected was deliberately lit, was started in the Booti Booti National Park near Janies Corner at the northern end of Seven Mile Beach. Around 1pm, emergency services, including local RFS crews, responded. The wind, blowing from a north-easterly direction made things difficult. Once the fire had jumped The Lakes Way, the RFS called for extra resources. The Lakes Way and the Green Point Drive access roads were closed, isolating the village residents.

(After starting as three small wisps of grey smoke, the fire had taken hold and the smoke soon developed into high dark brown plumes as it burnt through areas of Paperbark trees. Residents at that time may remember watching in awe at the sight of the dark smoke billowing towards the village.)

In total, there were around 120 firefighters from regional brigades in attendance and NPWS personnel who together battled the fire, assisted by five water-bombing aircraft. When the wind peaked, the fire jumped The Lakes Way on three or four occasions. Then it burnt towards Pipers Bay, with another front moving closer to Green Point. Knowing that the fire was unpredictable and could change direction at any time, back burns were conducted along The Lakes Way, Green Point Drive (200 metres east of the entrance to the village) and along the fire trail behind Seabreeze Parade – the fierce orange glow of the back burns, lighting up the evening sky well into the night and early hours of the following morning.

The fire was finally brought under control and the main road was reopened in a limited capacity, with police escorting vehicles through the danger zone. Around 11pm, the road was fully reopened and control of the site was handed back to the NPWS. An observation helicopter returned the next morning at 9.50am to collect water from the lake, and then work its way southwards to put out spot fires. As the fire ground was still smouldering and with occasional flare-ups, the local RFS continued to conduct 'active watch' patrols over the weekend. It was reported, that as a result of the 2013 bush fire, 757 acres of Booti Booti National Park had been affected.

For many months afterwards, these blackened tree trunks in the nearby bushland, on the northern side of Green Point Drive – east of the chicane, posed as a reminder of how close the fire had come to the village; and how fortunate our community is to have RFS personnel of such calibre, willing to give their time and risk their lives to keep our livelihoods and properties safe.

Community Association Goes Digital

On 14/4/2013 the Community Association arranged for an email address –

greenpointcommunityassociation@g.mail.com

When Gaye Tindall was appointed President of the Community Association in February 2014, she encouraged the development of an Association website, as a new way of information gathering and to bring the organization into the digital age. It was hoped that the benefits would help the Association to continue to grow in membership.

The goals of the website were to make it accessible, easy to navigate for users and easy for the Association to manage and update – most of all, to assist residents to keep up-to-date with the workings of the Association and to encourage them to be involved and engage in the community activities.

Malcolm Tompson, a then resident of Green Point, volunteered to design the website. He planned it to be informative, user friendly and interactive. By 19/11/2014, the new website – www.greenpointcommunity.com.au was launched, with an article published in the Great Lakes Advocate.

Association minutes of meetings are placed on the website, in draft form, prior to being ratified at the next meeting and the Green Pointer Newsletter informs readers of upcoming events. Originally, the heading of the web page showed beautifully painted scenes of Green Point (mimicking the Association letterhead) supplied by local artist – Ron Davis. More recently colourful photographs have been used. Other changes include a change over of web host in August 2015 and in February 2017.

JOB WELL DONE: Web designer Malcolm Tompson from Green Point.

Website for Green Point Community Association

The Community Hall – A Meeting Place

Since the establishment of the early Community Hall, it has shown to be a welcome addition to the village and proved it's worth, providing a meeting place for the Association, as well as a venue for community events.

In 1991, in order that resident's views could be expressed, a Public Meeting was held at the hall. Richard Powell, the Water/Sewerage Engineer from Great Lakes Council, visited Green Point to explain to residents the need for the introduction of the sewerage scheme and the effect on the cost of Council rates.

On 15/4/1994, The Green Point Sewerage Scheme was officially opened by The Hon. Ian Armstrong, Deputy Premier and Minister for Public Works. Due to lack of space in the tiny hall, the Government dignitaries addressed the crowd of assembled residents from the hall veranda.

Since 1995, in March each year, the hall has been the meeting place for volunteers, before setting off on their walk around the village – collecting rubbish for 'Clean Up Australia Day.'

Due to lack of space in the Brigade Hall, in February 1995, March 1997 and September 1998, the Fire Brigade held day/evening training sessions and First Aid resuscitation courses at the hall.

Public Meetings were held in 1995, 2000 and 2013 with residents and their families, which enabled community consultation in the decision-making process regarding the proposed children's sporting facilities in Green Point Park.

For four years, from around 1996, the 'Green Point Grubs' play group used the hall – being the perfect venue close to the children's play area in the adjacent park.

For the convenience of residents, the Association negotiated for the hall to be used as an Electoral Polling Station on voting days – for Federal, State and Council elections from 1996 through to 2013.

In 2007, the Green Point Fishing Club's inaugural AGM was held at the hall, also wet weather meetings and a Club Christmas party.

In early 2008, Council's manager for Strategic Planning, Roger Busby, attended a Public Meeting at the hall to discuss the Draft Plan to Rezone Land at Green Point – regarding the proposed residential development adjacent to the hall.

Over many years, the State Government Member for Myall Lakes, Stephen Bromhead, has met with residents at the hall to discuss current needs, give advice and help where possible.

.... Social Get-Togethers

Since late 1993, when the Green Point tennis courts were completed, residents have been encouraged to come and use the courts. Wednesday and Friday became social tennis days and many lasting friendships have been forged over the years. Due to shortage of courts available, Forster Youth Tennis Competitions preliminary knockout matches were held at our courts. More recently, residents and holiday makers and their families come to enjoy the game. Over the years the local tennis group has enjoyed their Christmas parties held at the hall.

For less energetic residents, who wished to exercise with friends, Pirate Croquet was available between 1996 and 2000. Participants used the croquet court which was situated at the northern end of the original hall building.

In April and May 1995, local residents Bob Currans and Don Craig organized a couple of Disco Dances in the hall as an activity for the 32 children of the village. All dressed up for the occasion and with the mirror-ball in place the young boys and girls enjoyed the fun.

From May 1994 until May 2008, the 'Crazy Whist' card club played cards and socialized at the hall. The friendly company was enjoyed by locals and visitors from Forster.

Since the extension to the original building and with new modern kitchen facilities available, the number of people hiring the hall for social events has increased.

Get-together activities included short-term Modern Dance lessons and relaxation classes, Choral Club practice and regular Tai Chi classes. Also, a Council run special needs group which allowed its youth to enjoy each others company and share fun activities. These activities were held once a week over a number of terms in 2019.

The hall has proved popular for children's birthday parties, having the park play equipment close by. Many young families return each year as their children's parties were so successful. The hall has also been hired for such occasions as a 50th Wedding Anniversary gathering, two Wedding Receptions, family birthday parties and a memorial luncheon to celebrate the life of Lana Raward, a much loved resident of Green Point. Some Social Club Christmas parties were also held at the hall.

The Association continues to engage with the residents of the village through social activities and functions. At Christmas time it reaches out by extending an invitation to attend the Community Christmas Party held at the hall, and encourages residents to partake in the 'Christmas Lights' competition - an enjoyable way to meet and welcome new and existing residents.

.... *A Fundraising Venue*

The Green Point Community Hall has always been the hub of operations in the village. In the past, community fundraising efforts such as Fetes, Market Days and Fun Picnic Days have been held in the hall and surrounding grounds. The events have raised much needed funds for projects within Green Point and have all been generously supported by the local residents.

Over many years, the hall was used by Association members to produce over 1,200 dozen lamingtons which were sold throughout the area, as a fundraising exercise. For ten years Lana and Bill Raward and Elaine Wilmott organized and conducted a monthly 'Card Club' afternoon in the hall. This proved to be a most successful social activity, enjoyed not only by Green Point residents but also an enthusiastic group from Forster. All credit to Lana, Bill and Elaine as the money they raised was used to finance various items for the benefit of the community.

After a community meeting to discuss the proposed Green Point residential subdivision, it was established that a 'fighting fund' would be needed. A 'Picnic Day' fundraising event was arranged by the then President, Margaret Blackwood, for 24/8/2008 and as a result the amount of $3,200 was received as a buffer against unexpected costs.

.... *A Caring* Community

Other organizations have also benefited when their fundraising events have been held at the hall. For example, since 2002 the Cancer Council's 'Biggest Morning Tea' was held for many years at the venue. For the 2013 event Robin Jones and Carol Stockham worked tirelessly arranging additional raffles and a trading table full of handmade goods, all of which culminated in a donation of $900 for Cancer Council Research. The women of the community have always been generous with their time and willing to help – the cooks of Green Point once again coming to the fore. The 2015 event raised $961.

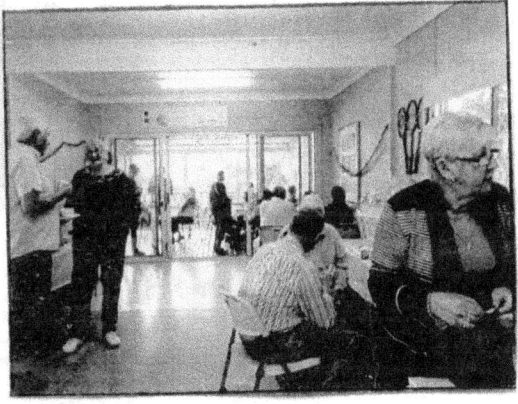

In 2009, the 'Black Saturday' Victorian bush fires, caused by arson and lightening strikes, burnt from 7/2/2009 until 14/3/2009, destroying 3,500 buildings and sadly, 173 people lost their lives. In response to this devastating event, Melissa Bawden, a Green Point resident, approached Margaret Blackwood, the then President of the Association to see if a 'Car Boot Sale' could be arranged for Saturday 28th of February to raise money for the Victorian Bushfire Appeal. Goods of all description were quickly gathered for sale and on the day, cars (with boots overflowing) were lined up on the grassed area adjacent to the skate park. Clothing stalls were also set up and tea/coffee and a variety of homemade cakes were available in the hall. The Fishing Club set up their barbecue for a sausage sizzle – which proved so popular Rod Bell had to drive to Forster to get more sausages. It was a mighty effort, raising a total of $3,500. A letter of thanks and a certificate from Wildlife Victoria to the Green Point Assoc. were received **"Well Done Green Point!"**

On 13/7/2014 a Garage Sale was held by members of the Great Lakes Hospice Auxiliary and the Riding for the Disable Association to raise needed funds for these worthy causes.

In 2019, at the Community Association Christmas Party, a 'giant raffle' was arranged to raise funds for the local Brigade. As a result over $200 was raised for much needed equipment.

When community fundraising events were taking place at the hall, the Green Point RFS was at times invited to man the barbecue and sausage sizzle to raise funds for their Brigade.

Since 2012, over 100 damaged children's bicycles were dumped at the park and Council's garbage collectors were unable to continue to take them. Seeing an opportunity to transform these broken items, John English, a Green Point resident, set up a collection point just outside the chicane for residents to leave their unwanted bicycles – there were another 2 collection points at Pacific Palms. Once collected the bikes were taken to the Men's Shed at the Tuncurry Tip to be restored - as a youth project by High School boys and with the help of older gentlemen mentors. The bikes were then sold for up to $40 and the funds raised were used for buying new parts for ongoing work. This thoughtful community service was curtailed in June 2019 when suitable transport was no long available.

Again, in early 2018, being inspired by a need within the area, John initiated a bottle and drink can collection depot at his home, with funds raised to benefit the 'Great Lakes Womens Shelter'. Another depot for the 'Return and Earn' fundraiser was situated in front of the Green Point RFS precinct. Over time, with the generous co-operation of the community, the scheme helped raise much needed funds for the project.

Wallis Lake – Island & Foreshore Clean Up

Appreciation and sincere thanks go to Dr. John Van Dyck and his grandson, for their efforts in cleaning the rubbish from Little Snake Island.

When called upon to participate in the Wallis Lake Clean Up, Green Point Coastcare group accepted the challenge and collected lakeside rubbish from Camp Elim to Pipers Bay – later to receive a Certificate of Appreciation from Great Lakes Council.

There have been, and remain, many other individual unsung heroes from Green Point, who have worked hard for the benefit of others. Over the years, a number of these residents have been acknowledged publicly and received Awards and Certificates of Appreciation from Council and Government representatives - some of whom are featured below for their long and dedicated service, through the Lions Club , the Green Point Community Association, the Great Lakes Hospice Auxiliary, the Arts and the Creative Network for Great Lakes, and the Riding for the Disabled group.

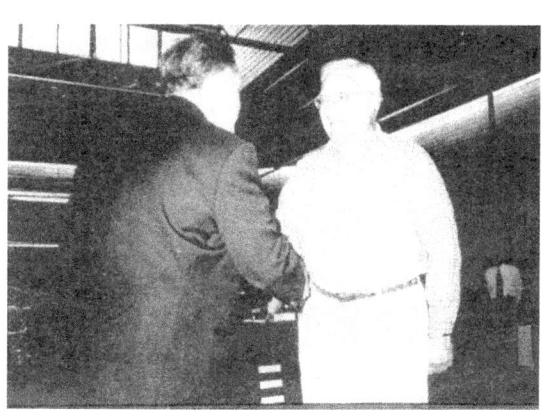

'Artistic Flairs' Of Green Point

As in the past, the Community Association continues to have close ties with the local bushfire brigade and regularly supports it with donations. Soon after the 2013 bush fire, which threatened the village, the Association donated $200 on behalf of the community to the Green Point RFS as a 'thank you' for their invaluable help. Whenever opportunities arise, the Association and the community are happy to work together to further support the local RFS.

Over the years, Green Point has had and still has a number of talented artists within the community, many of whom have won awards and prizes for their work. The newly extended Community Hall promised to be the perfect venue to promote a local Art Show, raise funds for the local RFS and fully involve the community. Local artists, Helen Cooper and Denise Dunsterville initiated this exciting event and invited artists, sculptors, potters, photographers and multi media, woodworkers, craft workers and mosaic artists from Green Point, to participate.

The date for the 'Artistic Flairs; event was set for 22-24 November 2013 with the official opening from 6-8pm on the Friday evening. On opening night, drinks and nibbles were served before the President, Margaret Blackwood opened the exhibition. Later, two bottles of fine wine from the 'Lakes Folly' vineyard in the Hunter Valley, were auctioned with the proceeds going to the local RFS – which had a small display throughout the exhibition. There were also two raffles: a painting by local artist Ron Davis, with the proceeds also going to our RFS and a huge Christmas hamper, with the proceeds going to the Association to help with overhead costs. This event was well attended and enjoyed by all. Many sales were made with a healthy outcome of $1,300, which was donated to the Green Point RFS for much needed firefighting equipment.

Due to the success of the first event, the organizers decided on a 'repeat performance' in November of 2014. This time an entry fee of $10 for exhibitors would apply – with maximum of 4 paintings allowed. Guests were asked to donate a gold coin on entry and 'encouraged' to buy a ticket in the raffle with first prize of an enormous hamper. The artworks were again hung on stands on loan from the Great Lakes Art Society, and were greatly appreciated. The President of the Art Society, Vicki Bullard, opened the exhibition and expressed her surprise at the depth of artistic talent within Green Point. Auctioneer, Green Point resident Trevor Cooper, displayed his skills and the participants, encouraged by the plentiful supply of food and wine, were generous in their bidding for the list of donated gifts from various sponsors and donors. Again, the exhibition was well appreciated and many items of value were sold during the weekend event. Overall, the amount of $1,357 raised, was designated towards essential radio equipment of our RFS. An article on the 'Event' was later featured in the November 2014 issue of the district's 'Focus Magazine'.

2014 Green Point Artistic Flairs Event

2014 Green Point Artistic Flairs Event

When 2015 came along it was decided to continue to have an 'Art Show' at the Community Hall; but this time the fundraising event would 'have a different twist'. As plans had already been made for new playground equipment and to repaint the existing facilities in the play area, it was decided that funds raised should contribute to this project. Also, as the event was to benefit the children of the area, they should be invited to enter into the Art Show by participating.

The 'Green Point Creative Flairs Art & Craft Exhibition', as it now became known, was held on 24-25th of October 2015, to coincide with the Pacific Palms Markets and to benefit from passing traffic and avoid the constraints of the Triathlon as in previous years.

With the same entry fee and the previous arts and craftwork continuing to be on show, organizers widened the scope of creativity to include creative cooking, creative gardening, craft and a Kid's Corner. The added attractions brought a varied collection of work to the exhibition. Amongst the items on display were – a beautifully iced cake, crafted sewing, handworked fabric, ceramic jewellery, hand painted gift cards, donated glassware and exquisite examples of perfectly manicured Bonsai. The Kid's Corner displayed the creative pottery and colourful artwork of the extremely proud students from Lilly Pilly Pre-School. Volunteers manned the front desk and a record amount of raffle tickets were sold for the two Christmas hampers. Tea/Coffee and homemade cakes were available and also a plant stall outside. With good publicity in 'The Advocate' the event drew a large crowd, successfully raising $1,810 towards the new playground equipment.

Outside the hall the Green Point RFS ran their fundraising barbecue and were quite satisfied with their takings. To help raise funds for the Great Lakes Womens Shelter in Tuncurry, John and Cheryl English set up, the yet to be challenged, 'World's Biggest Scrabble Set' – at 50 times the normal scale.

Apart from being fundraising events, the three 'Artistic' shows gave artists and crafters, a venue at which to display and sell their work and give the community, in general, an insight into the wealth of creative talent within our village.

The Green Point Creative Flairs Art & Craft Exhibition

Hang'n Glide Park Equipment

On 9/11/14, the Challenge Forster Triathlon was held and with the event, six hours of road closures were experienced by the Green Point and Pacific Palms areas. Elite Energy sponsored the race and as compensation, the Pacific Palms Community Association received $3,000 towards children's sports equipment. Later in 2015, as a good will gesture, $300 was shared with the Green Point Community Association – on the understanding that the funds would benefit the health and fitness of the youth in our area. This then became the 'seed money' for the next Green Point project. Initiated by Gaye Tindall, who was President of the Association at the time, the children's project was to add another play structure to the variety of existing equipment in the park.

After canvassing some local children, it seemed a 'flying fox' style apparatus was a popular choice. Association research, along with Great Lakes Council's recommendation, resulted in Forpark Australia being selected. The proposed structure was a Free Standing Motion 'Hang'n Glide', part of the Fitness Track category. To enable this proposal to go ahead, the Association took the advice suggested by Stephen Bromhead MP, on 20/5/15, to apply for a Community Building Partnership grant from the NSW Government for $3,000. With the proceeds from the Art & Craft Exhibition held in October 2015, which raised $1,800 and the grant received in 2016, the Association was able to pay the $1,030 deposit required, towards the total cost of $4,130 for the new play equipment. Council was allowed $2,000 for the cost of installation and the Association matched it with $1,000 plus volunteer work-in-kind.

The play apparatus, built in Western Australia, was delivered to Council and then installed at the park in early April 2016. When the concrete was set the local children were eager to try out the new device and enjoy the 'freedom of the ride'. The achievement of securing the additional play gym activity was celebrated at the Green Point Christmas party where it was hoped many families would attend.

Hang'n Glide Park Equipment

Park Upgrade

In 2016, a 'Volunteers' Government grant for $3,000 was awarded by The Hon. Christian Porter MP, Minister of Social Services, for the refurbishment of the children's playground, upgrading the outdoor furniture and surrounding structures in the park. As the name implied volunteer work was to be used on the project.

In early 2017, local resident, David Lamb, replaced damaged woodwork in the children's play area and repaired any park picnic tables and benches where required. Due to the unseasonal weather conditions at that time, the planned repainting of the play gym was delayed until later in May. Many tins of brightly coloured paint, sandpaper and paint brushes were purchased and soon the nine-resident volunteer team was hard at work preparing and repainting the wooden structures. Care was taken to retain the delicately painted fauna and flora motifs that were originally painted by Ron Davis and Susan Blackwood. The little 'cottage' was also repaired and repainted in bright colours. The damaged 'Dave Breen' memorial bench, near the skate park, was replaced and painted to match the existing benches and picnic tables. The bollards and fence encircling the carpark were repainted in 'Paperbark' green to match the hall colours. Working for four hours one day a week – weather permitting – it took over two months to complete the detailed job.

A History of Green Point

Further Maintenance –

When the team discovered that the basketball hoop had rusted badly, Council quickly replaced it and the backboard was repainted a bright yellow – ready for the September school holidays. A worn tennis net was replaced from Community Association funds and later, storm damaged wire fencing on the northern side of the courts was replaced and minor repairs done along the east facing side. In 2018, when the weather was suitable, volunteers set about cleaning the surface of the twin tennis courts with a chlorine solution.

In 2019, Gaye Tindall suggested, as part of the popular 'Street Library' project, that Green Point should become involved. Members of the Association organized a colorful 'Book Swap' cupboard which was placed adjacent to the play gym, so children could be encouraged to use it as well as adults. It brings joy and satisfaction to see so many parents and young children enjoying the Green Point Park, whether it's a Dad or Mum teaching children to ride a scooter, bike or skateboard, or to throw a basketball through the hoop. Some grandparents travel a distance with their small grandchildren to experience the surrounding natural and peaceful environment, which allows them easy interaction. Young mothers also regularly get together as friends for picnic lunches, whilst watching their little ones conquer the different play gym activities. A sight that justifies the care and effort put in by the village volunteers.

Green Point Rural Fire Brigade

.... *Community Concern*

After the recent January 2013 bush fire, RFS Fire Captain, Phil McAsey, was invited to address the Community Association meeting on 14/4/2013 to discuss the concerns of Green Point residents and explain the issue of fire mitigation, especially along the lake shore and adjoining National Park firebreak areas.

As a follow-up to this meeting and to personally connect with interested residents, the RFS arranged a number of 'Open Days' at the Fire Hall, which included a family friendly barbecue. 'Get Ready' weekends were also held, just prior to the commencement of the fire season. Many residents attended the meetings, where literature was distributed; informing them how to protect their homes in case of fire. Hot and dry summer weather persisted and the local RFS crews were often called out to assist when needed.

.... *Local RFS Assist Elsewhere*

When large fires take hold and exhausted firefighters need to be rested, other brigades are often called up to help out. An example was in late October 2013 when Fire Communications in Sydney requested that RFS Captain, Phil McAsey and four of his crew be deployed to a large bush fire burning in an area eighty kilometres north of Windsor – known as the 'Howes Swamp' fire. When they arrived on 25/10/2013, the fire had already burnt out 14,000 hectares of land. After fighting the fire in extreme conditions, the group returned home – but, the rest was short lived. Headquarters 'again' requested that Phil and another four Green Point crew members be involved. RFS reports later showed that by 8/11/2013 more than 35,000 hectares had been burnt out. At this time, Fire Captain Phil McAsey, had been serving the community, with the RFS, for over 30 years (Advocate News). Since then, in times of emergency, firefighters from Green Point have been called to help out at large fires in our region, and as far away as the Hunter area in NSW and up to Laura in Queensland.

.... Heightened Awareness

The local RFS continued to reach out to the community and on 14/1/2014 a special event was organized with Carole Manners, FireWize Workshop consultant, from Gloucester Great Lakes RFS brigade. Many residents attended the meeting at the Community Hall. The presentation included alarming videos of recent fires, shown on a large screen, expert instruction and answering of questions, and the distribution of informative brochures. After the meeting the crowd went outside to the carpark area, to learn about the workings of the Canter 7 twin-cab tanker truck and its equipment on board. When given the opportunity some residents were able to man the fire hose. All involved with the event declared it a great success.

Through the Green Pointer newsletter, the Community Association regularly informed residents of RFS reports, with guidelines on how to protect their properties and how to prepare emergency check lists in case of an approaching bush fire.

.... RFS Radio Replacements Needed

Back in the mid 1990's, John Mauger, the then RFS Equipment Officer explained in The Advocate, that their analogue hand held radios, which were essential communication tools in emergency situations, needed to be replaced. The RFS group didn't have the funds available to purchase replacement radios and was then appealing for assistance. Retailer, Brian's Bedding, was only too happy to provide one radio and obtained it at a generous discount from Dick Smith Electronics. The brigade still needed another three new VHF digital hand held radios, valued then at around $200 each.

Times have changed and so too the cost of the hand held short range radios – present day value of which is around $900 each.

Volunteers seek help to obtain new radio units

A Great Lakes volunteer organisation dedicated to looking after other people and their property is itself seeking a helping hand.

Green Point's Rural Fire Service brigade is appealing for assistance in buying three badly needed new VHF hand held radios.

Brian's Bedding was only too happy to provide one and obtained it at a generous discount from Dick Smith Electronics.

But the brigade still needs another three of the radios, valued about $200 each.

The radios will replace units which have "had it", according to equipment officer John Mauger.

The Rural Fire Service says it doesn't have the funds to help buy replacement radios, which are essential communications tools in emergency situations.

The Green Point brigade has been working at a disadvantage during the current bushfire emergency, because of the sad state of its existing radios, John says.

Anyone who feels they could help is asked to contact him on 6555 6346.

☐ *John Mauger with a radio of the type the Green Point bushfire brigade needs to operate safely and efficiently.*

.... RFS Fundraising

At this time the local RFS was still in need of new and replacement firefighting equipment. Fundraising efforts included 3-4 hours once a month at Pacific Palms Markets and the Farmer's Market in Forster, in conjunction with an RFS display and a 'donation helmet'. Sausage sizzles outside Bunnings always proved popular, as did the ones held at Green Point community events.

Our RFS has always been generously supported by residents at Community Association fundraising events. The Artistic Flairs Art Shows in 2013 and 2014 jointly raised $2,657 for RFS equipment and later, Phil McAsey said "The members of our Brigade were overwhelmed by the support and generosity we received and the funds raised will be put to good use for equipment we need to help us perform to our best ability."

.... Modern RFS Radios

For safety, and man to man communications during firefighting operations, portable hand held fire ground radios are issued to firefighters in the field. Each fire truck has a number of radios installed on the dashboard for communications with their fire control. There is also another radio control in the fire hall office, which has state wide reception. The duty officer for Mid North Coast oversees operations in the event of a large scale bush fire.

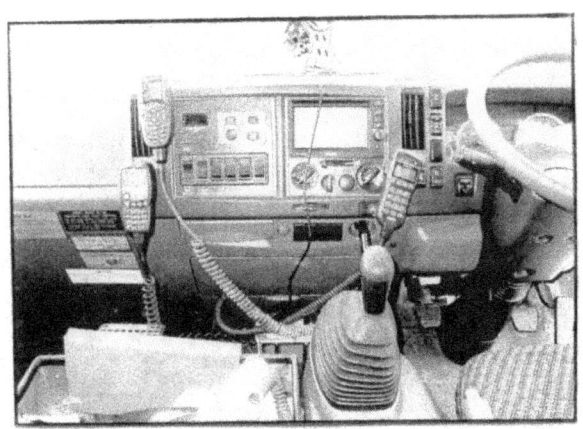

.... Being Prepared

- Despite a short-wet spell in 2014, the commencement of the fire season was brought forward from the previous year's September 2013 to August in 2014 – such were the extreme weather conditions that year.

- In January 2015, Bushfire Authorities erected a Fire Danger Rating sign at the entrance to the village, making residents and visitors aware of the fire danger for that day.

- By mid 2015, the new RFS Fire Control building in South Street, Tuncurry was completed. The Station Headquarters covers the Gloucester and Great Lakes areas and is fully equipped to back up the regions firefighters, ensuring a rapid response where needed.

- Record high temperatures during the year, together with extreme fuel loads on the ground, brought the threat of another bush fire. On 17/10/15, to liaise with residents, the local RFS held another 'FireWize' meeting – this time at the fire hall, where Carole and Rob addressed the many concerned residents who attended.

.... *New Bay for Fire Shed*

Over the past few years, the local RFS brigade had grown in strength as more volunteers completed their firefighting training and it became apparent that, sometime in the future, an additional tanker truck would be needed. However, in order to house a new vehicle, an extension to the fire hall would be necessary.

The proposed new truck bay was to be 6 metres wide and 12 metres long. With project management in place, anticipation was growing. In June 2016, the site was cleared adjacent to the existing building and a safety guard fence was erected. The concrete floor was poured in July and the steel frame, roof and outside metal cladding were completed in August. The large front roller door was installed and for convenience, a side entrance door was placed on the eastern side of the building. In November, the two concrete driveways were completed, one for the existing fire hall and the other for the new bay extension. A wooden dividing fence and retaining wall was constructed between the driveways, and later, pavers laid nearby. The ground on the eastern side of the building was levelled, allowing an area for the maintenance of the fire hoses.

.... Replacement Fire Truck

In order to build up the firefighting capabilities in the area, Great Lakes Council and the local RFS district office, decide what vehicle is required for the local region; which is then submitted to the Sydney RFS for ratification. As a result, the current twin cab CANTER 7 fire truck was replaced by a 'brand new' twin cab ISUZU 7 fire truck in 2016.

.... An Additional Fire Truck

As the new extension bay was now completed, the RFS members eagerly awaited the delivery of the additional firefighting vehicle. Fortunately, in June 2017, an RFS brigade west of Wingham had recently been issued with two new fire trucks and was able to pass on their older single cab CANTER 7 tanker truck to the Green Point brigade. The newly acquired support vehicle further enabled the local brigade to increase its primary role of bush fire protection in the area adjoining the Green Point village. The tanker's water holding capacity is 1,400 litres for the twin cab cat 7 and 1,800 litres for the single cab Canter 7.

Considering the sandy soil conditions of our area, it was important that the category sevens and no larger vehicle be used – as the friability of the ground is such, that there is less chance of bogging the vehicle. Also, the fact that there is a reticulated water supply in the village means that the category 7 vehicles enable the brigade to fulfill its role of defensive firefighting, in the event of a house fire. Green Point brigade is trained to carry out firefighting roles for structure fires supported by either Pacific Palms brigade or Tuncurry brigade (who have the necessary specialist equipment and training) and also by the NSW Fire & Rescue from Forster.

Today's equipment, with the new modifications, ensures as much as possible, the safety of the volunteer crew. Firefighters in the truck are issued with an essential hand held radio to keep in close contact with other members on the ground, appropriate personal protection equipment and the roll down heat resistant curtain in the cabin, protects the occupants in case of an extreme fire event. Radio connection through RFS Headquarters guarantees backup when needed.

....

.... More Fundraising Needed

The RFS, as a nonprofit organization, carries out a certain amount of fundraising activities. As a special event our RFS brigade arranged 'The Fireman's Ball' which was held on 3/3/2017, at the Tuncurry Memorial Hall. This 'black tie' event featured entertainment by 'The 'Albert Quartet', followed by 'The Big Fins'. Plentiful supplies of tasty food and fine wine, donated by Great Lakes Winery, along with many raffles and a photo booth, insured a great night was had by all. The event raised $1,600 towards the insulation of the fire hall and to improve the facility in preparation for the hall to be used, in the future, as a community Fire Evacuation Centre.

.... Bushfire Awareness & Increased RFS Membership

The extreme hot and dry weather conditions persisted and as part of the Rural Fire Service annual 'Get Ready Weekend' events, Green Point brigade held a 'Get Ready Day' on 17/9/2017, which was well attended. The information session informed residents on fire safety around their homes and how they could prepare their properties in the event of a bush fire. Firefighting demonstrations were performed in the grounds and small children were allowed to see the fire trucks up close. The brigade also ran a junior firefighters obstacle course, in which visitors could participate. The renewed interest by the community resulted in two new members joining the service – soon to become fully trained 'active' firefighters.

The brigade was kept busy in 2018 with over 50 calls, starting with two deployments to Singleton and ending with the brigade going to Salt Ash, Hawks Nest, Middle Brother and 2 members going to Queensland for 5 days. On the evening of 20/12/2018, a severe storm hit the coast of our region bringing down trees and damaging homes in Green Point. Together, with residents and the SES, the local brigade worked to clear the debris and make the area safe.

Since the 2013 fire, which threatened Green Point, residents have shown a greater interest in the local brigade and a number of young people have joined the organization. Around 2016-2017 there were 20 members, of whom 7 were 'active' members, helped by associated volunteer clerical staff. By 2020, another 8 new members had been trained to become 'active' firefighters – bringing the total to 15 active members and 6 auxiliary support members.

As part of the ongoing fire protection commitment to the village, the local RFS performed hazard reduction burning of the bushland south of Green Point. After years of negotiation, permission was eventually granted to carry out the work on block 306. Two sections were burnt in 2019 and due to adverse weather conditions, the last section couldn't be carried out until mid 2020. In the 6 months to August 2020 there were 58 hazard reduction burn operations carried out by the Green Point brigade. The number of call outs from July 2019 to May 2020 increased to 192 – most to fires and to other incidents, e.g. Ambulance Assist.

All men and women over 16 years of age are welcome to join the RFS, which offers training ranging from basic village firefighting, to first aid and breathing apparatus operation and rural fire. Also, it is an opportunity to train in life skills which benefit the volunteer and the community. Commencing August 2020, during school terms and in conjunction with the Education Department, Green Point brigade ran a Cadet Training Course at Forster High School – accepting cadets aged 12-16 years. The local brigade also accepts cadets aged 12-16 years, with parental permission.

.... Fireman's Fun

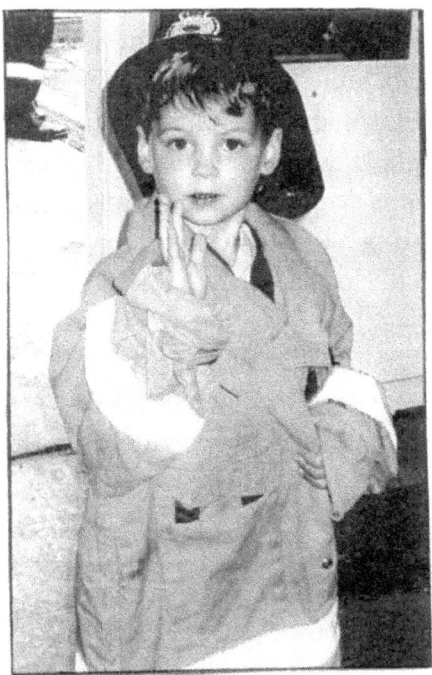

.... Increased RFS Membership

.... *Bushfire Prevention – Control Burn*

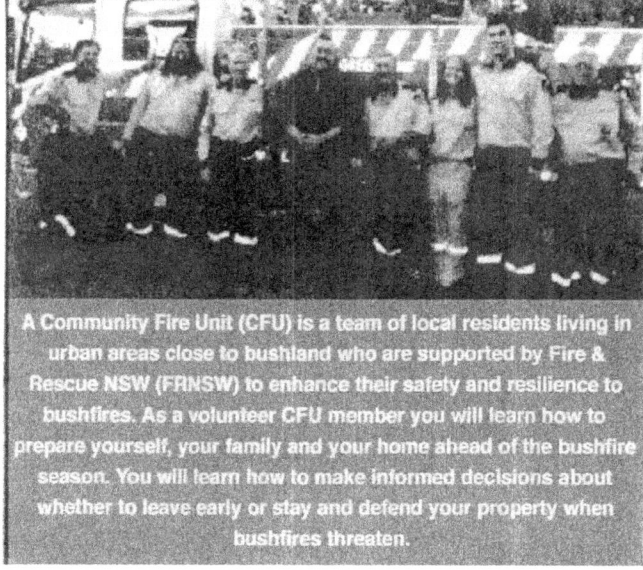

A Community Fire Unit (CFU) is a team of local residents living in urban areas close to bushland who are supported by Fire & Rescue NSW (FRNSW) to enhance their safety and resilience to bushfires. As a volunteer CFU member you will learn how to prepare yourself, your family and your home ahead of the bushfire season. You will learn how to make informed decisions about whether to leave early or stay and defend your property when bushfires threaten.

Council Amalgamation

In order to centralize local government administration in our region the NSW Government made a proclamation on 12/5/2016, that there would be a three-way merger between Gloucester Shire Council, Greater Taree City Council and Great Lakes Council – to become known as MidCoast Council. The merger was to create a stronger and more efficient council. MidCoast Council was to receive $15 million to invest in community projects or services and the community would decide how those funds are spent. In addition the new council was to receive approx. $5 million towards streamlining their operations. On 27/5/2016, The Green Point Community Association held a community consultation workshop to discuss priorities for a strategic plan for the future. The plan was presented to the Community Engagement Officer, Tracey Farrant, on 6/6/2016.

Council Management -

By July 2016, Glen Handford, who had had 35 years government experience, with 22 of those at the former Great Lakes Council, became the interim General Manager and John Turner, who had had 23 years as NSW Member for Myall Lakes, was appointed by the NSW Government as the Administrator, until such time that council elections were held.

On 1/7/2017, MidCoast Water was dissolved and water and sewer services were integrated into MidCoast Council – then to be known as 'MidCoast Water Services', a division of MidCoast Council. It continues to provide the same services that the community previously received.

On 9/9/2017, there were only two new councillors elected – the other nine being from previous councils. Glen Handford then invited the new councillors to participate in several workshops prior to the council meeting, to assist them in their new roles and provide background on MidCoast Council since May 2016. On 27/9/2017, the eleven new councillors elected to MidCoast Council took their oath of office at a ceremony in Taree, which was followed by the inaugural council meeting. The councillors voted in David West (who had had 32 years of council experience) to the position of Mayor. In October 2017, community meetings were held in 10 regional centres, where Council covered their plans to address the issues that residents identified as priorities.

An extraordinary council meeting was held on 24/1/2018, to address the replacement of Glen Handford, who resigned with an effective date of February 2nd, 2018. As Mayor, David West opened the meeting held at Forster Council Chambers (with more than 40 residents in attendance) during which, the MidCoast Council adopted a strategy for the selection of a new General Manager. After a long search, Adrian Panuccio was appointed to take up his position on July 9th 2018. He came with significant local government experience, recently working as Chief Operating Officer for North Sydney Council. (The Advocate, 18/5/2016, 31/1/2018, and 6/6/2018.)

The population of Forster/Tuncurry has increased significantly in the last 10 years – 2005-2007 total was 24,000 and by 2015 the number had increased to 36,171 – with 26% aged over 65 years in the Great Lakes Shire. The area of the newly amalgamated MidCoast Council became over 10,000 square kilometers, with a population of around 90,500. As it was considered that operating and maintaining a single Head Office location would be significantly more cost-effective than continuing to operate across multiple sites, plans were made in December 2017 to establish a Head Office in Biripi Way, Taree – at the former Masters site. In the meantime, Council's customer service points will be maintained. Forster's Customer Service Centre will relocate to the new Civic Precinct in Lake Street, Forster. (MidCoast Council)

MidCoast Community Stronger Together

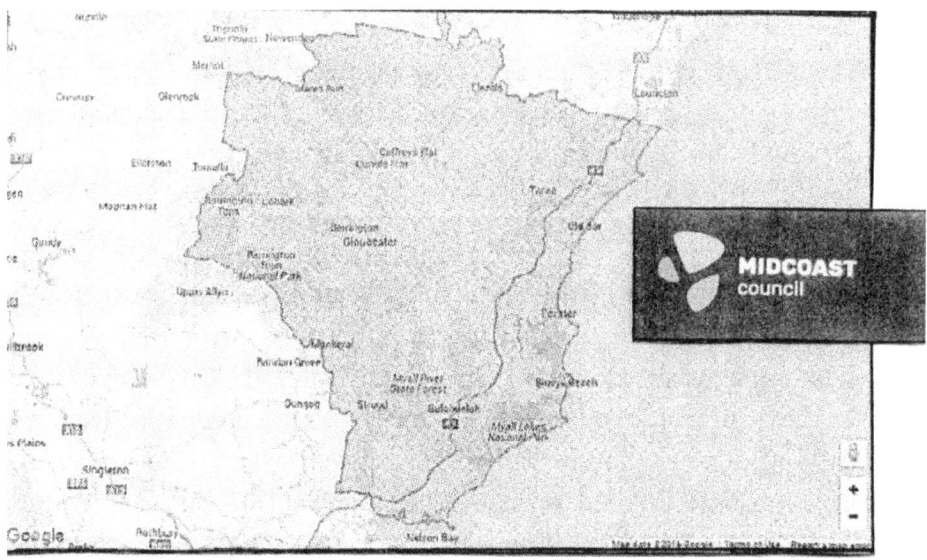

The boundary of the new MidCoast Council. Source: Local Government(Council Amalgamations) Proclamations 2016

Above: Yalawanyi Ganya (MidCoast Council's central administration building) on Biripi Way, Taree.

Housing Development

In early 2007, Hardie Holdings Pty. Ltd. proposed a housing development on a rural site at No. 1 Bottlebrush Close, Green Point. Originally the developer intended to construct a subdivision with 85 home sites, however, this was later reduced to 78 small blocks of land. The residents of Green Point strongly objected to this proposed development. After almost two years of devoted hard work by a subcommittee of the Community Association, outlining their reasoning for their objection, in December 2008 Great Lakes Council advised that the necessary rezoning of the property from RU2 (Rural Landscape) to Residential 1 was refused. Accordingly, in February 2009, Hardie Holdings withdrew their Development Application.

New Challenge – Manufactured Home Estate

In early 2017, MidCoast Council sent a letter of notification to those Green Point residents whose properties were adjacent to, or affected by, a newly proposed development in the area. The proposed housing estate was discussed at the Association meeting held on 12/2/2017 and follow up enquiries were duly made to Council. In reply, Council advised on 8/5/2017 that the location was Lot 312 DP 774361 and Lot DP 1012758, 1 Bottlebrush Close and that it was zoned RU2 Rural Landscape, which had a minimum Lot Size of 40 hectares. This particular property was found to have an area less than 40 hectares - therefore a Torrens Title subdivision was not possible on the site. As an alternative proposal, and being zoned RU2 Rural Landscape, the area was deemed capable of accommodating caravans and portable buildings. This enabled Oxford Street Holdings Pty. Ltd. to propose a development with 87 affordable housing sites for manufactured homes, a clubhouse, recreation facilities and caravan/RV parking. Village residents were then advised of this proposal through the Green Pointer newsletter – including a plan of the area and a reminder that residents had only 30 days from 21/6/2017 to lodge an objection.

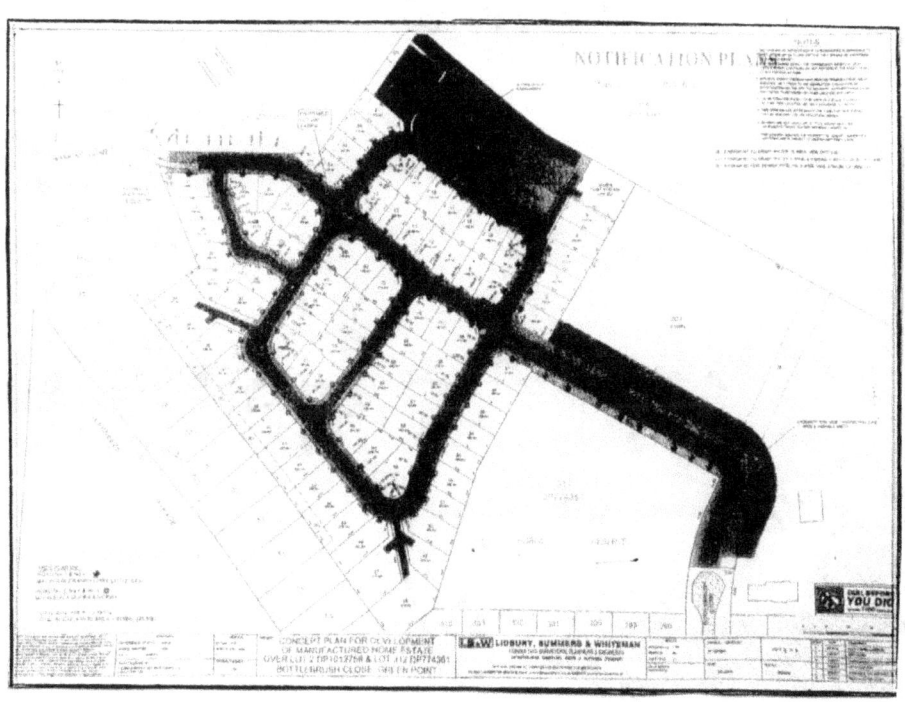

Public Meeting

On July 9th, the Community Association held a Public Meeting at the Community Hall where approximately 150 residents attended. The growing crowd spilled out into the grounds to hear key speakers from the Association review the development proposal. They encouraged residents to put forward their opinions whether they were for or against the development; however, the Association advised that it would be strongly opposing the application for the high density housing. Any submission made by way of objection was required to be specified in the submission. An example letter quoting the necessary reference – DA545/2017, was supplied to residents, to aid with their submissions to the General Manager of MidCoast Council. A petition, in opposition to the development gathered 165 signatures. Council later advised that 73 submissions in opposition to the development had been received from residents, covering 30 different concerns detailing why the project should not go ahead. Only one submission was received in support of the application.

Association Submission

The Community Association was fortunate to have the deadline for submissions extended beyond 21/7/2017. This allowed more time for detailed research and argument against the development which was finally lodged with MidCoast Council on 10/8/2017.

The Association's submission targeted five main issues:-

- Maintaining the RU2 Rural Landscape character of the village.

- The site is within a bush fire prone area, adjacent to a high fire zone, with only one road in and out – noting the recent bush fire in 2013, sweeping in from the National Park.

- Pollution of the lake due to stormwater run-off – proposed measures to prevent contamination from heavy run-off are inadequate and in the event of failure to meet standards, Council will have to pay for remedial measures with a cost to ratepayers.

- Traffic conditions – the T-intersection of Green Point Drive and The Lakes Way. Narrow road with blind corners. Pollution and noise effect on homes in Green Point Drive and Seabreeze Parade.

- Environmental health hazard – building adjacent to mosquito infested swampland is a serious health issue to such a proposed densely packed home site development.

The Association acknowledged that whether the DA was rejected or accepted, that there was a need to develop separate strategies, to either consolidate their position or to influence Councillors. To highlight the proposed subdivision at Green Point, The Advocate ran an article on 20/9/2017, headed 'RESIDENTS SAY NO'. It described the Public Meeting held at Green Point on 9/7/2017 with background information and the Association's arguments against the proposed development.

Association Meeting - On 12/11/2017, approximately 50 Green Point residents attended the Association meeting in the Community Hall, in order to hear speakers from the 'Tallwoods Action Group' to outline their strategies against the proposed development of 287 manufactured home sites, adjacent to the entrance on Blackhead Road. The main point was the impact of 'People Power', with huge attendances at Public and Council meetings and its effect on the Councillors. Circumstances became more worrying as it was discovered that Dunns Creek DA279/2016 (Follyfoot Farm) had its appeal upheld in the Land and Environment Court on 14/11/2017 – MidCoast Council would no doubt have to pay the high cost of fighting the development, which would ultimately be paid for by the ratepayers. This in turn could have ramifications for all DA refusals in Manufactured Home Estates in the Council area. On 15/11/2017, the Association's subcommittee had a meeting with Councillor Stephen Andrews at the Council Chambers.

Council Workshop - On 18/11/2017, the Association was notified of an upcoming 'Workshop' for Councillors, to be held at the Council Chambers on 29/11/2017. The meeting was to be open to the public, but oral presentations were unlikely. The focus was to be on the planning controls for the Manufactured Home Estate Strategy across the newly amalgamated Council area. The difficulty was to harmonize the three former Council areas, which all seemed to have different definitions and regulations relating to planning controls for Manufactured Home Estates, and to resolve the problems so that standard decisions could be made throughout the new Council area.

Council Report - Councillors were then provided with information on the current legislation from the NSW Dept. of Planning and Environment so that a report could be prepared, detailing the relevant legislation, the difficulties presented, and the options available to MidCoast Council. The report for the General Manager was due in late February/early March 2018 and no Manufactured Home Estate decisions would be made until Council had deliberated upon the report. By April 12th the Green Point development proposal was still under assessment and the Association awaited the report before determining any further course of action.

Development Refused - On 18/7/2018 Council advised that the matter would be considered at Council's Ordinary Meeting to be held on 25th July at the Taree office and that a copy of the report would be made available to view on Council's website. Three Green Point residents spoke up at the July Council meeting where their strong arguments were heard by the Councillors. On 30th July, residents were advised that the Council had resolved to REFUSE the development application based on eleven main reasons considered to be contextually inappropriate and not consistent with the various planning controls. The list of reasons for the recommendation to refuse the proposed development was reported in the 'Green Pointer'. On 1/8/2018 the welcome news became the front page story in The Advocate.

Growing Opposition - On 15/10/2018, a Preliminary Hearing was held between MidCoast Council and Oxford Street Holdings, before going to the NSW Land and Environment Court. On November 11th the "Stop Manufactured Home Estate Group" was formed to urge Council to look closely at what was happening to the people, the land and the environment with the development of Manufactured Home Estates. The Group was aiming towards a moratorium on MHE Development and residents were encouraged to log onto MidCoast Council Surveys on the website. Manufactured Home Estates were planned for other communities within the Council area and by early 2019 many residents were objecting to the planned DA's. This gave rise to a group called 'MAD' standing for MidCoast Appropriate Development. The Group had 1,000 followers on Facebook and looked into issues such as Developer's use of SEPP 36, loopholes in SEPP 368 MHE limiting where MHE can be constructed and the environmental, cultural and economic affects on the area.

An Appeal Lodged - On 10/4/2019, Local Government Legal (solicitors for MidCoast Council) advised that they had been instructed to defend an appeal lodged by the Applicant against the refusal of Development Application No. DA545/2017. The DA was before the NSW Land and Environment Court and the Court would proceed to redetermine the Application, having regard to the merits of the proposal. .Proceedings were set down for Hearings on 3, 6 and 7th May, 2019. Residents were advised of the impending Court Hearing and that the Commissioner of the Court would be in attendance at The Hearing, which was to be held in the carpark at Bottlebrush Close at 10.30am on May 3rd to undertake a site view and to hear any evidence from those persons who made submissions. It was emphasized that the attendance should be respectful of the Court's proceedings, without any interjection or disruptive behaviour. There was a limit of six persons who could give evidence and their details were to be given to the Solicitor by 24/4/2019. The Association subcommittee liaised with MidCoast Council and the legal counsel to determine the best course of action to defeat the appeal and co-ordinate speakers to present the case under their guidance.

Court Hearing

On the morning of the Land and Environment Court Hearing a large crowd of determined residents poured into the carpark area to listen to the proceedings. The Commissioner of the Court addressed the residents regarding the solemnity of the Court Hearing and then went on to hear the reasons put forward by the representative speakers, for not wanting such a development in the village area.

To fully comprehend the effect on residents bordering the proposed estate, the Commissioner accompanied the homeowners to inspect the proximity of their dwellings to the proposed development. As a result, it was recommended that three of the manufactured home sites be removed from the plan, to allow for a buffer zone between the properties.

To better understand the impact of stormwater drainage pollution running into the low level bushland environment, adjacent to the proposed estate, the Commissioner inspected the wetland water hole and saltwater marshes nearby – which demonstrated how close the area's water table was to the surface.

It was evident that the bushland beside the proposed estate was a bush fire hazard zone as the area had been burnt out a number of times in the past,

Driving into Green Point, the Commissioner would have been made aware of the dangerous intersection at the corner of The Lakes Way and the narrow roads leading to the site. Damage to these roads, due to the movement of construction equipment and the large vehicles needed to transport the pre-built homes would also have to be taken into account.

Proposal Rejected. On 21/6/2019 the legal department from the MidCoast Council informed the Association that the proposed MHE for our village had been REJECTED by the Land and Environment Court. (C.A. records). It was a joyous and pleasing outcome for the residents of Green Point whose combined tireless efforts achieved the desired successful result.

Socioeconomic Changes Many changes have occurred over the past 50 years since the early development of the Green Point subdivision. Originally a fishing holiday village where keen fishermen built their rough shacks and early holiday makers camped on their properties – namely the Schmakeit family in 1965 and the Mueller family in 1969. Nowadays, Green Point has grown into a vibrant community with around 300 dwellings – including some dual occupancy.

It was inevitable that the area would increase in popularity as land prices at Green Point were much more reasonable compared with areas like Pacific Palms. By 2018, there were only a handful of vacant blocks available for development in the village. However, there was a change in the 'type' of buildings being constructed, which in turn, changed the socioeconomic structure of Green Point.

A number of small older-style dwellings, with commanding views of the lake, were demolished to make way for new multi-storey up-market houses, and many older homes were extended and tastefully renovated. In order to take advantage of the expansive views over Wallis Lake, blocks of land which had earlier been dismissed as being too difficult to build on (because of the extremely steep terrain) now exhibit large multi-storey homes.

During construction, many of the larger homes had allowed for the possibility of holiday rental facilities in the future, whilst others were constructed purely for tourist accommodation purposes. Being situated near to the holiday activities in Forster, and within close proximity of a number of famous surfing beaches (including our own stunning Seven Mile Beach), Green Point soon became a chosen area for holiday rental potential. As roads and travelling time from Sydney have been improved many holiday makers have managed a relaxing break at Green Point, away from their hectic city life style.

Tourism

Name Change – Barrington Coast

Council meetings were held in July and August in 2018 to discuss future tourism planning, including an appropriate 'destination' name, which included all tourist areas within the 'new' MidCoast region. After extensive debate, 'Barrington Coast' was adopted as the most 'uniting' option and since then beautifully designed tourist brochures have been produced and distributed throughout the area. No doubt this promotion, with its map covering all regional destinations, will encourage more holiday makers to visit our beautiful village in the future.

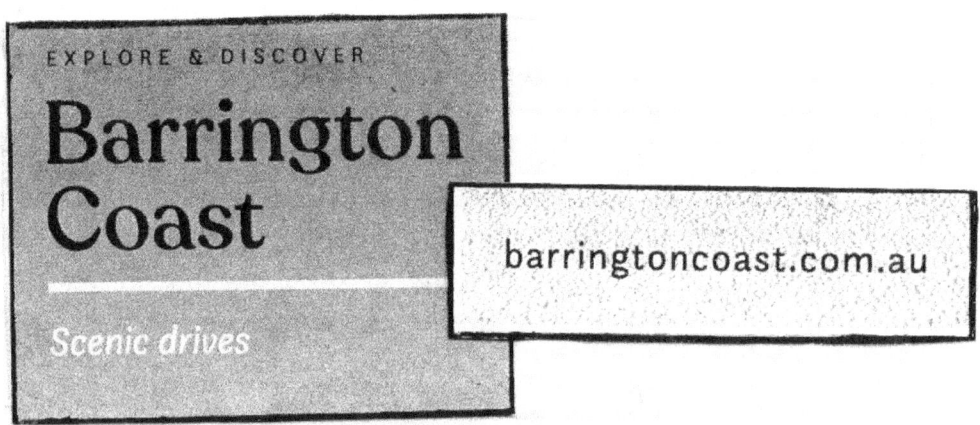

Weather Cycles Continue

As we are aware, weather cycles continue to follow roughly the same pattern – floods, droughts and on occasions, fire! Since the 1981 fire, Green Point has continued to experience a series of bush fires – namely, in 1991, 1997 and 2013. Leading up to these events, temperatures were high and the environment extremely dry.

The next cycles experienced after the bush fires were the extended periods of heavy rainfall. Between 1990 and 2016, our area has experienced many times of high rainfall, resulting in localized flooding around the lakes shoreline. Some long-term residents may recall the foreshore picnic area being extensively flooded in the early 1990's. As seen in these photographs, (courtesy of Leanne Legge), the water level rose a long way up towards the roadway, making it difficult for fishermen to get to their boats.

Lake Levels Rise

In 1927 it had been raining off and on for several weeks, when, instead of fining up, an easterly gale and torrential rain hit and the heavens opened, especially in the Wallamba area. According to Owen Mathias this caused the biggest flood and the lake level rose by 5 feet in height.

In May 2001, the water level in the lake rose by 500mm and a number of unsecured boats were found to have floated away.

The adjoining lowland area in nearby Booti Booti National Park also floods when the water table rises and storm surges occur – damaging the lakeside environment. Over the years, the shoreline has been dramatically eroded leaving tree roots exposed and at times, large trees uprooted.

Lowland areas of properties around Green Point have also been flooded. During heavy rain events the excess water is channelled from the higher areas via road drains down to the lowlands. In 2011, the Community Hall area and carpark, the children's play area and some nearby horse farm paddocks, were inundated with flood water.

In more recent years the mid north coast region had been affected by the ongoing 'drought' and by 2019 there was a dire shortage of water in the dams. The MidCoast Council introduced severe Level 4 water restrictions - according to protocol - based on river flows and groundwater levels. By late 2019 the weather became so dry that the main source of water in the region, the Barrington River, ceased to flow. As the hot dry weather persisted so did the ever present threat of bush fires.

Black Summer Bushfire Season (2019-2020)

Over the summer months many bushland areas on the coast of our region experienced horrific bush fires – mainly started by lightening strikes and prolonged by the existence of underground peat deposits which often smouldered and later reignited.

As early as May 2019 there was a bush fire at Coomba Park and later, in July, there was a fire on a small island in Wallis Lake and the fire-boat from Tuncurry RFS was employed on this occasion. Fires were also burning at Minimbar and in the Nabiac area. In August, the Big Island fire threatened homes and businesses in nearby Forster and. Stocklands shopping centre had o be evacuated due to flying embers.

Multiple fires were burning at Hillville (30 klms northwest of Forster), Bobin, John's River, and the Harrington Road fires threatened many homes. In late October there were fires burning near the Tuncurry Racecourse, the Tuncurry Tip, and at Failford Road/Darawank - where many homes were threatened and roads closed. Rainbow Flat was extremely hard hit with a number of homes lost and on the 8th November the RFS building was also destroyed. In all, thousands of hectares were burnt as the fires spread over long distances. The main highway to Taree was closed to traffic due to the vast forest fires burning each side of the roadway. Overall, in the MidCoast area, the bush fires had claimed 1214 dwellings and damaged 14 facilities. All the Emergency Services were employed along with the help of interstate firefighters and aerial support – resulting in an excess of 980 homes and 64 facilities being saved. The fires covered more than 3960 hectares.

.... *Fire in Forster – Goldens Road/Southern Parkway*

Finally, the large bush fire areas were brought under control, to the great relief of nearby residents – but this reprieve was short lived as another fire broke out on 3/11/2019, this time threatening many homes and businesses in the centre of Forster.

Apparently, the fire was alleged to have been started by a burnt-out stolen car in bushland at the corner of The Lakes Way and Cape Hawke Drive – opposite the Forster High School Campus. Forster's Fire and rescue promptly put out the blaze, but as is often the case, the peat below the surface continued to smoulder and the next afternoon the Green Point RFS was called to attend the fire ground. In order to protect the Golden Ponds Retirement Village the RFS carried out a back burn adjacent to the facility to the relief of the residents.

Later the fire reignited, took hold, and continued northward on its course along the bushland corridor behind homes in Goldens Road. The fierce flames climbed high into the trees with embers exploding over house tops and starting spot fires on footpaths in the nearby Southern Parkway. Continuing on it sway through bushland the fire quickly reached the corner of Southern Parkway and Breese Parade, threatening the back boundaries of the Council Chambers, Library and other auxiliary buildings. Live embers flew across Breese Parade starting spot fires in the carpark gardens of businesses and burning some advertising bill-boards. The bushland at the corner of Likely Street and Kularoo Drive was also affected. The fire then crossed near the roundabout and threatened commercial businesses in Boundary Street South and came dangerously close to the Baptist Care Kularoo Centre.

Firefighters were kept busy as the strong winds continued to carry the burning embers ahead of the fire, eastward and up towards the ridge. A number of spot fires started in bushland reserves adjacent to residential areas and homes were threatened in the vicinity of Karloo Street, Zamia Place, and Forster Grange, off The Southern Parkway. The bushland reserve behind Burrawan St. was also on fire and the NPWS was quick to extinguish a spot fire on Cape Hawke hillside.

Dark smoke billowed high into the air and from Green Point residents watched intently as two small fixed-wing aircraft flew overhead, just metres above their homes – each plane alternatively collecting water from the lake, then returning quickly to Forster to douse the fire. Thanks to the early response of the Green Point RFS and other fire control personnel, the area's assets were saved from harm. The water bombing invigorated the bushland soil and soon signs of new growth appeared as the vegetation started to regenerate. This incident is a continuing reminder that, during the summer fire season, there is always a danger of fire wherever there are bushland areas close to homes.

.... *Bushfire Threat*

On 30/12/2019, fires broke out south of Green Point at Topi Topi (west of Mayers Flat) then later at Tarbuck Bay. Then, on 1/1/2020 another fire started on the northern side of the entrance road to Camp Elim – which if not controlled quickly would threaten Green Point village.

Booti Booti National Park, between Camp Elim and Green Point, had not had a major fire through the area for decades and the undergrowth at this time was tinder dry. Authorities anticipating the worst had taken the bush fire threat extremely seriously. The NPWS responded immediately and within half an hour firefighting personnel and appliances were in place. Two small fixed wing aircraft and one helicopter were deployed from the Giro fire (around 30 klms west of Gloucester) to water bomb the blaze from above and a bulldozer employed to clear a fire-break around the fire ground area. Forming a line of defence and stopping the spread of the fire advancing towards the populated area, regional firefighters and their tanker trucks lined up along the Green Point track (which runs from The Lakes Way, up over the hill and west towards the lake). RFS brigades from Green Point, Coomba Park, Bungwahl, Pacific Palms, Tuncurry and Diamond Beach plus Forster's Fire and Rescue team, all attended in readiness.

In the meantime, Forster's Fire and Rescue personnel had alerted residents along the flat in Green Point Drive of the danger, and to be ready to 'evacuate'. As news spread it became a worrying time for residents and holiday visitors. Many watched anxiously from the roadways as the thick dark smoke reached up into the sky. Others gathered near Smokehouse beach – trying to assess how close the fire actually was to the community.

Thankfully, the evacuation of residents was not required due to the thorough dousing of the fire by the dedicated firefighting planes and follow-up work done by the RFS volunteers. The fire was extinguished quickly and the smoke died down. The very relieved community settled back to normal – all residents truly appreciative of the quick response to the emergency by all the personnel of organizations involved.

.... *Drought Broken*

With many bush fires in the mid north coast region still smouldering it was a great relief for the area to receive 17" or 425 mls of rain between the 7th – 14th February 2020. At Green Point, the showers became downpours – mainly between the 7th – 9th February. Lowland areas flooded as the king tides increased the water levels close to the lake. At last, the 'wonderful news' – all the bush fires were extinguished and water storage dams would soon be filled. The drought, on the eastern coast of NSW, had broken.

.... *Planning for the Future*

Being almost surrounded by bushland and with only one access road, Green Point remains vulnerable to summer bush fires.

Hopefully, in the event of another major bush fire threatening our village residents will stay calm and have their Evacuation Fire Plan ready – deciding whether to stay and defend their property, or to leave.

Following the recent bush fire which could have seriously affected our area, the Association requested a meeting with the Green Point RFS to discuss a draft Evacuation Plan for the future. On 21/2/2020, at a meeting held at the Fire Hall, RFS members detailed their proposed comprehensive Bush Fire Emergency, Management and Evacuation Plan for Green Point.

The planned procedures were outlined to ensure that residents were cared for in an orderly manner. Residents and their vehicles would be marshalled along Bottlebrush Close and directed onto the grassed area in the park nearby. The evacuees would then be ushered to the comfortable facilities within the Community Hall. Any pet owners would be responsible for their pets. For contact tracing, residents would then be required to register their names and details.

In the event of the electricity supply being cut off due to the bush fire the Green Point RFS has acquired a 7kw diesel generator enabling the refrigeration of residents' essential medical supplies on site. With the help of a government grant, the Fire Hall was fully insulated in mid-2019 and to ensure an adequate water supply, a new 22,500 litre water tank was installed in October 2020. The local RFS has purchased hydrant standpipes and extensions for the fire hoses, to enable firefighters to protect and defend the Community Hall and the Fire Hall if needed.

The RFS has a Local Emergency Management Officer (LEMO) in charge of Green Point. Also an incident Control Officer, who is able to deputize leaders in the event of an evacuation, and help keep the people calm. When necessary, the RFS is authorized to close off streets and ensure that no parked vehicles block the progress of speeding fire trucks. (In an emergency, sirens would be blaring as firefighters attended to any outbreaks.) Members from the RFS, SES and Police would be doing door knocks around the area, checking on residents. In times of extreme danger, local fishermen and boat owners would be asked to share their boats and to ferry residents out to the 'Amaroo' or other large marine craft on the lake.

Before Green Point Bush Fire Management and Evacuation Plan can be formally approved, other organizations, such as the Council, SES, Police and NPWS have to be contacted. Where these groups have similar plans already in place, consideration had to be given and agreed to, by all parties concerned. Due to the Covid-19 Pandemic, negotiations were suspended for the time being.

Regardless of the outcome, if Green Point experiences a major bush fire in the future, residents can be assured that our local RFS and other supportive organizations will continue to be prepared and all work together for our protection and safety. Later, the Emergency Evacuation Plan for Green Point was made available to the Community Association.

EMERGENCY EVACUATION PLAN
GREEN POINT

Below is a guide only to assist in the event of an evacuation required at Green Point and can be overridden by higher authority.

- Green Point Community Hall (location: Bottlebrush Close, GREEN POINT) and Green Point Rural Fire Brigade shed (location: 110 Green Point Drive, GREEN POINT) to be joint evacuation points.
- The Community Hall and Green Point RFB are to appoint one (1) person each to oversee the respective evacuation locations (i.e.: "Co-Ordinator)
    - It would be recommended that more than one (1) person each be trained up in the role/s. This will cover in case of an absence.
    - It is recommended that identifiable tabard-vests be purchased to identify the person controlling the situation.
- In the event of a Fire Emergency, Green Point RFB will appoint a person to take overall control for fire protection control of both the Community Hall and Fire Shed.
- The area in the paddock near the Hall (approx. Latitude: 32 degrees, Longitude: 152 degrees) would be suitable for helicopters to land if required.
- If Green Point and The Lakes Way roads are open, people will be directed out of the village via Green Point Drive and which way to go (North or South on The Lakes Way).
- In the event of an emergency, people with boats are to be asked to launch ready to evacuate people by water.
- It will be recommended that those persons leaving the village will register that they have left town. This will assist in identifying those houses that may have people still in attendance.
- At each evacuation location, a register is to be kept by both locations as to all persons in each location
    - Register to be separate to normal sign in books.
    - Register to contain place for Name, Address, Number of People in Group, Time In, Time Out, any special needs (e.g.: Medication, Infant Food requiring refrigeration)
- In the event of a power blackout during the event, Green Point RFB shed has its own generator and will be used to store all medical and baby milk requiring refrigeration.
    - All refrigerated supplies to be clearly labelled
    - Refrigerator will be off limits to general attendees and controlled by Co-Ordinator
    - **No Normal Food will be stored in Refrigerated Facilities.**
- Assistance animals will be allowed inside on proper handling gear
- All other pets will be the sole responsibility of their owners and will not be allowed inside the evacuation centres (e.g.: Cats are to be in their cat boxes)

Evacuation notice will be given as soon and as early as possible. Please remain calm and await instructions.

Any or all of the above may be alternated or changed without notice.

Thank you, Paul Constable

Community Officer Green Point Rural Fire Brigade

Changes To Booti Booti National Park at Green Point

Boat Access

The natural boat ramp in the Booti Booti National Park area at the end of the Green Point peninsula, has for many decades been used by local and professional fishermen to launch their boats. Being close to the deep channel on the western side of the area, this boat access is more conducive for the use of larger vessels – compared to the long length of shallow water and soft sand close to the Foreshore Reserve.

Due to the ever increasing size of recreational fishing boats and marine pleasure craft, more local and visiting boat owners in recent years have been using this natural boat ramp – regardless of the fact that it was in an area of Booti Booti and regulated by the NPWS.

Earlier, the NPWS planned to close off the bush track access with a metal rail – allowing for bushwalkers only, to visit the area beyond. Since then, in July 2020, at a meeting arranged by the then President of the Community Association, Gaye Tindall, with National Park Rangers, representatives of the Association and a resident recreational fisherman, Wally Paszyn, alternative plans were proposed. The need for a large turnaround parking area for eight vehicles and boat trailers was discussed – also the necessity for bollards to be installed to protect the surrounding pristine environment and the bush track access road to be improved. In August residents were informed at a meeting, in the Community Hall, of the proposed work to be carried out.

Turnaround / Parking Area Completed

Eager to work with the Green Point community, the NPWS promptly had plans drawn up for the parking area and by late September early October, the work was well on its way and the bush track made easier to negotiate. (C.A. records) The completed facility no doubt fully appreciated by local residents and visitors alike.

Over the years, much of the National Park bushland had been destroyed by vandals and the lowland area extensively damaged. The use of heavy vehicles had churned up the sensitive wetland, resulting in the destruction of many native plants. It is hoped that the newly positioned bollards will protect this valuable asset from further degradation and that, in the future, plant regeneration will occur – stabilizing the forest floor and bring more wildlife to the area.

Epilogue

This work recalls the courage, determination and good humour of the early residents of Green Point as they faced life's difficulties in the early days of the development. Working with the (then) Progress Association they formed the foundation of the present community. Together, with the Bush Fire Brigade, they were an integral part of community life.

In more recent times, the Progress Association has become known as the Community Association, whilst the Bush Fire Brigade has become a member of the Rural Fire Service. It is with the help of residents, in co-operation with these organizations and in conjunction with the local Council and the Booti Booti NPWS, over the years, that many worthwhile goals have been achieved.

It is thanks to the many years of dedicated voluntary service to the community by the members of these organizations – coupled with the tireless efforts of Coastcare and village mowing and park maintenance groups – that residents and visitors can continue to enjoy the picturesque lakeside environment and appreciate the hard-won community facilities at their disposal.

Although we have to move on and keep up with these modern times, it is hoped that we will remain a cohesive community and willing to continue to work together to maintain the legacy – started so many years ago.

Jo Currans – Green Point resident since 1990

A History of Green Point

About The Book

After many years of detailed research local resident Jo Currans recently completed this informal history of Green Point. To date, no previous large-scale history had been written about the area so hopefully this work will contribute to local records.

Beginning with an early historical background of the area the work continues with the development of Lachlan Fraser's Green Hill farm from 1928.

By interviewing many close friends of Lachlan Fraser, the author was able to build a picture of the farmer and the workings of his Green Hill farm up until when the property was sold to developer C.H. Degotardi in 1960.

The story progresses with recollections of the early residents who bought land and settled in the newly formed subdivision, their struggles to build a village community and their resilience and determination to overcome hardships and obstacles, all of which proved successful.

By 1973 a Progress Association was formed and in 1974 local residents started a volunteer Bush Fire Brigade to patrol the area. Over the years, residents working together and with the help of local Council, enabled many community projects to be completed which have achieved positive change to benefit the village as a whole. Being a village by the shores of Wallis Lake. Green Point Coastcare group ensures that efforts have been made to care for the lakeside environment and the village parkland areas continue to be maintained by volunteers.

Over the last 50 years Green Point, with its increased population, has developed into a unique and self-reliant outer suburb of Forster.

Hopefully readers will find this book interesting and informative.

Jo Currans

Newspaper Article – Forster Fortnightly Publication.

An Accidental Author – Jo Currans.

It all started in early 1996 when local resident of Green Point, Jo Currans, accepted the challenge to compile a pictorial display of the transportation of a tiny tennis shed from Tuncurry to Green Point, to show community residents.

As a fundraising venture a community fete had been arranged to raise funds for the needed improvements to the newly delivered building, which was to be used as a Community Hall. On the day of the fete the display of recent photographs was set up on a large board to show how the building was delivered from the original site and deposited on the newly acquired land at Green Point.

From this initial involvement it was suggested that I build upon the collection of photographs to form a local history. Not realizing how large the project would become or how time consuming it would be I accepted the challenge.

By collecting information and photographs from earlier residents who had bought land in the subdivision developed by C.H. Degotardi I was able to form a picture of how the village developed. Further enquiries led me to seek out residents who had known the previous landowner, Lachlan Fraser, a dairy farmer who had worked the area from 1928 until the development of the subdivision in 1960.

With the generous help of Owen Mathias, who was a great friend of Lachlan Fraser, I was able to learn about the details and workings of the earlier dairy farm and its relationship with the area today.

The story progressed with the recollections of the early residents and their struggles to gain services to build the village community – their resilience and determination to overcome hardship and obstacles, all of which proved successful.

By 1973, a Progress Association was formed and in 1974 local residents started a volunteer Bush Fire Brigade to patrol the area. Over the years residents working together and with the help of the local Council, enabled many projects to be completed which have achieved positive change and benefit to the community as a whole.

Being a village by the shores of Wallis Lake, Green Point Coastcare group ensures that efforts have been made to look after the foreshore environment. The parkland areas are also maintained by volunteers.

Over the last 50 years, Green Point, with its increased population has grown into a unique self-reliant outer suburb of Forster.

Thanks to the Green Point Community Association for allowing access to their records and the Green Point Rural Fire Service for their contribution and support, I was given insight into the 'life and times' of our small community and provided detailed information on many of the significant events and projects which have been undertaken since 1973.

The book would not have been able to be produced without the contribution of many residents, the tireless assistance of Margaret Blackwood who typed the information from my hand-written notes and Michael Davies who assisted in its publication.

To date, no previous large-scale history has been written about the area of Green Point, so hopefully this work will be able to contribute to local records. Although this work has been a time-consuming exercise (over many years) I have found it to be greatly rewarding. Hopefully readers will find the book interesting and informative.

For purchasing enquiries – phone Jo Currans (02) 6555 5432.

Index

	Pages
Green Hill' Farm 1928-1960	10-38
Green Point Subdivision	39-46
Residents' Struggles	47-51
Residents' Stories	46, 53, 59-62, 66-68, 71-79, 85-89, 97-98, 108-111, 118, 167-168, 247-248
Progress/Community Association	49, 70, 211-212, 268
Bush Fire Brigade	54-58, 64-65, 70, 90, 124-126, 213-218, 249-252, 265-267, 282-292, 305-309
Community Hall & Building Extension	80-81, 91-96, 111-116, 253-264, 269-278
Sporting Facilities	70, 82-83, 99-107, 131-139-144, 154-166, 237-238, 279-281
Roads & Drainage	127-128, 227-236
Fishing from Green Point	219-226
Flora & Fauna	191-210
Struggles Against Proposed Developments	69, 239-246, 293-300
Care for the Environment	63, 120-123, 129-130, 140, 145-153, 169-190, 301-304, 310-311

www.ingramcontent.com/pod-product-compliance
Lightning Source LLC
Chambersburg PA
CBHW080855010526
44107CB00057B/2582